HMS BERMU

Also by Peter Broadbent
HMS GANGES DAYS

HMS BERMUDA DAYS

An Ordinary Seaman's Log

PETER BROADBENT

CHAPLIN BOOKS

www.chaplinbooks.co.uk

Admiral J G Hamilton, Captain Lumby and Ordinary Seaman
Peter Broadbent were onboard *HMS Bermuda* in 1961-62. All
others who have a part in this story are fictional characters
and in no way represent actual crew-members of the time.

A CIP catalogue record for this book is available from The
British Library

Design by Michael Walsh at The Better Book Company

Chaplin Books
5 Carlton Way
Gosport PO12 1LN
Tel: 023 9252 9020
www.chaplinbooks.co.uk

CONTENTS

FOREWORD

In 1961 the Royal Navy was the second largest naval force in the world. It had 816 armed ships at sea and an additional 122 under construction. That same year it was decided to place all the Home Fleet's criminals, villains, rogues, thugs and malcontents on board one ship.

HMS Bermuda, the Home Fleet's Flagship, was the chosen ship: a World War II armour-plated veteran. If any ship could deal with a difficult and decadent crew, '*Bermadoo*' could.

I wasn't a malcontent, a villain or in any way corrupt: I was just one of the youngsters required to make up *Bermuda*'s quota of Junior Seamen. I'd completed my 386 days of basic training at *HMS Ganges* and been bundled off to *HMS Dryad* to be trained as a Radar Plotter.

When first drafted to *HMS Bermuda*, I lived a cocooned existence in the Juniors' mess, sharing accommodation with a well-established community of mutinous cockroaches. My life changed dramatically on the day I turned 17½ years old and was transferred to *Bermuda*'s notorious For'd Seamen's Mess. There, totally unprepared, I grew up – thanks to living with the Home Fleet's most colourful, self-indulgent and accommodating characters.

In the 1960s, the authorised way of keeping trouble-makers in line was to keep them busy. For *Bermuda*'s final year in service, she was continually exercised – defending herself against constant air attacks from the Royal Air Force and underwater threats from our own Submarine Service. *Bermadoo* and I travelled 34,000 eventful and unforgettable nautical miles together.

Peter Broadbent

ACKNOWLEDGEMENTS

I acknowledge the help and assistance of Les Burrill (www.hmsgangestoterror.org) for details of *HMS Bermuda*'s final commission, which I had forgotten or overlooked; Rob Guyatt for some of the photographs; Douglas Carr for the photograph of *Bermuda*'s superstructure and Dave Johns for the picture of *Bermuda* being scrapped at the end.

1

A TIN HAT, A STICK AND A PUSSER'S TORCH

With my kit bag balanced precariously on my shoulder I stagger the short distance from Portsmouth Harbour Station to where the RN bus stands waiting on The Hard. I am focused on a group of waving, welcoming girls on the black-iron balcony of a building directly ahead of me. If I were to look to my left, I'd see the masts of Nelson's Flagship *HMS Victory* showing above the Victorian red-brick buildings of Portsmouth Dockyard ... but I don't.

I am one of a group of Junior Seamen, fresh out of *HMS Ganges*, on my way to *HMS Dryad* for the specialist part of my naval training. I sneak a final look at the waving girls before dragging my kit bag up the steps of the bus and dumping it onto a seat near the front.

I slump onto my seat: take my cap off, wipe my brow, unbutton my uniform jacket cuffs and try to massage some life back into my numbed shoulder. I look up at the black-iron balcony: the girls have gone.

'Lash' Trainer is the last one of us to board the bus. He drags his kitbag along the central aisle, kicks it and slumps down in the seat opposite me. 'Shit Pete, that was a walk wasn't it?'

'It's the kit bag, mate, it's got heavier since this morning.'

'I think I've sprained my ankle or something,' he says, rubbing his foot.

'The girls have gone.' I point out of my window.

'What girls?'

'Didn't you see them on the balcony ... the waving ... the girls?'

'Balcony ... what balcony?'

I point. 'That one. That one up there ...'

There is a noise from the front of the bus as a large uniformed bloke trips up the step. A flying clipboard hits the driver on the back of the head and a uniform cap skids across the deck.

'Bugger,' mumbles the sprawled heap on the deck as he clambers back to his feet.

Lash and I look at each other. I shrug my shoulders.

The driver massages the back of his head.

The large uniformed bloke recovers his clipboard and pats the driver a couple of times on the shoulder. Coughing, he recovers his cap and places it squarely on his head before turning to face us. He's wearing a black eye-patch. He counts us and scribbles on his clipboard. 'Six. All present and correct,' he mutters to the driver.

Tossing the clipboard on the front seat, he faces us, takes a deep breath and removes his cap. 'Welcome to Portsmouth. My name is Leading Seaman L J Silver.' He pauses to allow his introduction to sink in.

Lash and I look wide-eyed at each other. I've read 'Treasure Island' and by the look on Lash's face so has he.

'Only joking.' He pokes a finger at his eye-patch. 'I've got a stye. My name is Leading Seaman Potter ... known as 'Potter the Plotter'. I'm one of the staff who looks after the Juniors' Division at *HMS Dryad.* The final leg of your journey this afternoon will take approximately 45 minutes depending on traffic.' The looks at his wrist: there isn't a watch. 'Hopefully we can beat the Dockyard rush.'

I take a final look at the black-iron balcony as the bus slowly pulls away: it's still empty.

Leading Seaman Potter loses his balance briefly. 'On arrival at *HMS Dryad* you will be allocated a bunk and locker in the Juniors' accommodation before being taken to the Dining Hall for something to eat. The remainder of the evening will be yours to unpack your kit and settle in. Petty Officer Wilkinson, Leading Seaman Jones and myself will be available throughout the evening should you have any problems settling in.'

It's getting dark as a torrent of cyclists emerges from the large gates in front us. The bus has to give way as we are surrounded by a weaving phalanx of blokes on two wheels: they are jam-packed in the side streets waiting to pour out onto the main road.

We leave Portsmouth town as dusk turns to night and the street lights come on. The bus grumbles and splutters as we climb to the top of a steep ridge. Looking out of the window on Lash's side I can see the lights of what I assume is Portsmouth, laid out below me.

Leading Seaman Potter stands and braces himself against the backs of two seats as he points downwards. 'That's the dockyard down there.' He swings an arm. 'And that's Gosport over there to the right. Over there in the distance somewhere is the Isle of Wight. Somewhere over there ... they haven't switched their light on yet.' He sits down.

HMS Dryad nestles alongside the 'chocolate box' village of Southwick in a fold of land on the north side of Portsdown Hill, the high chalk ridge overlooking Portsmouth and Gosport. In this quiet, rural setting, tucked away at the end of a long, unmarked approach road, members of the Radar Plotting branch are trained to operate the Royal Navy's most sophisticated Radio Detection and Ranging Equipment.

Messdeck accommodation at *HMS Dryad* consists of single-storey, badly insulated prefabricated huts: they look like terraced pigsties. The bathrooms are a long cold walk way, outside the Juniors' accommodation, which is protected by a Petty Officer and a couple of Leading Seamen. The rest of *HMS Dryad* is a bewildering array of admin blocks and classrooms, some of which have been designed to look like the Operation Rooms onboard ships.

I have barely got my bearings when it's time to start my course. All six of us from *Ganges* join up with a similar number of Juniors from *HMS St Vincent*. The 'switching on' part of our course is done at a place called Fort Purbrook, a pleasant bus-ride away, set right on the top of Portsdown Hill and commanding a huge vista that encompasses the Isle of Wight and the Solent.

The Fort's history is explained to us the moment we arrive and are mustered on the small quadrangle immediately inside the main entrance gate. 'Fort Purbrook is one of a chain of seven forts known as Palmerston's Follies, built to protect Portsmouth Naval Base from a land-based attack by the French in the nineteenth century. The attack never happened because it took so long to build the forts that, by the time they'd finished, the threat had gone away. All the forts are connected by tunnels and it rumoured that Purbrook has a direct underground link to The George Inn.'

We laugh obediently.

Then we are given the Fort tour. Within the thick-walled interior are a variety of small windowless rooms. Some contain pulsating hot radars, others house rows of radar screens. Tucked away in the most inaccessible of places is our small, intimate classroom. Our course Instructor has a couple of medal ribbons on his jacket and a crown above the spider's web badge on his arm. 'Welcome to the start of your basic Radar Plotters course. My name is Petty Officer Pinkerton. You may have been told when at *Ganges* or *St Vincent* that you were selected to be Radar Plotters because you are the cream of the Seamanship branch. How many of you believe that?'

I look around. Nobody else is putting their hand up ... so I don't.

Petty Officer Pinkerton scans our faces. 'Good. Because you are no better or worse than other members of the Seaman branch. The Radar Plotting branch has its fair share of idiots and nincompoops, believe me. If you successfully complete this course ... and when your Mummies have sewn your badges on for you ... you can be justly proud that you are a member of the Royal Navy's newest branches. This course is the foundation stone of your future career. Any questions so far?'

'Why aren't we doing our course in *Dryad* itself sir?' asks Lash.

'That's a very good question, lad. What's your name?'

'Junior Seaman Trainer sir.'

'*Ganges* trained?'

'Yes sir.'

'Thought so. To answer your question: we are not allowed to operate modern, high-frequency radar equipment from *HMS Dryad* because the local villagers complain that it interferes with their radios and televisions. We are not so restricted at *Fort Purbrook*, although we can only operate some of our really powerful, long-range radar at certain times of the day, as they could interfere with marine navigation equipment. Any other questions?'

Bogey raises his hand.

'Yes, lad.'

'Can we smoke, PO?'

'I'm glad you asked that. What's your name?

'Junior Seaman Knight sir ... err PO.'

'To answer your question Junior Seaman Knight ... no.'

'How long will we be ... in *Fort Purbrook*, PO?' asks one of the *St Vincent* lads.

'Exactly two weeks. You will then be tested on what you have been taught. Those who attain the required pass mark will then transfer to *HMS Dryad* proper for the second and final part of the course.'

'What is the pass mark sir ... err, PO?' asks Muddy.

'That, young man ... is our secret.'

'That's not fair is it?' I whisper to the *St Vincent* lad sitting alongside me.

Petty Officer Pinkerton hears me. He points his stick menacingly at me. 'What's your name, lad?'

'Junior Seaman Broadbent sir.'

'What isn't fair, Junior Seaman Broadbent?'

'Nothing sir.'

'Petty Officer will do.'

'Nothing Petty Officer.'

'Don't whisper in my class young man ... understand me?'

'Yes PO. Thank you PO.'

Petty Officer Pinkerton looks at his watch. 'Stand-easy in ten minutes. I'll show you the way.'

The NAAFI canteen is located in the very bowels at the end of a bewildering series of steps and turns. While we queue to be served we unanimously name our Course Instructor 'Pinky'. On the end of the counter is a pile of steaming-hot steak-and-kidney pies. A pair of grey-haired ladies in powder-blue overalls serve us. They have their names on plastic tabs pinned to their fronts: one is called Maud and her companion Mary.

As Maud looks up at Lash, she stops pouring teas. 'Are you the new course?'

'Yes,' replies a surprised Lash.

'Which of you is Peter?'

Lash turns and points at me. 'He is.'

'Jump the queue, young man,' says Maud as she waves me to the front. 'I want a word with you.'

I stroll forward and present myself opposite Maud.

Maud looks at Mary and points the spout of her teapot at my nervous chest. 'Can't see what she sees in him, can you Mary?'

'Nope.'

'Back to your place then.' She waves me away.

I'm confused and I've forgotten where I was in the queue so I play it safe and go to the back.

When I make it to the front, Maud smiles and offers me the last of the pies.

The tea is stewed, but my steak-and-kidney pie is brilliant.

Two weeks later we get the results of our Fort Purbrook studies: we all pass. The top of the class is 'Swotty', a *St Vincent* lad. It is rumoured that I'm near the opposite end of the scale and have only scraped through.

On the second day of the *HMS Dryad* part of our course, the class is corralled through the porticoed entrance of the Wardroom (Southwick House) and into a room that has a huge map of southern England and northern France covering one wall. Pinky explains that in 1943, with the planning of D-Day already underway, this room was the Advanced Command Post of the Supreme Headquarters Allied Expeditionary Force. In 1944, in the months leading up to D-Day, the house was the headquarters of the main allied commanders: Naval Commander-in-Chief Admiral Ramsay, Allied Supreme Commander General Eisenhower and the Army Commander-in-Chief General Montgomery. The large wall map still displays the markers showing the positions of the forces on the day of the first D-Day landings, along with the weather charts for 5 and 6 June 1944. I stifle a yawn. Historically, I suppose it is significant but not as important to me this morning as my 10:15 Stand-easy. Along with my classmates I'd queued in the Canteen to be served by 'Wilco', an attractive young lady who, it is rumoured, wears nothing significant beneath her powder-blue NAAFI overall.

Southwick House

As Easter approaches, I become a fully-fledged member of the Radar Plotting branch and am presented with my spider's web badges. It isn't the only remarkable thing to happen this month: a Russian bloke called Yuri Gagarin becomes the first man to travel beyond the earth's atmosphere, England beats Scotland 9-3 at football, I have a green-winged eagle tattooed on my right forearm, and Wilco and I start 'seeing' each other.

While I'm awaiting draft, I am regularly part of the notorious Duty Watch Emergency Party. *HMS Dryad* is a secretive place and each night a select group of qualified Radar Plotters sleep fully clothed in a tin Nissen hut behind the Main Gate. This small group of fearless individuals, each armed with a badly fitting tin hat, a metal-tipped wooden night-stick and a Pusser's torch, is *Dryad*'s principal line of defence. As a junior member of the ship's company, I spend every fourth night in the tin hut, apprehensively prepared to do my bit in defence of Queen and Country.

One night, instead of sleeping in the tin hut, I am the 'back-drive security sentry' from 22:00 until midnight. Dressed in an issued greatcoat that is a couple of sizes too small, and armed with a metal-tipped wooden night-stick and a Pusser's torch, I am stationed in a white-painted sentry box located at the junction of two mud tracks in the empty part of the Southwick Estate. I am surrounded on all sides by dark, deserted and cold fields. My sentry-box is open at the front and has large chest-high openings on either side; only the back offers any protection against the wind that within minutes makes a mockery of my protective coat. I wrap my scarf around my lower face and stroll up and down the frosted, crunching track, swinging my metal-tipped wooden stick and always keeping the sentry-box in sight. The torch only works after it's given a good thwack on top of a fence-post. It is the longest two-and-a-quarter hours of my life.

The Able Seaman who relieves me is a quarter of an hour late. 'Anything to report, young 'un?'

'Nope.' I unbutton my greatcoat and hand it over, along with the torch and the metal-tipped stick.

'Not even a rabbit?'

'Haven't seen anything.'

'Or a hare?'

'Nothing.'

'Ferkin' cold isn't it?' he says as he struggles into the coat.

'Yep.'

'Was that your first sentry duty?'

'Yep.'

'Enjoy it?'

'Nope.'

'Waste of ferkin' time, isn't it?'

'Yep.'

'Are you the Junior who I've seen sniffing around Wilco?'

'Me? ... Naah.' My teeth are chattering. It's freezing and I'm not in the mood for conversation: all I want is a reasonably warm bed.

During the day Muddy and I work in *Dryad*'s range of pigsties. Along with a couple of Able Seaman Radar Plotters, I learn how to cement and lay concrete blocks in order to build a south-facing extension for the two camp 'studs'.

Back home in Pudsey, on Easter leave, I'm surprised to discover that Mum is not particularly impressed with my newly acquired Radar Plotting or pigsty-construction skills. The West Yorkshire weather is terrible. On Easter Monday I go to Elland Road to see my team beaten by a superior Scunthorpe United 3-2. It is a disappointing leave and after a week I am looking forward to going back to *Dryad* and getting to grips with Wilco. A few days before the end of my leave, however, I meet a blonde girl from

Wakefield who promises to write to me while I am away. I feel like a real sailor ... now I've got a girl in two 'ports'.

After Easter leave I am told that, along with a number of other Radar Plotters, I am to join a ship called *HMS Bermuda*, a Second World War Battle Cruiser. In May I begin my Pre-Commissioning Training, but I take an instant dislike to *Bermuda*'s Senior Radar Plotter and he doesn't seem to think much of me, either.

Tuesday 16 May is my last day at *Dryad* and I am yet again a member of the elite Duty Watch Emergency Party. The only time I can say goodbye to Wilco is during the afternoon Stand-easy in the Canteen. She slithers over her counter top and gives me a lingering, two-arm hug.

'I shall miss you,' she says.

I sneak one final look into the now-familiar depths of her gaping NAAFI overall. 'I'll miss you both too.'

'Cheeky.' She taps my chin.

'Mmm.'

'You watch yourself onboard that *Bermuda* ship. Home Fleet Flagship and all that,' she says, rolling her shoulders. 'I want you back here safe and sound.'

'I will,' I reply, suddenly feeling myself welling up.

'Ship full of bad lads apparently.'

'I've heard.'

She kisses me full on the lips. 'You'll survive, Pete. See you when you come back to *Dryad*.' She gives me a final, sloppy kiss.

The lads waiting in the queue to be served look on, open-mouthed.

2

SMELL OF THE BARMAID'S APRON

Along with the rest of *Bermuda*'s Radar Plotters, I wrestle my bulging kit bag into the back of a Naval truck parked alongside the clock tower and, resplendent in my best uniform, board a bus bound for *HMS Victory* in Portsmouth. It is Wednesday 17 May 1961. A few of my classmates have not yet got a 'draft chit' and earlier, over breakfast, I said a very blokish goodbye to them. From around the edge of the canteen building Wilco, in her powder-blue overall, waves me a very feminine farewell.

HMS Victory Barracks is located near to the centre of town and is a large assembly of imposing red-brick buildings behind ornate, wrought-iron railings. Peering out of the bus window, as I pass through the elaborately gilded Main Gates for the very first time, I set eyes on the largest and most intimidating Parade Ground I have ever seen.

Today 'Vicky Barracks' is the assembly point for the new crew of *HMS Bermuda*. As soon as we disembark, we are organised by strutting Petty Officers of the Gunnery branch and marched to the dining hall for an early dinner.

There are grumblings from those who are old enough to draw their tot.

'Rum will be issued after all the ceremonies of the day are complete,' a Petty Officer explains.

Ceremonies? We have to do ceremonies?

'I can't do ceremonies without mi' ferkin' tot inside of me,' says someone.

'Nor me.'

'Me neither.'

'I need mi tot.'

'I'm not doin' ferk-all till I've had mi tot.'

'Rum will be issued as soon as the Commissioning Ceremony is finished,' decrees a barrel-chested Chief Petty Officer.

'What a load of bollocks this is,' whispers someone from the back of the queue.

After dinner we assemble in our respective specialist groups on the Parade Ground. I'm in the Seaman group: a large body of individuals only second in size to the Stokers.

I'm pleased to see an old friend from *Ganges* who had joined the TAS branch and spent the last three months at *HMS Vernon*.

'Hiya, Tug.'

'Hello, Pete.'

'How's life in the TAS branch then?' I ask.

'Shit. How's life in the Radar Plotting branch?'

'Shit.'

We both grimace.

'Anybody else here from *Ganges*?' asks Tug.

'Four of us. Muddy, Bogey, Lash and Stumpy.'

'All from *Dryad*?'

'Yep.'

'I've seen Blacky,' says Tug, pulling a face.

'Oh shit! Not with you at *Vernon* was he?'

'No, he went to Whale Island … a Gunner.'

We both look around but neither of us can see him.

'It's a load of ferkin' bullshit this is,' says the bloke standing alongside us, a wrinkly-faced Able Seaman who introduces himself as 'Soapy'. I notice the marks of recently unstitched badges on his sleeve.

'Yeah it is,' I agree.

'Absolute ferkin' bullshit.'

'Sure is.'

'Sure is,' confirms Tug.

'A load of ferkin' bollocks. First ship?'

'Wha?'

'Is this your first ship?' asks Soapy.

'Naah. Spent a bit of time on *HMS Petard*.'

'How long?'

'A week.'

He smiles: he has blackened teeth. 'You'll find this grey funnel bastard a lot different.'

'OK then.'

'She's a big ugly bastard,' explains Soapy.

'Is she?'

He nods to the front. 'Here we ferkin' go!'

A Chief Petty Officer clamps a black stick under his arm, takes a deep breath and bellows ... '*Bermuda* Ship's Company ... *Bermuda* Ship's Company ... Atten ... Shun!'

The band of the Royal Marines appears and comes to a boot-banging halt directly facing the Main Gate.

I find it difficult to concentrate on what the Parade Chief Petty Officer is saying, but I hear snippets. 'March Smartly ... Queen's Street ... South Railway Jetty ... Smell Of The Barmaid's Apron ... Silently ... IS EVERYTHING CLEAR?'

He doesn't expect a reply and he doesn't get one. There are a few grumbling noises within the ranks.

'Typical big-ship ferkin' bullshit!' says Soapy.

'You can say that again.'

'Typical big-ship ...'

'SILENCE IN THE RANKS!'

As the senior branch, we march behind the Wardroom contingent who follow the band. All the way down Queen's Street, Soapy comments as we pass each Naval tailor's and each pub. 'Three Crowns, that's a good 'un: great barmaids. That pub's great on a Saturday. Don't use that Naval tailor: it's a load of bollocks. Home Club: great place for a couple of jars before heading off into town. Ship & Castle: that's only for the really desperate until about 21:00 when it calms down to a roar.'

'SILENCE IN THE RANKS!'

At the bottom of Queen's Street we 'right-wheel' in through the impressive gates of Her Majesty's Dockyard Portsmouth and march up towards the masts of *HMS Victory* that angle skywards above the small-boat repair shops on our starboard side. The Royal Marine band leads us around to our left and under a large wooden canopy painted a brilliant white and supported by a phalanx of highly decorated blue and gold stanchions. On a raised platform area at one end is a large gathering of dignitaries milling around searching for their reserved seat. According to the Order of Service, His Worship the Mayor of West Bromwich – the town that adopted *HMS Bermuda* when she was first commissioned in 1942 – is here. In addition, there is a crowd of Portsmouth's local worthies, a variety of thick-ringed Naval Officers, their wives in large-brimmed hats and an array of robed clerics.

Alongside us, silent and grey, sits a monster. I suppose I expected something larger than *HMS Petard*, but I didn't expect anything this size. *HMS Bermuda* is the largest object I've ever seen. She is immaculate, her paintwork is unblemished, her lines of polished brass scuttles sparkle in the spring sunshine. Three brows, each with white canvas screens, angle up to her decks from the jetty. At the bottom of each brow are a pair of ornate lifebelts on stands of varnished wood. In the centre of each is *HMS Bermuda*'s crest: an intimidating-looking red figure holding a trident. I read more of my Order of Service. It's four pages long and looks like it is going to take ages.

And it does. Everybody has something to say to us. The microphone system isn't brilliant and although I am near the front, I find it difficult to hear everything that is said. We pray when instructed to do so and we sing a variety of rousing hymns. I particularly enjoy the one about 'Those in Peril on the Sea' – it seems appropriate somehow and I join in enthusiastically.

It all comes to a thankful end with the Captain's wife and a Junior Cook, the youngest crew member, cutting a Commissioning cake. The cake looks nice enough to eat, as does the Captain's wife dressed in a flowing, flowery dress.

We stand silently as the dignitaries disperse. Many of them go onboard *Bermuda* while others are whisked away in black official cars or stand around not knowing exactly what to do.

The band marches smartly away and we are divided into smaller units by the men in peaked caps. There are about 40 Juniors from different branches: Seamen, Stokers, Cooks, Stewards, Electricians, Stores Assistants, Writers and Communicators. We are called to attention and a small, barrel-chested Petty Officer with ginger hair and a face full of freckles addresses us. 'My name is Petty Officer Batten. I am the Juniors' Petty Officer onboard *HMS Bermuda*. Once the remainder of the ship's company have made their way onboard we ... my two Leading Hands and I ... will arrange for you to collect your hammocks, and show you to your new mess.'

'Bloody hammocks again,' whispers Tug.

'Sounds like it.'

We collect our hammock components from a large storage container on the jetty, and under the watchful eye of Petty Officer Batten and a couple of Killicks, we are corralled onboard. We stagger up and down a seemingly endless number of ladders and along a bewildering range of passageways until we end up in our new mess. I sling and make up my hammock. We *Ganges* boys definitely have the edge over most of the other lads. The Writers, Stores Assistants and the Junior Cook don't have a clue what to do. Eventually, with plenty of assistance and encouragement from Petty Officer Batten and his two Killicks, we all lash up a reasonably tight hammock: tight enough to fit through one of our messdeck scuttles and keep us afloat until help arrives in the event of an 'abandon ship'. We mark our hammock with our name and official number and stow it in the designated hammock stowage in the corner of the mess.

The Juniors' mess spans the width of the ship with a couple of portholes on either side. Small silver lockers, in banks three high, separate the two halves down the ship's centreline. On each side of the mess is a long wooden-topped mess table flanked by long wooden benches topped with a thin burgundy-coloured plastic cushion. Directly below the mess entrance hatch is another hatch and a ladder leading to somewhere dark. In a corner of the starboard mess is a small Juniors' Office where Petty Officer Batten, now known as 'Freckles', lives.

We are officially introduced to our Leading Seamen: McKlusky, a corpulent man with ginger hair and a large, matching beard, and Thomas, who has a tidy, dark beard with flecks of grey. They are responsible for the efficient day-to day running of the mess, its cleanliness and general discipline.

We queue up at the Juniors' Office and are each issued with a locker key. The location of our lockers indicates on which side of the mess we are to live. I am on the starboard side with about 20 others and Leading Seaman Thomas.

Petty Officer Batten stands at the end of the table. 'Just so there is no confusion, particularly for those of you who went to *Ganges* and had to call everybody, including the ship's cat, 'sir' ...' There are sniggers from those who haven't been to *Ganges*. 'Let me tell you how you should address us. My name is Petty Officer Batten – you can call me Petty Officer, PO or Petty Officer Batten. Leading Seaman Thomas and Leading Seaman McKlusky are to be addressed by their full rank and name or 'Hooky' or 'Leading Hand'. They will no doubt let you know when you overstep the mark.'

Behind their backs, the two Killicks have already been nicknamed 'Tommo' and 'Mac'.

Outside Freckles' office is a notice board and pinned to it is a copy of Daily Orders. Freckles explains to us that this sheet is issued daily and it is our duty to read it. It lists all the duty personnel and the events of the forthcoming day. Apparently, during our impending 'Work-up' period it will not detail all daily activities, as these will change as the situation demands. Alongside Daily Orders is the 'Mess Duty Roster' that details all the messdeck duties for the forthcoming week. There will be no excuse for not knowing our duties. Exchange of duties is allowed with the approval of the Killick of the mess. We can swap duties, but we can't sell or buy them.

I see that I'm going to be mess 'Gash party' the day after tomorrow and 'Cook-of-the-mess' a couple of days after that. Then it looks as though I have about six days clear before I am on something called 'Mess Traps', whatever that is.

The Junior Cook, who helped to cut the Commissioning cake, is also in the starboard side mess. A *St Vincent* lad has the next locker to mine. His name is David Rutherford and is nicknamed

'Margaret' after a popular actress of the day. He doesn't appear to be the type to complain about being called Margaret.

The Tannoy has been broadcasting continual instructions, none of which register until one broadcast stiffens Freckles. 'Back onto the jetty everyone. Back onto the jetty and collect your kit bags!'

I've forgotten all about my kit. I assess the size of my recently allocated locker and decide that it's much smaller than my kitbag. I'm not going to be able to fit everything in. Tommo guides us back to the upper deck. On the jetty we Radar Plotters collect our kit bags from the back of the *Dryad* truck.

By the time my kit bag pulls me down the mess ladder I am soaked: my best uniform suit is like a crumpled rag and my white front is wet through. I stow my kit away as best as I can and put my suit and Burberry in one of the small hanging cupboards. Surprisingly, with some clever adjustments, my entire kit fits into my locker and I jam my footwear into a small sliding tray underneath. I feel more comfortable when I change into my Number 8s.

I notice 'Blacky' on the other side of the mess. Blacky's real name is Bill Yardley and he has a reputation for having done everything better, faster and more often than anyone else. If you have a black cat, then Blacky has a blacker one: that's how he got his nickname. He is an irritating individual who, sooner or later, gets up everybody's nose.

Tired, and more than a little confused by everything, I sit with the rest of my messmates at the starboard side table while Tommo gives us a run-down on the most important thing of the day – feeding ourselves. We will eat all our meals in the mess. All food is prepared in the Main Galley and placed in large mess trays to be collected by each mess. The main galley Cooks have been onboard for a few days and are scheduled to flash-up the galley equipment first thing tomorrow morning. Today we will be given sandwiches and cake for tea. As from breakfast tomorrow, we will draw hot, *Bermuda* nosh from the galley along with everyone else.

We are all taken on a brief tour to show us where the main galley is. From behind the closed and clipped doors we can smell and hear something being prepared. I'm not the only one to take a wrong turning on the way back to the mess and for a while I am completely lost.

At 17:30 a couple of the lads are detailed off to collect sandwiches from the galley. I wait expectantly but am disappointed with the greasy, yellowed slices of corned beef that I eventually place between slices of dry white bread. There is no cake: that was a 'Tommo' joke apparently.

On the after bulkhead we have something called a Mess Trap locker which contains a couple of bags of sugar, some coffee, a brown paper bag full of loose tea and about half a dozen tins of condensed milk known as 'Tinned Cow' according to Tommo, and 'Canned Cow' according to Mac.

I'm sent to the galley to get some boiling water so that we can make some tea.

'Just knock on the galley pantry door and ask the Chef if you can have some hot water for tea,' says Tommo, as he hands me a large, battered container. It sounds a simple enough task.

My mistake is confusing the main galley door with the door to the galley pantry. After knocking twice, the main door is opened by a bloke wearing food-encrusted whites and a silly white cap. 'What the ferk do you want?'

'Can I please have some hot water for tea ... for the Juniors' mess ... please?'

'Piss off!'

'Pardon sir?'

'Piss off!

'But Leading Seaman Thomas has just sent me up ...'

'Don't give a shit who ferkin' sent you. The Admiral of the bastard Fleet couldn't get hot water from this door. The galley pantry's next door. Now piss off in short, sharp, jerky movements.'

'Thank ...'

The door slams shut.

Next door is clearly marked 'Galley Pantry': I'd missed that. I knock and knock again on what I hope is the right door.

The same bloke opens it.

'Leading Seaman Thomas has sent me to ...'

'Piss off.'

'But you said ...'

'Give me your ferkin' kettle then.'

'I've only got a ... a.' I don't know what to call my container.

'That's what's called a fanny, lad. Give me it then.'

I hand my fanny to him. He snatches it and slams the pantry door shut.

Fanny eh? I stand there for what seems like five minutes. Eventually the door opens and a grubby white arm plonks my container full of steaming water on the deck. 'Now piss off.'

'Tha ...'

Carrying an un-lidded fanny full of steaming water is not that easy and it is a while before I manage to negotiate the messdeck ladder and place it gingerly on the end of the mess table. The handle is hot.

'Any problems?' asks Tommo.

'Naah sir ... Hooky. It was easy.'

Pusser's tea, when you make it yourself, is not for the faint-hearted. Maybe we don't get the proportion of tea to water correct because the liquid we pour into chipped Pusser's cups is almost black and has a strange, unidentifiable smell to it.

'Is there bromide in the tea?' asks Muddy.

'Not unless you've put it in,' replies Tommo.

Mac, the red-bearded Killick from the port side of the mess, appears cradling a part of the commissioning cake. It is much larger than it appeared during the cutting ceremony. Freckles uses the rusted blade of his Seamen's knife to help the Junior Cook cut it into the correct number of pieces. 'Specially for the Juniors' mess: courtesy of Mrs Lumby ... enjoy!'

I don't have a clue who Mrs Lumby is, but she's made a nice, iced cake: my sliver is delicious and I am content with the fact that I've consumed an unexpected piece of Naval history to end what has been a momentous and confusing day. I write a short letter to Mum and Wilco giving them my new postal address. I also send a photograph of *HMS Bermuda* to the blonde from Wakefield.

I am a bit slow in getting my hammock out of the stowage and miss getting myself one of the best slinging points that are traditionally above the mess table. I eventually find myself a space directly above the hatch leading down to the deck below. It takes a while for everybody to sling their hammock correctly and longer for those who have never used a hammock before. I have a large black valve wheel to help me swing up and into mine, which is a bonus. Once settled, I find that there is a lagged pipe labelled FW-H only inches from my face and a vent trunk with a Punkah Louvre that blows cold air directly onto my groin and is stuck in one position by liberally applied coats of paint.

The lights are switched off and my first day onboard *HMS Bermuda* is over. It has been a day chock-full of new experiences. My bedding smells of rank Naval stores. From the glow of a conveniently placed red night-light I read the back of the commissioning pamphlet that gives me the vital statistics of my new home. *HMS Bermuda* is a Fiji Class Cruiser. She displaces 10,450 tons fully loaded. She has Parsons geared turbines and four Admiralty three-drum boilers that can develop 72,500 horsepower and a top speed of 31.5 knots. She has a range of 10,200 miles at 12 knots and can store 1,700 tons of fuel oil. Her armament consists of three triple six-inch turrets and a mass of other smaller guns. Structurally she has a 3½" armour plated hull belt: two-inch-thick deck, turrets and bulkheads. She was built by John Brown of Clydebank Scotland: laid down on 30 November 1939, launched 11 September 1941 and completed 21 August 1942. She is home to 729 crew ... and me!

As soon as we have all stowed our hammocks away the following morning, Tommo places the duty mess roster on the mess table. He identifies the two unfortunate individuals who are 'Cooks-of-the-mess' for today along with the pair who are responsible for washing up mess traps and those in charge of ditching the gash. I'm not on any list. Tug is on gash duty.

Tommo accompanies the two 'Cooks' to the galley while Freckles ensures that all the mess traps are ready for breakfast. Our mess knives, forks, spoons and plates are far from new.

Breakfast is a tray full of hard-boiled cackle berries, some crispy slices of fatty bacon and something yellow and static that, after lengthy examination, Tommo declares to be scrambled egg. I've seen manky galley trays onboard *HMS Petard* but they were nothing compared to the dark-brown encrusted trays now placed before us. The battered edges have obviously clashed with *Bermuda*'s armoured structure many times. Tommo throws a solid white loaf on the table and someone finds a blunt carving knife and hacks off a couple of ragged slices. Breakfast is a hurried affair as Freckles tells us that we have to clear lower deck at 08:30. I hack off a couple of slices of white bread and mash up a couple of cackle berries that I season with large, damp salt crystals. It is surprisingly tasty.

Tommo sprinkles some blue Daz dhobi-dust into buckets of hot water and those on washing-up duty clean the plates and eating utensils, dry them and put them away. Trays are returned to the galley with a warning from Tommo that they may be refused if they aren't considered clean enough. All the uneaten food is scraped into the mess gash bucket and Tug and one other lad, accompanied by Leading Seaman Thomas, are shown where they are to be emptied.

On his return, Tug tells us that 'The main gash bin is on the ferkin' jetty, ferkin' miles away!'

At 08:30 the entire crew of *HMS Bermuda* assembles under the canopy on the jetty to be addressed by the Captain (M G R Lumby, DSO, DSC) who I figure is probably the husband of Mrs Lumby: her who made the delicious iced cake. He describes *Bermuda*'s role as Flagship of the Home Fleet and formally welcomes us onboard. He ends by telling us that we have a difficult 'Work-up' period ahead of us.

Freckles explains to us later in the day that when a ship starts a new commission, particularly when it has a completely new crew, it has to be trained and tested to ensure that all its equipment is working correctly and that every member of the crew knows what their individual duties are. For a ship this size, our 'Work-up' period could take months, during which time we will be deprived of sleep, worked to the limit and beyond. If we thought that Naval life was tough ... that would all change in the weeks and months ahead. I am more than a little apprehensive: all I want to do is see the world – I don't want months of 'tough'. On a more practical note, he explains to us that no other members of the Ship's Company are allowed in the Juniors' mess or our designated bathroom or heads. We are as isolated as is possible on a large warship.

Before dinner, Freckles tells us all to grab a piece of paper and a writing implement and follow him to a large open passage area directly under the boat deck. This is the Canteen Flat, so called because it is where the small Canteen shop is located. One bulkhead is covered in large sheets behind perspex. Freckles explains this is the main Watch & Station Bill that lists every crewmember and his duties. I'm listed on the red side of the sheet, in the second part of Port watch. At sea I will keep Radar Plotting watches in the Operations Room. My 'part-of-ship' is the Quarter-deck, which is where I will work during the day. In addition to standard watch-keeping duties, there are a variety of other roles to be filled: each member of the crew has a number of emergency tasks that are tabulated on the extreme right of the Bill. At sea, my Defence Station is in the Ops Room but during Action Stations I am part of the forward ship's fire-fighting team that assembles in HQ1 ... wherever that is. Thankfully, none of us Juniors are tasked with anything remotely complicated.

'Note your duties down,' instructs Freckles.

Behind us, crew members wait patiently for us to finish taking notes.

Back down the mess Freckles explains to me what HQ1 is. It's where all damage-control activities for the forward part of the ship are co-ordinated.

'Interesting place to be during Action Stations. Interesting place,' he says.

'Thanks PO,' I reply, not one hundred per cent convinced. It sounds like it could be hard work.

'What's my abandon ship station, PO?'

'What did the Station Bill say?'

'Starboard boat deck.'

'Should the ship be in danger of sinking, and you are ordered to abandon ship, you're in a Carley raft.'

'A Carley raft?'

'You're part of a team of Seamen responsible for releasing the starboard side row of Carley rafts, and ensuring that they are thrown over the side and correctly secured in order that those mustered on the boat deck can scramble over the side on nets, into the rafts and get away to safety. Get away to safety.'

'Including me?'

'Including you.'

'Thanks,' I say.

'Any more questions?'

'No, PO. Thanks, PO.' I don't have a clue what a Carley raft is.

Today's dinner is the first hot meal supplied by the main galley. Tommo accompanies the mess 'Cooks' to the galley while the remainder of us sit around the mess table waiting patiently for the food to appear. I am starving.

Eventually the mess 'Cooks' appear, each slowly negotiating the hatch and the mess ladder with two battered and badly bruised trays. I remember *Petard* and how difficult it was to carry trays full of food when the ship had a 'roll' on. The trays are placed at the head of the table. Tommo, who is carrying a fanny full of thick brown gravy, seats himself at the head of the table and issues the distribution instructions. 'Equal shares all round. Eat as much as you can. Only 'Cooks of the mess' are allowed to dish out the contents of the trays.'

One tray contains what I guess is a mound of boiled potatoes alongside a much smaller pile of sliced grey meat edged with thick bands of yellowed fat. To give the tray some badly needed colour the chefs have added a pile of green and yellow vegetables alongside some carrots. The second tray contains something that looks like solid, unmovable rice pudding topped with a couple of curly-edged apple slices.

I am one of those strange individuals who enjoyed 1950s school meals: my epicurean needs have always been simple. To say that my first onboard dinner fills my empty stomach is praise enough. The meat is tepid, stringy and tough: the vegetables are undercooked and the spuds are greasy and cold. Not everybody is as easily satisfied as I am, consequently both mess gash buckets are filled to the brim with unwanted food. The unidentified green-and-yellow vegetable combination goes into one of the gash buckets more or less in its entirety. Apparently the 'duff' is the Chief Petty Officer Chef's favourite and is a mixture of cold sago, tepid rice and tapioca.

Another designated member of the mess is responsible for collecting a large fanny full of hot water for washing up. It takes him half an hour wielding a Pusser's dirk and a paint scraper to clean the galley trays to Tommo's satisfaction. There remain some WWII encrustations that just can't be removed short of shot-blasting. The table is washed and the bucket full of cold and greasy washing-up water ditched in the Juniors' bathroom. Each mealtime involves a certain amount of organisation and the roster is drawn up so that the mealtime duties are distributed fairly. It is also a very effective method of keeping everybody in line: minor messdeck misdemeanours regularly earn you an extra 'Cook-of-the-mess' or 'gash party' duty.

Later that afternoon I flick through the Admiralty Manual of Seamanship until I find something about Carley rafts. There is a section that details the Carley raft's unique propulsion equipment and exactly where the two oars are stowed. At 17, my 'abandon ship station' is just for information: there is never going to be a time when I'll have to scramble over the ship's side and into a Carley raft. *Bermuda* is armour plated – too well-built for anything to happen to her. What I don't realise at the time is that the Carley rafts themselves aren't built to the same indestructible standard.

A number of us ask Freckles if we can go ashore in the evening but he firmly says 'No.'

We slink away. He has given no explanation or reason why we can't. The phrase 'Leave is a privilege lad ... not a right' comes to mind.

That evening we sit around the mess table while Tommo tells us about the difference between harbour routine and sea routine. In harbour, in addition to our daily work, the crew is divided into four watches; the first and second part of Port watch and two parts of Starboard watch. One of these watches is duty each day and as Juniors we are responsible for providing back-up support to the gangway staff, cleaning up after the normal working day finishes and cleaning and reporting the mess 'Ready for rounds, sir' for the Officer of the Day's inspection at 19:30 each evening. In order to improve and broaden our seamanship skills, our upper deck duties are subject to regular change: we will be moved about between the Quarter-deck, Fo'csle and the Top part-of-ship. The Fo'csle, or to give it its full name, Forecastle, is all anchors, chains and capstans and is the place where the real Seamen work. The Quarter-deck is the wooden deck area down aft and onboard the Flagship of the Home Fleet is where all the ceremonial bullshit takes place. The Top part-of-ship is for those who like boats, cranes and davits. Tommo warns us not to be disappointed in the early days if we spend a lot of our time with a tin of bluebell and a rag polishing brass tallies: there are millions of brass tallies onboard *Bermuda*.

I turn in that evening with information buzzing around my head. I spend some time scraping the paint from around the edges of the Punkah Louvre so that I can move it. I almost do it: one more attempt tomorrow should fix it. I sleep soundly with my clasp knife under my pillow.

3

A SPOT OF PILFERING

Next morning, after 'Stand-easy', I muster for the first time on the Quarter-deck with all the other members of the Quarter-deck part-of-ship. We are a mixture of old, middle-aged and young. Petty Officer Gander introduces himself along with a Leading Seaman called Collins. The older lads have already christened them 'Goosie-Goosie' and 'Jumper' respectively.

Petty Officer Gander gives us a brief tour of our part-of-ship. Apparently, because *Bermuda* is the Flagship of the Home Fleet and has a very senior Captain onboard, our wooden-planked Quarter-deck is very different from the Quarter-decks on smaller ships. *Bermuda*'s Wardroom opens directly onto the Quarter-deck that is used as a patio and recreation area for Officers. Consequently it receives extra special treatment. All large, practical fixtures, such as bollards and fairleads, are covered with wooden gratings, smaller fittings are hidden from view by chrome fittings of various shapes that have to be polished daily. The triple six-inch 'Y' turret is on the Quarter-deck and while the other two six-inch turrets forward are regularly washed and painted, 'Y' turret is painted with a super glossy paint and polished daily. The end of each barrel is plugged with a fancy chrome tampon sporting the ship's crest. In addition to the vast wooden expanse of the Quarter-deck itself we also look after a number of cabin 'flats' that include the passageways outside the Captain and Commander's cabins. 'Goosie' assures us that we will quickly become acquainted with the wooden deck as our first scrub-down is scheduled for 15:30 this afternoon.

Goosie is surprised when a couple of tugs arrive. He cranks the handle of the bridge telephone located on the main screen bulkhead.

He listens and slams the phone back in its cradle. 'Get a heaving-line over to that tug, someone.'

The Tannoy crackles into life ...

'DO YOU HEAR THERE ... PREPARE FOR AMMUNITIONING SHIP.

PREPARE FOR AMMUNITIONING SHIP.

IN TEN MINUTES' TIME SMOKING AND NAKED LIGHTS WILL BE BANNED THROUGHOUT THE SHIP.

CLOSE ALL UPPER DECK SCREEN DOORS, SCUTTLES AND DEADLIGHTS.'

Ten minutes for a smoke. Goosie throws his hands in the air as almost everybody lights a cigarette. Even the bloke with the heaving-line lights his cigarette before throwing a perfect line onto the after-deck of the tug.

I play my part in the removal of our berthing wires and ropes. Little do I know at the time, but this is to be the most tiring day of my young life.

The Tannoy crackles ...

'DO YOU HEAR THERE! ... AMMUNITIONING SHIP.

NO SMOKING OR NAKED LIGHTS THROUGHOUT THE SHIP.

I SAY AGAIN ... NO SMOKING OR NAKED LIGHTS THROUGHOUT THE SHIP.

CLOSE ALL UPPER DECK SCREEN DOORS, SCUTTLES AND DEADLIGHTS.

CHIEF GUNNERY INSTRUCTOR REPORT TO THE GUNNERY OFFICER.

GUNNERY OFFICER REPORT TO THE BRIDGE.'

Tow lines are secured and as *Bermuda* is dragged away from South Railway jetty, 30 or so partially smoked cigarettes are tossed over the side. The journey up the harbour takes about an hour: *Bermuda* is a large chunk of metal to manoeuvre. We busy ourselves laying down coir mats and generally preparing everything in accordance with some obscure plan. We connect to a buoy opposite the long wooden ammunition jetty. Lighters, packed to their gunwales with a variety of ammunition and explosives, come alongside. Radial arm davits are rigged and individual working parties organised. Apparently there is no stopping the ammunitioning process once it gets underway. It is scheduled to be completed in one day, and we are told 'It Will Be Completed In One Day No Matter How Long It Takes!'

People in peaked caps scuttle around making encouraging noises and notes on pieces of paper. I am placed on the forward side of a large coir mat. A Petty Officer Gunner tells the 'coir mat team' what is required of us. 'When The Crate Is Landed On The Mat You Will Remove One Shell At A Time And Carry It Over To The Ammunition Hoist.' He points to a hole in the screen bulkhead. He doesn't tell us that each shell weighs 112 lbs.

Crates full of shells are hoisted onboard and land gently on the coir mats. As instructed, we remove the shells one by one and carry them to the mechanical hoist where a technically superior member of the Gunnery Branch pushes a large red button and lowers each shell to the magazine somewhere far below.

After an hour, everything is brought to a sudden halt. We remove the mooring ropes of the lighter and let it drift a short distance away. Someone appears with a fanny full of bright-green lime juice and a couple of tin mugs. I sit on the deck rubbing life back into my under-developed biceps and wait my turn with a mug. We are all issued with a set of chalk-white 'Anti-Flash' gear that consists of a pair of elbow-length gloves and a hood that covers the head and shoulders leaving only a small opening for the eyes. They are impregnated with an irritating dust that smells awful, making a bad job even worse.

'Put Your Hood On Correctly, Lad!'

Then it is back to work. Approximately every hour we are moved around from the upper deck to magazine. The magazine is hot and humid, much worse than being out in the fresh air. There are occasional breaks when we empty one of the ammunition lighters and have to wait for its replacement to arrive. We have a short stop for a sandwich dinner and a then a mid-afternoon mug of lime-juice. The lack of nicotine is stressing many of us: even the supervisory staff are displaying irritable signs of cigarette deprivation.

The 112 lb shells just keep on coming. By teatime even the most burly of our team are flagging. Our teatime sandwiches are Spam and dry bread. A Petty Officer tells us that there are lighters still to be emptied and if we don't finish today we will have to stay on the ammunition jetty overnight. Nobody fancies a cigarette-free night.

We are assured that 'If You Put Your Backs Into It!' we can finish by 19:00. Not many of us have much of a back left.

The last shells are finally stowed in our magazines as the sun casts lengthy shadows from behind the skeletal masts of *HMS Victory*. The mooring lines of our final lighter are released and I slump onto a spare piece of deck. We wait ages for our tugs. Eventually, a fully ammunitioned *Bermuda* is slowly pulled and pushed in to the centre of the harbour.

'DO YOU HEAR THERE! ... SMOKING IS NOW PERMITTED THROUGHOUT THE SHIP! I SAY AGAIN ...'

The striking of matches and the clicking of cigarette lighters is deafening.

'...SMOKING IS NOW PERMITTED THROUGHOUT THE SHIP!'

A series of cigarettes have never tasted so good.

My day is far from finished: I am Duty Watch and my first taste of duty is as Bosun's Mate's Runner from 20:00 to midnight. I miss tea.

Back in the mess, as I sling my hammock, I overhear part of a Tommo explanation about the origins of the term 'fanny'. Apparently it is connected with the brutal murder of a young Hampshire girl called Fanny Adams in the middle of the last century.

I eventually turn in just after midnight and as instructed hang my towel over the clews of my hammock with my name showing so that I can be shaken early in the morning for a Duty Watch muster before breakfast. I don't bother doing any maintenance work on the Punkah Louvre.

The following morning, the duty watch muster on the Boat Deck and we are checked off and allocated duties. I am one of a small band told to skirmish the Fo'csle. Between the four of us we find two dog-ends and some empty beer cans that have been stuffed behind the breakwater.

The rest of the forenoon I spend polishing the brass tallies on the after screen bulkhead. By dinner time the tallies look exactly the same as when I started. Jumper is satisfied with them, though.

That evening Freckles says that we can go ashore if we're not duty. Tug and I arrange to go with a *St Vincent* lad called 'Streaky' Bacon, whose home is just over the other side of the harbour in Gosport. We learn that everybody below the rank of Petty Officer has to go ashore in uniform.

Tommo asks those of us going ashore if we can find some ashtrays for the mess and promises that if we do, we can be excused 'Cook-of-the-mess' for a week. 'Don't steal them, just permanently borrow them. Your Burberry has that convenient inside pocket.'

It sounds like a good deal to me.

At the forward brow, Tug, Streaky and I hand our Station Cards to the Bosun's Mate and suffer the indignity of an inspection by the Officer of the Day.

'Does it forecast rain?' the Officer of the Day asks the Quartermaster.

'Don't think so sir,' he replies.

'So why are you three wearing your Burberrys?' he asks us.

Streaky is quickest. 'Just in case it might rain later, sir.'

The Officer of the Day smiles and waves us away. 'Be good, don't drink and don't forget Juniors' leave expires at 23:00.'

We stroll over the brow and ashore. At the Home Club we are refused a beer so we have a coffee and a game of snooker instead. Tug and Streaky both know the rules of the game: it wasn't a popular Pudsey pastime.

I spot a large blue-glass ashtray in the Home Club's entrance lobby and as we leave I scoop it up, empty it and stuff it inside my uniform jacket in one beautifully co-ordinated movement. I wrap my Burberry tight around me as I negotiate the steps outside. At the bottom I am stopped by a two-man Naval Patrol, both of whom are wearing *HMS Victory* cap tallies and dressed in uniform with white webbing. They both have night-sticks hanging from their belts and a less than sociable approach.

'What you got there lad?'

'What?'

'What you got under your raincoat lad?' says the largest of the two.

'Better not be alcohol,' says his companion. They grin at each other.

'Nothing, sir.' I am confident that the blue ashtray is hidden and well secured inside my jacket and open my raincoat with a flasher-type flourish. There is a crash. I look down to see a mass of shattered blue glass around my feet. There are a few glistening blue shards on the boots of one of the Naval Patrolmen. Streaky and Tug have disappeared. They have adopted the first rule of 'mates ashore': if your run-ashore oppo' gets into trouble with the Naval Patrol, weigh up the possible consequences and leave them to it.

'You *Bermuda* bastards are on an ashtray-collecting run aren't ya?' the largest patrolman asks.

'Not really sir.' I don't know what else to say.

'Fresh out of *Ganges* this one.'

His mate nods.

They march me up the steps and back into the Home Club where they organise me a broom and dustpan and stand over me until I have cleared the pavement and a good length of Queen Street's gutter of glass, dog ends, turds and anything else that there is.

I return onboard ashtray-less. To rub salt into my wound, Tug and Streaky appear half an hour later both having purloined perfectly acceptable Brickwoods ashtrays from the Trafalgar Club near to Aggie Weston's. Tommo promises to take them both off the 'Cooks' roster for a week.

I sling my hammock. Tonight I sleep the sleep of the absolutely and completely knackered. What a day it has been. Once again, no repair work on the Punkah Louvre.

4

SOUTH-SOUTH-WEST OF THE NEEDLES

Sunday is the worst day to be 'Cook-of-the-mess' and it is my turn. I've been onboard for almost a week now and am slowly getting used to the routine. Half an hour before dinnertime, a Junior Steward and I queue outside the galley pantry to collect the trays of Sunday dinner along with a fanny of custard and another full of gravy. *Bermuda* is stable, but descending ladders with both hands occupied is still a less than easy task.

Tommo examines the trays as we lay them at the head of the mess table. During the past week 'Cooks' have been sent back to the Galley for a replacement. This is an impossible task. Chefs who have spent long hours cooking the food under horrible conditions don't take kindly to a snotty-nosed Junior nervously asking for a replacement tray.

It is the most complicated Sunday dinner I have ever had: there are far too many tepid components. The beef is a strange, unnatural colour, but the roast potatoes are fabulously crunchy and warm when smothered in gravy. For pudding we have a crumble-crumble: this is a crumble with no discernible filling.

The poor buggers who have the job of cleaning the remnants of the crunchy roast potatoes spend ages removing what they can from the trays.

Three or four times during the day I am sent to the galley with an empty fanny for boiling water.

'Can I please have some boiling water please, Chef?'

'Piss off!'

'Please, chef.'

'I'm busy. Can't you ferkin' see. Busy! Ferk off!'

'Please, chef.'

'Piss off!'

'Please, chef.'

'Give us your fanny then ... quickly ... give the ferkin' thing here!'

It is the job I hate most.

Later in the evening I have to collect our 'nine-o-clockers' and fresh provisions. I rub shoulders with older crew members.

'What mess?' the miserable duty chef asks.

'Juniors' mess. Starboard side.'

'Anything left of the last issue?'

'No.' Tommo has told me to say that if I am asked.

I'm given a brown paper bag of loose tea, a couple of bags of white sugar and some tins of sardines.

According to Tommo, if we need anything sophisticated, like coffee, we have to buy it ourselves and he will collect money from each of us and buy it from the Canteen. Few of us have yet developed a taste for coffee.

It is nice to snuggle down that night knowing that my 'Cooks' duty is almost over. According to tomorrow's Daily Orders, we are going to sea.

I find a visitor in my hammock on Monday morning: it's about an inch and a half long, scaly brown with long, swaying tentacles. Creepy-crawlies don't bother me, but I don't like sharing my hammock with them, so I scoop it out and toss it down the ladder leading to the deck below.

Bermuda vibrates with excitement and for the first time we hear...

'PREPARE FOR LEAVING HARBOUR.

HANDS FALL IN FOR LEAVING HARBOUR, DRESS NUMBER 2s WITH CAPS AND CHIN STAYS DOWN.

HANDS OUT OF THE RIG OF THE DAY CLEAR OFF THE UPPER DECK.

SPECIAL SEA DUTYMEN TO YOUR STATIONS.

CLOSE ALL UPPER DECK SCREEN DOORS AND SCUTTLES. ASSUME DAMAGE CONTROL STATE 2 CONDITION YANKEE BRAVO.'

Unberthing the ship and connecting *Bermuda* to her tugs is exclusively a Seamen's job. The Quarter-deck Officer is in contact with the bridge via a Junior Seaman, who mans the bulkhead telephone.

'The bridge says single-up sir!' shouts the Junior Seaman on the telephone.

'Single Up!' shouts the Quarter-deck Officer.

Goosie and Jumper yell 'Single up!' at slightly different times.

We reduce the number of ropes and wires connecting us to Portsmouth.

One of the harbour tugs is waiting for a line. I spot an opportunity.

'I can throw a heaving-line, sir,' I say to Goosie.

'Don't call me sir. PO or Petty Officer will do.'

'I can throw a heaving-line, PO.'

'Ex *Ganges* boy eh?'

'Yes ... PO.'

'Go on then.'

I unhook a grubby heaving-line from the guardrail. Goosie stands and watches me while keeping an eye on the tug that is patiently waiting. Then I throw my very first proper heaving-line. It's a perfect throw: my Monkey's Fist flies true and straight into the outstretched gloved hand of one of the tug's crew.

'Get ready to haul in the tow wire,' bellows Goosie. He turns to me. 'Beginners luck, lad!'

We haul the wire in as instructed. Someone else throws a heaving-line to the other tug ... and it falls short.

I am about to volunteer to throw another when an Able Seaman with a couple of stripes on his arm steps forward and, without any apparent effort, tosses a perfect line onto the stern of the second tug.

There is a yell and a clattering of boots as the Royal Marine Band takes up position on 01 deck, forward and above us.

We line up, tallest forward and shortest aft, on both the port and starboard side. Two ABs wait patiently to haul in the only remaining stern line once the order is given.

'Let go aft, sir,' says the Junior manning the telephone.

'Let Go Aft!' repeats the Quarter-deck Officer.

Goosie waves a sweeping arm at the group of Dockyard-mateys who are crowded around a large dockside bollard. They scoop the eye of our final rope up and over the top of the bollard. The ABs pull on the rope before it has the chance to drop in the water.

'Quarter-deck Part-of-ship Atten ... shun!'

We stand ramrod straight while *Bermuda* is towed out into the centre of the harbour as the Royal Marine band plays something military and rousing. We release our tugs. Alongside the Harbour railway station, and on a large round tower structure where the harbour entrance is at its narrowest, people have gathered to wave us farewell. In the distance is Billy Manning's fairground and the sweeping green expanse of Southsea Common.

We are at sea ...

'FALL OUT SPECIAL SEA DUTYMEN.

RETAIN DAMAGE CONTROL STATE 2 CONDITION YANKEE BRAVO.

GASH CAN BE DITCHED IN APPROXIMATELY TWENTY MINUTES' TIME.

HANDS KEEP CLEAR OF ALL UPPER DECK WORKING PARTIES.

MEN UNDER PUNISHMENT MUSTER ON THE BOAT DECK. AFTERNOON WATCHMEN TO DINNER.'

We stow our Quarter-deck finery away.

'Wash down decks this afternoon. Number 8s and gym shoes for those who have them,' says Goosie.

As we are walking forward and the Royal Marine band is being dismissed, the Able Seamen who threw a heaving line taps me on the shoulder. 'Right, lad. I'm Able Seaman Kayne, known throughout this man's Navy as 'Sugar'. I'm the heaving-line thrower for the Quarter-deck part-of-ship. Don't you muscle in on me.'

'OK,' I say, but I don't mean it.

I don't believe that those on the bridge of the Flagship of the Home Fleet would be so childish as to carry out manoeuvres immediately after broadcasting ...

'COOKS TO THE GALLEY.'

But they do.

According to Tug, who is looking out of our mess scuttle, we are opposite Seaview on the Isle of Wight.

At sea, our working routine is different. The working day is divided into seven watches, five of which are four hours long, and two watches two hours long. The Forenoon watch runs from 08:00 until noon, the Afternoon watch from noon until 16:00, First Dog watch 16:00 to 18:00, Last Dog 18:00 to 20:00, First watch 20:00 to midnight, Middle watch is midnight to 04:00 and the Morning watch from 04:00 to 08:00. Most of the crew are split into four watches and you stand your watch one in four: for example after the Afternoon watch your next watch will be the Middle, followed by the First Dog, then the Morning and so on. The best watch is the Last Dog because the next watch you do is the following Forenoon – which means you get an uninterrupted night's sleep. This is known as 'Last Dog and all-night in'. The normal daily working hours are 08:00 until 16:00 with an hour for dinner and a 15-minute 'Stand-easy' in the morning and afternoon. Watches are done over and above your normal Part-of-ship working duties. As Juniors we are not allowed to do the Middle watch. It all sounds confusing but Freckles assures us that we will soon get the hang of it.

Bermuda rolls and we lose a few messdeck plates. Our first seagoing dinner is an untidy affair. *Bermuda*'s movement is very different from *HMS Petard*'s: it is less sharp, more prolonged and sophisticated as befitting the Flagship of the Home Fleet. It will take a while for me to master it.

Down the mess during the afternoon Stand-easy, Freckles explains to us the watch-keeping duties for Radar Plotters, Sonar Operators and Gunners while we are at sea. I am in the Operations Room and my first watch will be the First Dog watch followed by the Morning watch. I double-check the time of the Morning watch ... 04:00 in the ferkin' morning!

Tommo shows me where the Operations Room is. It is up a bewildering number of ladders, located a deck below and aft of the bridge.

The hatch and the ladder below our mess leads to the Wheelhouse. I can clearly hear the commands coming from the bridge, the responses of the wheelhouse crew and the bells and whistles associated with steering an armour-plated Battle Cruiser.

I spend an interesting hour polishing the brass tallies on the outside of 'Y' Turret this afternoon. As it is the showpiece of *Bermuda*'s Quarter-deck, we are told to report any blemishes or stains to Jumper. I don't want to find any, so I don't.

At 14:45 Goosie assembles all the Quarter-deck team aft of 'Y' turret and tells us that as from today the final task of each day will be scrubbing down our wooden deck. *Bermuda*'s standing orders require the Quarter-deck to be scrubbed at least twice each day, weather permitting. As from tomorrow it is to be scrubbed before breakfast each morning by the Juniors Division and Men under Punishment. At 15:00 each working day it will be scrubbed by those who work on the Quarter-deck. Goosie suggests that we change into our plimsolls and we are sent away to get them. Some of the older lads don't bother and choose to scrub down in bare feet.

I run halfway down the Burma Road before I realise what I am doing and slow to a more sensible shuffle. It is illegal to run or whistle onboard Royal Naval ships and appearing to be enthusiastic about anything is frowned upon by most of the crew.

Back on the Quarter-deck I am allocated my scrub-down

task. 'Grab a broom and join them,' instructs Goosie, pointing to a line of people leaning expectantly on stiff brooms.

I collect a wide-headed stiff broom from a wash-deck locker and roll up the legs of my trousers. The elite Hose-Party rig hoses to the fire hydrants and 'crack' them open to spew freezing cold salt water over the deck. A specialist team of elderly ABs pour Teepol over the deck. We 'Scrubbers' form a line and slowly work our way forward wielding our brooms. My plimsolls offer absolutely no protection at all from the cold fire-main water. Within minutes my legs and feet are frozen. Behind us, a couple of ABs hose the dirty sudsy water into the scuppers.

As we reach the forward part of the deck the fire hydrants are closed and we exchange our brooms for squeegees. In a line, we squeegee from forward to aft, pushing the surface water over the side. A 'Mopping-Party', armed with mops and buckets, follow us drying the inevitable puddles and any water trapped in the scuppers. I squeeze water from my trousers. The 'Drying-Party' wipe any splashes from the bulkhead and 'Y' turret.

I waddle back to the mess, my footwear leaving wet marks all along the Burma Road. In the mess I wrap my soaking wet plimsolls and socks in a towel and put them on the top of the warm FW-H pipe that runs above my hammock-slinging point. Whether they will dry, I don't know.

'Pete, you've got the first dog haven't ya?' asks Tug.

'Oh shit!'

In my haste I take a wrong turn or the wrong ladder and get lost. Fortunately I bump into a Killick with a spider's web badge on his arm.

'Can you tell me where the Operations Room is please, Hooky?'

'Follow me.'

I'd taken the wrong ladder.

Outside the door marked 'Operations Room. No Unauthorised Entry', the Killick points to a set of letters and numbers on the bulkhead. 'Have you been shown what a ship's location marking means?'

'Not really, Hooky.'

'Who's the Killick of your mess?'

'Juniors' mess. Leading Seaman Thomas.'

'Ask him to explain it to you.'

'Thanks – will do.'

'Thank you what?'

'Err. Thank you, Hooky.'

'That's better.'

We both enter the Ops Room together, a small dark humming compartment lit by shielded ultraviolet lights. The brass clock on the wall shows one minute to four. Against the inboard bulkhead is a cabinet and behind a glass-panelled door glows a serious-looking valve.

'First time in the Ops Room?' asks the Killick.

'Yes. I did the course at *HMS Dryad* but ...'

'You're pretty ferkin' useless then ... and you've seen nothing like this, eh?'

'Nothing like this, no.'

'Right then. My name is Leading Seaman Lee and I'm the Senior RP of the watch. I have a team of three ... four with you. Our job is to plot all surface activity and keep the bridge informed of what is going on around us. One person is seated at the PPI ... you know what a PPI is don't you?'

'Err ... a Plot Position Indicator.'

'Correct. There speaks a lad fresh from *Dryad*. One person will sit at the PPI reporting the position, distance and bearing of every surface contact to the team of plotters at the table. You've used a plotting table before haven't you?'

I have, so I say a confident 'Yes.'

'I'm responsible for communicating directly with the bridge. Plonk yourself on the back side of the table, grab yourself a chinagraph pencil and let's see what kind of a plotter you are.'

I squeeze myself round the back of the table. It is the same as those we had used at *Dryad*: it has a glass top and a compass rose is projected from underneath. The centre of the compass rose is *Bermuda*'s actual position as it is connected in some way to the ship's compass. When a contact is reported by the bloke sitting at the PPI, it is plotted on the glass tabletop with a fluorescent chinagraph pencil that shows up bright blue under the ultraviolet light. Each contact is given an alphabetic letter and classified as a 'Bogey', a possible enemy, until visually identified otherwise. Because I am on the opposite side of the table to Leading Seaman Lee, I have to write everything upside down. I find that to be surprisingly simple.

It isn't a difficult business, this plotting of surface contacts, but it is relentless: Leading Seaman Lee is a nice bloke and keeps us amused and entertained for the following two hours, as well as keeping the bridge informed of the many 'Bogeys' that surround us. I don't have a clue exactly where we are. I ask Leading Seaman Lee, who politely asks the bloke on the bridge. The answer comes back that we are 24 nautical miles south-south-west of the Needles lighthouse on the Isle of Wight.

Before our watch finishes I have to write down exactly where my hammock is located and Leading Seaman Lee suggests that I hang something on my hammock with my name on it so that I can be found easily.

Bermuda begins a series of unbalancing manoeuvres as I make my way back to the mess ... having once again taken a number of wrong ladders.

Down the mess everybody is tucking into something yellow and brown from a battered tray.

'Cheese Ush!' explains an animated Tug.

'Great!' With a nod of agreement from Tommo, I serve myself a plateful. It tastes OK – even cold Cheese Ush is brilliant.

After tea it is time to clean the mess for evening rounds. Every Messdeck on the ship is inspected to ensure that it is clean and tidy after the evening meal and that everybody is dressed correctly. Normally Freckles inspects our mess. Occasionally an Officer comes down. Number 8s are worn during the working day, but as from 18:45 it is expected that everybody not on duty has showered and changed into night clothing: blue serge uniform trousers and a white front.

As I sling my hammock, Tommo suggests that I hang my

towel over the clews: it has my name on it. I am due a shake at about 03:45 for the morning watch and I don't sleep that well. The constant noise from the wheelhouse below doesn't help matters: neither does the regular coming and going of people up and down the ladder, all of whom shoulder my hammock.

I am wide awake by the time someone shines a torch light in my face and gives my shoulder a thump. 'Morning watch, it's 03:45. Get your feet on the ferkin' deck ... come on ... out of your smelly pit. Get your ferkin' feet on the ferkin' deck now!'

You can't resist such an invitation, can you? Others are crawling out of their hammocks, coughing, spluttering and trying desperately not to disturb their still-sleeping messmates.

'Ferkin' morning watchmen!' is heard more than once.

I only take one wrong turning and eventually make it to the Ops Room all by myself. During the next three and a half hours I move from the plotting table to the uncomfortable brown swivel chair that is screwed to the deck in front of the PPI. Leading Seaman Lee is in talkative mood and there aren't many 'Bogeys' for us to worry about. He tells those of us who haven't been to the Far East all about the opportunities that Hong Kong or Singapore has to offer. He also spends some considerable time telling us about a place called 'The Gut' in Malta, taking us on a detailed tour from the bottom of The Gut to the 'Greasy Spoon' at the top. It sounds a frightening place. In particular, I don't like the sound of the Bing Crosby Bar.

From 07:00 onwards we all take it in turns to return to the mess to stow our hammock away and to get some breakfast. I grab a couple of sausages and a slice of greasy bacon, wrap them in a couple of slices of limp white bread and eat them on the way back to the Ops Room.

'Do we start work at 08:00 with everybody else?' I ask Leading Seaman Lee.

'No. Morning watchmen have an hour to get a wash and shave ... you don't shave, do you?'

'Yeah! Almost every day now,' I bluff.

'You start work at 09:00. Just tell your part-of-ship PO or Leading hand that you've had the morning watch. Morning watchmen are normally mess cleaners until the morning Stand-easy.

While Leading Seaman Lee goes for his breakfast, one of the older Radar Plotters tells me that Leading Seaman Lee's nickname is 'Tansy'.

As our reliefs began to arrive, Tansy asks the bridge where we are.

There is a lengthy pause before a cultured voice says 'Approximately 10 nautical miles south of Bournemouth Dorset and four miles west of the Admiralty measured mile.'

Down the mess there are only a few morning watchmen.

'What's a measured mile?'

'I don't ferkin' know.'

On the Quarter-deck I have to wash and dry the screen bulkhead from the starboard side round to the port side. At first glance it is a monstrous job ... and so it proves. I dull all the brass tallies I cleaned only a few days ago.

The ship exercises something called a Gyro failure this forenoon which has people wearing overalls, trudging across our wooden deck in dirty shoes. By 11:30 the exercise is complete and those who have dirtied our deck just drift away.

Goosie tells us: 'Stop Whatever You're Doing, Roll Your Trousers Up, Grab Stiff Brooms And Wash These Marks Off Our Deck.'

So we do. It isn't a full wash-down but we remove the oily marks with a liberal application of Teepol and elbow grease.

'COOKS TO THE GALLEY.

WE WILL SHORTLY COMMENCE THE FIRST OF OUR MEASURED MILE RUNS.

CLOSE ALL UPPER DECK SCUTTLES AND SCREEN DOORS.

SHIP'S COMPANY ARE NOT TO USE THE UPPER DECK UNLESS INSTRUCTED TO DO SO.

NO GASH IS TO BE DITCHED.

THE FIRST MEASURED MILE RUN WILL BE AGAINST THE WEATHER AND WILL COMMENCE IN LESS THAN FIVE MINUTES TIME.

COOKS TO THE GALLEY.

THE PADRE IS REQUESTED TO REPORT TO THE CHAPEL WHERE A VISITOR IS WAITING.'

'This could be fun,' says Tommo. 'Make sure all the locker doors are closed correctly and anything that is loafing is stowed away. This old bastard is going to rattle like a badly stowed cutlery tray.'

We all rush our dinner. 'What's a measured mile then?' someone asks Tommo as he returns smelling of rum. Mac and Tommo have their daily tot inside the Juniors' office behind closed doors.

'Every ship that's been in refit, or had some work done on its engines and things, always does a fast run along a measured mile course to see that everything is working correctly. It's also a bit of a competition to see who's the fastest. At the moment *HMS Manxman* holds the speed record at about 40 knots.'

'How many measured mile runs will we do then?' I ask.

'Loads. Until the Stokers start dropping dead probably.'

'If we're not allowed on the upper deck, what will we do for work this afternoon?'

'Probably cleaning flats: the internal passageways. They're called passageways everywhere else on the ship but down aft near the Wardroom they're called 'flats' because that's what the Officers like to call them.'

For the next couple of hours, *Bermuda* vibrates herself to bits.

'DO YOU HEAR THERE ... OUR MEASURED MILE RUNS ARE NOW COMPLETE.

THE UPPER DECK IS NO LONGER OUT OF BOUNDS FOR

WORK APPROVED ACTIVITIES ONLY.
GASH CAN NOW BE DITCHED.'

Whoopee!

'DO YOU HEAR THERE ... INITIAL CALCULATIONS INDICATE THAT *BERMUDA* HAS ACHIEVED AN AVERAGE SPEED OF 31.5 KNOTS WITH A FOLLOWING WIND.
AN IMPRESSIVE SPEED FOR SUCH AN ELDERLY LADY.'

Another whoopee!

Down the mess Freckles calls us all together: 'In Her Majesty's Royal Navy gambling in any form is strictly forbidden.' There is a groan from somewhere.

'Who groaned?' Freckles scans the faces but nobody owns up. 'In Her Majesty's Royal Navy gambling in any form is strictly forbidden. There is however one important exception ... Tombola.' He turns to Tommo. 'Tell them all about Tombola, Leading Seaman Thomas.'

Tommo, taken a little by surprise, shakes himself, gets to his feet and coughs twice. 'Tombola is a method of raising money for ships' charities throughout the Royal Navy. Individual crew members ... including Juniors ... can buy Tombola tickets for a shilling each. Each ticket contains a series of random numbers between 1 and 99. Each day somewhere on Daily Orders there will be six Tombola numbers ...'

'A good way of making sure that you read Daily Orders,' Freckles interrupts.

'If any of the numbers coincide with any on your ticket you tick them off. The first person to tick all the numbers on one line will win a percentage of the Tombola pot, as will the person who is the first to tick-off all the numbers on his ticket.'

'How much can we win then, Hooky?' someone from the back asks.

'Could be as much as five pounds for ticking all the numbers on one ticket,' says Freckles.

'And a couple of quid for a completed line,' adds Tommo.

'Tickets are now available from my office: a bob each, maximum purchase five tickets.'

'What is the ship's charity, PO?'

'Orphanage in Portsmouth I think,' says Freckles.

I buy a couple of Tombola tickets. That leaves me with about three bob to my name.

That evening, Tommo initiates us into the delights of Uckers. Uckers is played on a standard Ludo board with counters of different colours and two dice. The object of the game is the same as Ludo. What is different, is the way it is achieved: terms like 'Mixi Blob', 'Blow Back' and 'Suck Back' are explained. By the time we turn in, a number of competitive games have been played. Tommo and Mac have only narrowly beaten Tug and I by a couple of counters on the last game of the evening. Tug and I are convinced that they are frightened of being beaten if they have to play us again. I don't know how Tug does it but he can throw more sixes than anyone else: using the same dice.

I am about to sling my hammock – I've been up since 03:45 – when ...

'MAN OVERBOARD!

MAN OVERBOARD!

AWAY EMERGENCY SEABOAT'S CREW.

WATCH ON DECK MUSTER PORT SIDE OF THE BOAT DECK.

CLEAR LOWER DECK OF OFF-WATCH SEAMEN, MUSTER ON THE STARBOARD SIDE OF THE BOAT DECK!

MAN OVERBOARD

MAN OVERBOARD!

THIS IS NOT AN EXERCISE.

I REPEAT THIS IS NOT AN EXERCISE!'

Freckles comes flying out of his cabin. 'Everybody Up Onto The Boat Deck! Doesn't Matter What You're Wearing ... Drop Everything And Get Up There. MOVE!'

We drop everything and scamper up the ladder following the

rush of Seamen who know the quickest way to the boat deck. By the time we are up-top the seaboat davits are already winched out, gripes removed, the boat's crew onboard and the boat's falls ranged out along the starboard waste. It isn't just raining, it is pissing it down.

'Man The Boat's Falls!' yells someone and we are waved towards the rope falls. We grab ropes.

'Take The Weight!'

We lean back.

'Pay Out Handsomely!'

We pay out slowly until the weight is off the falls.

The seaboat is slipped.

'Marry The Falls And Hoist To Deck Level!'

We walk the falls until we are told to stop and stand there staring out into pitch darkness. *Bermuda* is wallowing. Powerful, diagonal rain is soaking us, particularly those of us who are wearing only our number 8s. My feet are freezing, I only have my damp plimsolls on ... no socks.

'Don't Lean On My Guardrails!' someone yells.

Eventually the seaboat comes alongside and we lower the boat's falls.

'Marry The Falls!'

We hold both ropes together as the boats crew clip on.

'Two Six Heave. Walk It! Walk It! Stamp Those Feet! Keep It Moving! There Is An Injured Man In This Boat! Walk It! Walk It! Put Your Backs Into It! Walk It! Stamp Those Feet!'

Slowly the boat comes up.

'Handsomely! Handsomely!'

We slow to a crawl.

'Belay Hoisting!'

We stop.

We can see that the boat is at deck level; we hold the weight until all the crew disembark. The injured man is tossed onto the deck: it is a dummy dressed in dark blue foul-weather clothing with a faded yellow lifejacket draped over his shoulders. We hoist the boat to the davit head and it is secured. We let the falls drop and the Watch on Deck stows them away correctly.

Back in the mess someone asks about the dummy.

'Don't believe everything you hear from the bridge,' says Tommo. 'We're into a 'Work Up' period. They'll try every trick in the book to bugger us up.'

I sling my hammock. I string my plimsolls over the clews at the bottom of my hammock. There is a warm breeze coming up from the wheelhouse.

Over a microphone from below our deck comes the command 'Port Thirty!'

A clear-voiced replies: 'Port thirty. Thirty of port wheel on, sir.'

Our hammocks swing together as *Bermuda* heels over.

'Very good ... ease to ten.'

'Ease to ten. Ten of port wheel on, sir.'

Our hammocks swing back.

'Very good ... midships ... steer two six zero.'

'Midships, steer two six zero, sir.'

All hammocks return to their normal position.

'Course two six zero, sir.'

'Very good.'

From the glow of the red night-light I see the head and tentacles of another of those brown things looking at me over the lip of a flange on the warm FW-H pipe.

I have started sleeping with my Seamanship Manual: it gives my floppy pillow some support. I rifle through one of the sections on ships' services and I reckon that the FW-H pipe contains hot fresh water.

I spot a second pair of waving tentacles. Then I fall asleep.

The mess lights are switched on at 05:35 by the duty Petty Officer. It is my first experience of the early-morning Quarter-deck scrub-down. All Juniors, irrespective of branch, are rolled, prodded, pushed and dragged from their hammocks.

'Muster On The Quarter-deck At 06:00,' yells the duty Petty Officer. 'Officer Of The Day's Defaulters For Anybody Who Is Adrift. You've Got Exactly 22 Minutes.'

I grab my damp plimsolls. The grandfather of all tentacle-waving brown things has taken up residence inside one of them. I toss him down the hatch into the wheelhouse. There is no time to lash my hammock or have a wash, so along with the rest of the mess I shuffle down the Burma Road to the Quarter-deck where a small group of Men under Punishment are lounging on the lee side of 'Y' turret. On the weather side are bunched a small number of my messmates. Junior Cooks, Stewards, Communicators, Electricians and Stokers blinking in the unfamiliar morning light and inhaling lungfuls of early morning air.

The morning scrub-down proves to be a much less organised affair than our afternoon scrub. A Killick under punishment takes charge of us as we wield brooms with a distinct lack of enthusiasm. I arm myself with a squeegee and dry the deck behind those who are scrubbing. Within 30 minutes it is all over. I look around: if Goosie could see the state of the place he'd have a heart attack. There are puddles and splashes everywhere and no Teepol has been used.

I notice the familiar outline of Portland Bill on the horizon as we stow our gear away and point it out to one of the other Juniors.

He totally ignores me. I am only trying to be helpful. It doesn't seem that long ago that I had been here onboard *HMS Petard*.

No sooner have I finished my breakfast than the Tannoy crackles into life for the first time today ...

'HANDS FALL IN FOR ENTERING HARBOUR.

CLOSE UP SPECIAL SEA DUTYMEN.

CLOSE ALL SCUTTLES AND UPPER DECK SCREEN DOORS.

HANDS OUT OF THE RIG OF THE DAY CLEAR OFF THE UPPER DECK!'

On the Quarter-deck, Goosie has us 'Fallen-in' in a straight line. We put the chin-stays of our caps down as, according to Jumper, it is officially 'Blowing a bastard'. Goosie strolls up and down the deck shaking his head at all the puddles and splashes.

We pass the humped-back outline of the Island and manoeuvre our self in preparation to berth on Portland Harbour's wooden jetty with our bows pointing out to sea. There are no dockyard-mateys to help berth us. *Bermuda* wallows as near to the jetty as possible while a group of lads are hoisted in a basket by the boat-deck crane and lowered onto the jetty. An unexpected gust of wind catches us, our bows clatter the edge of the jetty and a large electrical distribution box explodes like a gigantic firework. The lads in the still-swinging basket are silhouetted against a backdrop of golden yellow sparks.

The basket bounces onto the jetty and the shell-shocked occupants climb out and scamper away from the still-exploding distribution box.

An AB who reckons he can throw a heaving-line misses the jetty that is only ten feet or so distant. I toss a casual Monkey's Fist towards one of the guys waiting for a rope and he catches it with a hooked arm.

Goosie taps me on the shoulder. 'Well done, lad.'

Once berthed, we rig a brow and a number of high-ranking visitors troop onboard.

I don't know if it is an exercise in berthing alongside an ancient wooden jetty without the help of dockyard-mateys, or if it is a quick visit to take onboard high-ranking visitors. Whatever the reason, we aren't alongside for long ...

'COOKS TO THE GALLEY.

BOTH WATCHES OF SEAMEN TO MUSTER.

PREPARE FOR SEA.

CLOSE ALL SCUTTLES AND UPPER DECK SCREEN DOORS.

HANDS OUT OF THE RIG OF THE DAY CLEAR OFF THE UPPER DECK.

SPECIAL SEA DUTYMEN REMAIN CLOSED UP.

WILL THE PADRE MAKE HIS WHEREABOUTS KNOWN.'

During our dinner hour, *Bermuda* performs a series of high-speed manoeuvres within Weymouth Bay. We lose one more messdeck plate.

'MAIN ARMAMENT TO ACTION STATIONS.

ASSUME DAMAGE CONTROL STATE 1 CONDITION ZULU ALPHA.

ASSUME DAMAGE CONTROL STATE 1 CONDITION ZULU ALPHA.

THE PADRE IS REQUESTED TO REPORT TO THE BRIDGE.'

The guns crews are closed up at Action Stations: dressed in full anti-flash gear to practise anti-aircraft tracking. While the gunners are tracking all sorts of invisible objects, the rest of the seaman branch launch the whaler along with a Dan buoy and spend hours performing ship- and boat-handling exercises with the Destroyer *HMS Diamond* and the Frigate *HMS Eastbourne*. None of us on the Quarter-deck understand exactly what we are doing: we just muster wherever required and do whatever we are told to do. I am getting good at mustering and finding my way around *Bermuda*'s complicated upper decks.

We anchor in Weymouth Bay as it is getting dark. Portland dockyard has no electricity and is blacked out. After a tidy-up of the Quarter-deck and a quick wash down we all slope off to our respective messes. In the Juniors' mess there is the cold remains of some cheesy-hammy-eggy.

Tommo is coming down the ladder as I am waiting to go up. I point to the FW-H pipe: 'What is it that the pipes are covered with, Hooky?'

'Asbestos.'

'I found a long brown thing with long tentacles in my hammock a few days ago ... and I've seen a couple of them, walking along that pipe.'

'Cockies.'

'Wha?'

'Cockies ... cockroaches.'

'Heck.'

'How long was it?'

'Inch and a half easy.' I exaggerate a little.

'Small one then.'

'Small one?'

'Youngster. Ship's crawling with 'em. They come onboard with the stores. Ship as old as *Bermadoo* will have millions of 'em ... everywhere.'

'Really?'

'If you ever find something crunchy in the gravy it'll be a young, adventurous cocky who's found his way into the urn to keep itself warm. They won't bother you though ... if you leave them alone.'

'But one of them was in my hammock.'

'Male or female?'

'I don't ferkin' know ... Hooky.'

It is the first time I have heard anyone refer to *Bermuda* as *Bermadoo*.

That night I imagine I see another pair of waving tentacles on the FW-H pipe before I wrap my blanket tightly around me and eventually fall asleep.

Thursday morning's scrub-down is a little better than Wednesday's as the Duty Petty Officer is a bit more organised. One of the Men under Punishment almost kicks one of the gratings over the side and we enjoy listening to the bollocking he receives.

When both watches muster at 08:00 we can see in the murky distance the impressive hulk of something large and flat. Sugar says it is an Aircraft Carrier.

We weigh anchor and once again ...

'MAIN ARMAMENT TO ACTION STATIONS.

ASSUME DAMAGE CONTROL STATE 1 CONDITION ZULU ALPHA.

ASSUME DAMAGE CONTROL STATE 1 CONDITION ZULU ALPHA.'

According to Daily Orders we are on our way to calibrate and test our four-inch weapons.

'DO YOU HEAR THERE ... FRESH WATER WILL BE RATIONED AS FOLLOWS.

BATHROOMS FORWARD OF SECTION GOLF WILL HAVE FRESH WATER UNTIL 12:15.

FURTHER DETAILS WILL BE BROADCAST IN DUE COURSE.'

It is my first experience of water rationing. Our bathroom is forward of section Golf so we won't have fresh water after 12:15 ... apparently.

HMS Eastbourne makes a couple of passes close down our starboard side as we steam into Weymouth Bay. Whoever throws *Eastbourne*'s first heaving-line is good and I watch as all the classroom theory about jackstay transfers is played out before me. I perch on a wash-deck locker and watch. Once everything is rigged we spend half an hour transferring a large concrete sinker back and forth between us. Once the concrete block is satisfied with our performance, we disconnect and *Eastbourne* swerves gracefully away.

Just before dinner we get paid. Freckles talks us through the routine. We muster aft of the Forward Capstan flat wearing our cap and, in no particular order, queue up along with the rest of the ship's company. On reaching the pay table we salute smartly, give our name and ship's book number and hold out our left hand showing our ID card. We are then handed money. Men in peaked caps patrol the pay queue looking for things to criticise. In front of me, a bloke is sent away because he is wearing overalls: apparently you can't be paid wearing overalls. It is the first time

I've seen the Master-at-Arms: he is a large barrel-chested man with a hooked nose, long bedraggled eyebrows and a ruddy red complexion. He's carrying one of those intimidating wooden sticks. I survive my first pay parade without incident. Back in the mess I count what Her Majesty considers I am worth for two weeks' hard graft: six pounds two shillings and nine pence.

The Ops Room watch is stood down as *Bermuda* secures herself to a buoy after the afternoon Stand-easy. The radar is switched off and lookouts are posted as an unexpected fog bank envelopes us. A bell is rigged up forward and Streaky gets the job of ringing it every two minutes.

'ASSUME DAMAGE CONTROL STATE 2 CONDITION YANKEE. ASSUME DAMAGE CONTROL STATE 2 CONDITION YANKEE.'

Back down the mess the lads who work on the Fo'csle complain about the complexities of securing to a buoy for the first time. The afternoon wash-down is more unpleasant than normal because the fog is clammy and cold and we can't see from one side of the Quarter-deck to the other.

At 16:00 we hear ...

'CLEAR LOWER DECK. HANDS MUSTER ON THE BOAT DECK WITH CAPS!'

Tommo explains that if we are told to muster with caps then it is to witness the reading of a Punishment Warrant. If the punishment is imprisonment or dismissal from the service this is normally read out in front of the entire ship's company. '*Bermuda* has more Punishment Warrants than the rest of the Home Fleet put together,' explains Tommo.

We line up on the boat deck. The offender stands facing us flanked by two members of the Regulating branch. The Juniors' Division are at the back so I don't hear the details of the offence read out by the Captain. We are told to remove our caps before the sentence is read out. I don't hear that either.

Back down the mess Tommo, who was near the front when the Warrant was read out, tells us that it isn't the first time that particular Able Seaman has been charged with theft. He has been sentenced to 90 days in the Royal Naval Detention Quarters in Gosport and dismissed the service. Apparently *Bermuda* has some prison cells in the bilges and he is being held there until it is convenient for him to be taken ashore.

'MAIN ARMAMENT TO ACTION STATIONS.
ASSUME DAMAGE CONTROL STATE 1 CONDITION ZULU ALPHA.'

We have water from 18:00 until 19:30, when our bathroom is locked again.

'You'll just have to go dirty for a while,' Freckles tells those who haven't showered.

As we are settling ourselves down for a Tommo lesson in the complexities of a card game called Crib ...

'CLEAR LOWER DECK OF ALL SEAMEN, RIG BOTTOM LINES.'

'What are ferkin' bottom lines?' asks someone.

'Get up top and you'll find out,' says Tommo as he pulls on his seaboots.

It is dark and all the upper deck lights have been switched off as Goosie divides us into small groups by torchlight. The rain has dispersed the fog. We work with divers and the whaler's crew to slide wires under the waterline so that our small complement of divers can carry out a search of *Bermuda*'s underwater hull. Of course we stay on the upper deck until the search is completed.

The non-Seaman members of the mess are asleep in their swinging hammocks by the time we return to the mess. We are soaking wet and covered in grease and gunge from the wires. Our bathroom is still locked. Tommo arrives with a fanny full of tepid, soapy water taken from the main galley and we all take it in turns to wash our hands. We make a lot of unnecessary noise as we rig our hammocks.

I am temporarily promoted this morning: instead of wielding a broom or a squeegee, I am on the end of a hose. Squirting water is better than scrubbing but my nozzle leaks badly and I am soaked from the waist down by the time I've finished.

Thankfully we have water in the Juniors' bathroom this morning. Following our 08:00 muster we remove all the portable gratings and lay our guardrails flat on the deck in preparation for a helicopter transfer.

Within minutes of us clearing everything a dark blue helicopter appears. We are ushered up to 01 deck while a mob of people stomp onto our recently scrubbed deck and stand against the screen bulkhead. A side door in the body of the hovering helicopter opens and a man wearing a crash helmet and a bright red lifejacket is winched down onto the Quarter-deck. As the bloke's feet hit our deck a couple of the welcoming party unclip him, remove his crash helmet and escort him towards the aft screen door. A number of Officers salute him as he passes. This is no ordinary visitor.

Apparently the bloke from the helicopter is the Flag Officer Sea Training (FOST) himself – an Admiral and the reason we've been doing all these exercises.

Putting the guardrails back up is a dangerous enough job without the comedians on the bridge thinking it is a good time to do some high speed zigzagging. Even Goosie remarks that we are probably showing off for the benefit of FOST.

'DO YOU HEAR THERE, WE SHALL COMMENCE SEA HANDLING MANOEUVRES SHORTLY.

SECURE ALL PARTS OF SHIP.

STOW AWAY ALL LOOSE EQUIPMENT.

NO GASH IS TO BE DITCHED UNTIL FURTHER NOTICE.

FRESH WATER RESTRICTIONS REMAIN IN FORCE.'

We spend time in the mess making sure that everything that can move is stowed away and lashed securely. I am posted as sentry on the gash chute located forward of the wooden deck. Fortunately nobody comes up to ditch gash.

Apparently our sea-handling manoeuvres are impressive. We skid, slew and slip all over the place: the 'Cooks' have a particularly difficult dinner-time. We leave the cleaning up after dinner to the none-seamen of the mess, as we are called to muster on the Quarter-deck for yet another helicopter transfer.

We mentally wave a two-finger farewell to FOST. Unfortunately our manoeuvres have used up so much of our fuel that we urgently need to replenish. I wonder whether the actual business of refuelling at sea will be as complicated as it appeared in the *Ganges* classroom.

Surprisingly, the whole refuelling process is much simpler in practice than in theory. A wire is strung between *Bermuda* and *RFA Black Ranger* and lengths of flexible fuel hose attached to the wire. The hose sections are connected to each other, one end is connected to *Bermuda*'s inlet, the other to the *RFA*'s outlet pump and the fuel is transferred.

We seamen lounge around just in case we have to pull or adjust something. Eventually the ship is fully fuelled. Hoses are pulled onboard and the Stokers department stow all the fuel transfer equipment in the upper deck storage racks.

RFA Black Ranger sounds a farewell salute on her horn and slews away.

'DO YOU HEAR THERE ... FRESH WATER WILL BE RATIONED AS FOLLOWS.

BATHROOMS FORWARD OF SECTION CHARLIE AND AFT OF SECTION UNIFORM ONLY WILL HAVE FRESH WATER UNTIL 12:45.

THE SHIPS COMPANY ARE REMINDED THAT THE JUNIORS BATHROOM IS STRICTLY OUT OF BOUNDS.

CHIEF SHIPWRIGHT REPORT TO THE BRIDGE.'

Brilliant! Our bathroom has no water anyway. *Bermuda* makes her sedate way back towards Portland ...

'COOKS TO THE GALLEY.

PREPARE FOR ENTERING HARBOUR.

CLOSE UP SPECIAL SEA DUTYMEN.

CLOSE ALL SCUTTLES AND UPPER DECK SCREEN DOORS.

HANDS OUT OF THE RIG OF THE DAY CLEAR OFF THE UPPER DECK.'

We are mustered on the upper deck as *Bermuda* slinks past the wooden jetty that she damaged a few days ago. A group of men are standing looking at the remains of the electrical junction box and two boats full of men are busying themselves underneath the jetty.

Once again, we use a boat launching crane to put a couple of lads onto the coaling jetty, a concrete structure separate to the wooden jetty. It seems, we have been banned from the wooden jetty.

Mail comes onboard. The letter from the Wakefield girl is surprisingly sloppy. I also receive a letter from Wilco. Everything at *Dryad* remains unchanged. She has been issued with a brand new overall and given her very own plastic name tag.

'ALL WATER RATIONING RESTRICTIONS ARE LIFTED.

CHIEF SHIPWRIGHT REPORT TO THE ENGINEERING OFFICER.

THE SHIP'S COMPANY ARE REMINDED THAT THE JUNIORS' BATHROOM IS STRICTLY OUT OF BOUNDS.'

There is nothing of tea left in the mess. Tommo accompanies those of us who have been working to the galley and organises a tray of warm pies for us. Apparently the galley sometimes has food available for those who miss normal meals. The pies are delicious. Tommo explains they are officially known as Cornish pasties, but known throughout the Navy as Oggies. I become an immediate Oggie fan.

I am convinced that life onboard *Bermuda* is one continual programme of exercises and jobs to do. So, I am surprised to learn that we are staying put for the whole weekend. There is leave for one part of the Starboard watch tonight, both parts of the Port watch on Saturday and the other part of Starboard watch on Sunday. No weekend leave is granted unless you can prove that you live within ten nautical miles of Portland Dockyard and find someone to do your duty for you. A number of the lads in the mess get changed into their best uniform and are going ashore to experience whatever delights Portland has to offer. Those of us in the Port watch are a bit disappointed that we have to wait until tomorrow. Mac tells us that Portland has little to offer. 'There's only a handful of pubs within staggering distance, none of which will serve you. There's a greasy-spoon at the top of the main drag, but I wouldn't let my mother-in-law eat there.'

Secure in the knowledge that I'm not missing much, I shower and settle down to a game of Uckers. Tug and I team up against our arch rivals, Tommo and Mac.

I take a break from a losing game at 21:00 and go down the galley to collect the mess 'nine-o-clockers'. They are the same as most nights: sardines-in, a tin of canned cow and a loaf of white bread.

My antenna-waving companions on the FW-H pipe look disturbed. I am formulating a plan to divert them away from the pipe ... and they sense it.

The following morning we are allocated our Saturday morning messdeck cleaning tasks. It is my job this morning to remove all the hammocks from the hammock stowage rack and re-stow them vertically. Those that are lashed up the best are to be placed at the front.

The lads who are sweeping the deck prior to it being polished are happily stamping on the pile of 'cockies' they have amassed in the centre of the mess.

'You can't kill 'em. Royal Navy cockies are the only living creature that they reckon will survive an atomic bomb,' says Tommo.

Those that have been stamped on by a number-nine-sized Pusser's boot look dead enough to me.

'Scoop 'em up and give 'em a float test,' says Tommo, pointing to one of the scuttles.

As one of the lads goes off to find a dustpan, I watch as a couple of the cockies drag their crumpled bodies towards the relative safety of a gap under a bank of foot lockers. They have obviously heard Tommo.

By 10:00 the mess is looking good. It smells of liberally applied Teepol and the hammocks are stowed perfectly. Freckles inspects both messes. He knows his way around and even strokes his finger along the bottom of the Mess trap locker where he expects to find granules of sugar. Thankfully it is clean. He does, however, find dust amongst the deckhead pipes, cables and trunkings. It isn't surprising that we've missed some.

His final verdict on the cleanliness of the mess is good and as we slump down on the mess benches for a well-deserved rest we are told to drag our hammocks up to the boat deck. Just what we want – to manoeuvre a hammock up through three decks and along passageways and through clipped doors. We do it, however, and once on the Boat Deck we are instructed to lay our hammocks on the side of the deck away from the jetty, unlash and open our bedding to the elements. Apparently this is called airing.

Freckles is surprised when he spots my seamanship manual beneath my pillow.

'I've never seen a Junior Seaman who sleeps with his seamanship manual before.'

'I read a bit before going to sleep.' I sound pathetic and I hope I've not been overheard.

I turn my mattress as instructed.

Most of us have a cigarette and when a disturbingly damp breeze gets up, we all grab our bedding, take it back down the mess, re-lash everything and stow our hammocks away.

'COOKS OF THE MESS TO THE GALLEY.'

After dinner Tug, Stumpy and I decide to go for a stroll to see what the Island of Portland has to offer three lads with a few bob in their pockets. Tommo explains to us the business of getting a mate to sling your hammock for you when you went ashore. 'Of course if you've got no mates then you're in the shit.'

We present ourselves at the brow where, as Juniors, we would normally be inspected by the Officer-of-the-day before being allowed ashore. The Officer-of-the-day isn't available: apparently he is in the Wardroom doing something important. After a 20-minute wait the Quartermaster, a Leading Seaman, takes our station cards, checks them and tells us to 'Piss off ashore. Don't run across the brow.'

Portland is all hills. We don't fancy the first pub we pass: the place is overflowing with *Bermuda*'s finest, all noisily drunk. We continue up the hill, reckoning that the more distant pubs will be empty. We are wrong. They are all full. The greasy-spoon at the top of a long hill is empty and despite the fact that we haven't long ago had dinner we each order a bacon sandwich and a cup of coffee. We all agree it is the worst bacon sandwich any of us have ever had. The coffee tastes like ground-up mouse droppings according to Stumpy, who has apparently tasted the real thing before.

The street fills with taxis taking those of *Bermuda*'s crew, who are falling out of the various pubs, to the distant delights of Weymouth. With a sudden rush of youthful innocence we decide to take a walk up yet another hill: I am enjoying the space and the feel of solid English ground beneath my feet.

We wander, eventually finding ourselves on a high point on the east side of the island where we can see out over the greyish waters of Weymouth Bay. Portland Race, a patch of disturbed and dangerous water, is quite plain to see.

We sit on a bench and smoke our cigarettes. We discuss girls and Stumpy tells Tug about Wilco.

'I got a letter from her the other day,' I say.

Silence. Stumpy lights another cigarette.

'She's been given a new overall and a plastic name tag.' I add.

'Blimey!' says Tug. 'Is that a promotion?'

'Dunno.'

Stumpy splutters. All three of us realise how pathetic I sound and we laugh until our sides ache. We have a further wander, skirting round the rim of a huge stone quarry and then stroll downhill back to the dockyard.

We make it back onboard in time for tea. I take my seamanship manual up top and find myself a washdeck locker on which to perch while I spend an hour or so reading about flags and their international meanings.

5

COCKROACHES 6 – PETER 0

I'm not an aggressive person but last night I noticed a couple of cockroaches on the FW-H pipe, waving their tentacles and quite obviously discussing an offensive strategy. So I decide to take action. I take a roll of strong, adhesive tape from the Quarter-deck cleaning locker and wrap some around the FW-H pipe, sticky side uppermost. Convinced that I have established an effective boundary, I fall asleep not worrying about my antenna-waving visitors.

Sunday wouldn't be Sunday if it was a day of rest would it?

'RIOT CONTROL PARTY WILL MUSTER ON THE STARBOARD SIDE OF THE BOAT DECK IN FULL RIOT GEAR IN FIFTEEN MINUTES TIME.
I REPEAT: RIOT CONTROL PARTY WILL MUSTER ...'

According to Tommo, an enjoyable Portland diversion is the Sunday Civil Disobedience Exercise. The Royal Navy is occasionally required to intervene to quell rioting, looting and general unrest when visiting some of the less disciplined parts of the Commonwealth. Every ship therefore has to demonstrate to the satisfaction of FOST and his staff that they have an efficient and well-disciplined body of men ready to step-in to restore law and order. *Bermuda*'s Riot Control Party consists mainly of Cooks, Writers, Supply Staff and Stewards. They are commanded by a Sub Lieutenant and managed by the Master-at-Arms. They are all kitted out in a tin helmet, No 8s, boots, gaiters and armed with an intimidating metal-tipped stick. They have undergone a short period of training at Whale Island before joining *Bermuda* and today is the day they have been dreading: the long-expected Sunday Civil Disobedience Exercise.

The locals of Portland and surrounding areas have an open invitation from FOST to act as rioters for the day. They aren't paid but they get a free mug of kye, a sticky bun and the opportunity to throw things at the ship's crews who wreak havoc on their peaceful community and their fair maidens. Work-up ships continually visit Portland and the local youth have plenty of opportunity to practice riotous disobedience. Off-duty members of the crew are also invited to be disobedient ... within strict limits of course and as defined by Queen's Regulations and Admiralty Instructions.

Tug, Streaky and I volunteer because it is our first chance to participate in the well-established naval tradition of dressing-up. The children's party equipment store is opened and we rummage around in the mountain of strange, unwashed clothing. I grab myself an Indian headdress and a suit of fringed buffalo hide to go with my Pusser's boots. Tug dresses himself as a pirate with an eye-patch. Streaky emerges dressed as an unarmed cowboy with an oversized ten-gallon hat but no side-arms.

Once the Riot Control Party has been bussed off to wherever the riot will take place, we congregate on the Boat deck to receive a briefing from a young-looking Sub Lieutenant who blushes violently when addressing us. 'The purpose of today's exercise is to test the effectiveness of *HMS Bermuda*'s Riot Control Party ...'

'He's going to tell us not to use excessive violence or bad ferkin' language,' whispers the bloke standing next to me who is dressed as a milkman.

The Sub Lieutenant coughs. 'While you are encouraged to make life as difficult and unpredictable as possible for the Riot Control Part, you are reminded that mindless violence and bad language will not be tolerated ...'

'See. Told ya,' says the milkman as he elbows me in the ribs.

'Can I swear in Welsh, sir?' asks someone from the back.

The Sub Lieutenant doesn't have an answer and tells us to muster on the jetty and wait for our transport.

He regains his composure as we form an untidy group opposite the forward brow. 'When we arrive at the riot site you will be divided into teams: each under the direction of a member of the Flag Officer Sea Training's staff. Remember, that in any riotous situation there is always a leader. Enjoy yourselves and remember if you are captured you only divulge your name and official number – nothing else.'

'I'm going to get myself the Petty Officer Writer who refused me an advance of pay a few months back,' says someone as we queue to board one of the buses.

Blacky sits alongside me on the bus. He is dressed in his Navy overalls.

'See you made an effort with the dressing up then, Blacky?' I say.

'Don't know where all that dressing-up stuff has been do ya?' He pokes a finger at my fringed jacket. 'Who's worn it before and all that.'

'Suppose not.'

'I've done something like this before you know.'

It doesn't surprise me. 'Really?'

'Anyway, how's things with you?'

'OK.'

'Life as a ferkin' gunner is no joke.'

'Isn't it?'

'I'm one of the six-inch turret team. The best team in 'A' turret, the team with the best practice times and the least misfires.'

'Are ya?'

'Always ferkin' closed-up we are. The ship would fail this whole work-up thing without a team like ours.'

I look out of the window as we approach a collection of deserted buildings that apparently were once occupied by quarrymen. I wish Blacky good luck: I don't really mean it.

The Civil Disobedience Exercise lasts all morning with only a brief break for a cup of refreshing tea and something that could have been distantly related to a pork pie. The bloke in charge of us disappears part-way through the morning so we reclassify ourselves as Guerrillas. Being a Portland Guerrilla means finding a quiet, elevated spot, lying down, smoking fags and taking it easy. From my elevated vantage point I watch as the Portland rioters outwit the professionals. The rioters have armed themselves with bags of flour and eggs and are setting up ambushes and generally making life impossible for *Bermuda*'s finest.

The end of the exercise is signalled by the arrival of buses. All of a sudden everything stops. The Portland rioters give the Riot Control Party an impromptu three cheers as they throw what is left of their flour and eggs in the air. A few of our crew are stretchered back onboard by the Sick Bay staff. We hear rumours that some of the mock interrogations got out of hand. Apparently this is a crucial assessment, the result of which will determine if *Bermuda* will be sent to deal with any disobedient civilians in the future.

On the bus I remove my headdress. I sit behind a couple of mud-covered cowboys who brag that they have been unfairly treated during an interrogation by a couple of female rioters. The Sub Lieutenant takes a seat directly behind the driver: his back is covered in yellow and green egg stuff and he looks severely dishevelled. From the window I spot Blacky nursing what looks like a twisted arm.

We are warned that it will be an early start on Monday, and it is. We are just starting our Quarter-deck scrub-down when reveille is bugled at 06:00. Both watches are mustered at 06:45 and a stream of FOST's staff troop up the brow minutes before it is pulled onboard.

The remainder of the day is given over to the firing of guns: a noisy and disruptive day. I polish hundreds of brass tallies in one of the cabin flats. I am particularly proud of a tally I have brought back to life. This morning it was covered in paint, now it shines brightly, clearly identifying its adjacent hose rack.

In the evening we run out of fresh water during a tense game of Uckers ...

'THERE IS NO FRESH WATER THROUGHOUT THE SHIP.
I SAY AGAIN THERE IS NO FRESH WATER THROUGHOUT
THE SHIP.
WE SHALL SHORTLY BE REPLENISHING FROM RFA BLACK
RANGER.
REPLENISHMENT PARTIES MUSTER ON THE STARBOARD
SIDE IN THREE ZERO MINUTES.
ENGINEERING OFFICER REPORT TO THE BRIDGE.'

A well-illuminated *Black Ranger* greets us like a long lost friend. We refuel and just before midnight she is disconnected and slews away with a farewell blast on her horn.

'DO YOU HEAR THERE, THERE IS NO FRESH WATER
THROUGHOUT THE SHIP.
I SAY AGAIN THERE IS NO FRESH WATER THROUGHOUT
THE SHIP.
CHIEF PETTY OFFICER COOK REPORT TO THE BRIDGE.'

The Fo'csle part-of-ship is mustered for anchoring. We must be anchoring in the deepest part of Weymouth Bay as the rattle of the anchor cable appears to go on for ages. I am snuggled up in my hammock by the time the Fo'csle lads come back down the mess, smelling of fresh salty air and telling us all what a ferkin' job it had been 'bringing this bastard to anchor.'

This morning we are up early again! According to Daily Orders we are doing more manoeuvres, a transfer, a full power trial, a boiler room shut-down, gun and radar tracking and calibrations, finishing with a Starshell firework display after dark.

I do a relief watch in the Operations Room for the forenoon, so I miss the thrills and spills of manoeuvres and the full power trail. Even in our elevated position, just below the bridge, *Bermuda*'s vibration at high speed causes deckhead fittings to rattle and cabinet doors to unclip themselves. The door to the throbbing and pulsating cyclotron valve flies open.

'COOKS TO THE GALLEY.

WE SHALL SHORTLY BE DOING A SERIES OF MANOEUVRES, ENSURE THAT ALL LOOSE EQUIPMENT IS CORRECTLY STOWED.

CLOSE ALL SCUTTLES AND UPPER DECK SCREEN DOORS.

CHIEF PETTY OFFICER STEWARD REPORT TO THE BRIDGE.

FRESH WATER WILL BE AVAILABLE AFT OF SECTION MIKE FOR THE NEXT TEN MINUTES.

I SAY AGAIN FRESH WATER WIL ...'

Back down the mess, during dinner, I am able to tell everybody who is interested that we are about 20 miles south of Bournemouth and doing a series of predetermined zigzag patterns. Apparently we will be returning to Portland tonight. It is good being in the Ops Room: I get to find out all sorts of important things.

This afternoon we do a transfer with *HMS Grafton*; a Blackwood type Anti-Submarine Frigate. *Bermuda* sends the concrete test weight over first to ensure that everything is in working order. Then the Regulating staff appear. The bloke who was sentenced to a period of imprisonment is transferred over to *Grafton* who is on her way back to Portsmouth, having completed her Work-up. The Regulating staff watch intently as the prisoner is landed on the deck of *Grafton* and into the hands of a couple of large crew members who slip a pair of handcuffs expertly onto his wrists. As he is manhandled through one of *Grafton*'s screen doors he manages to give *Bermuda* a handcuffed 'two finger' salute before disappearing completely.

'HANDS TO TEA.

COOKS TO THE GALLEY.

STOW ALL LOOSE EQUIPMENT.

WE SHALL BE PERFORMING A SERIES OF ZIGZAG MANOEUVRES WHILE HEADING WEST INTO THE PREVAILING WEATHER.

WE SHALL BE ANCHORING IN WEYMOUTH BAY OVERNIGHT. OUR ETA IS APPROXIMATELY 02:00.

FRESH WATER IS AVAILABLE IN THE MAIN GALLEY AND PANTRY ONLY UNTIL APPROXIMATELY 01:45.

CHIEF SHIPWRIGHT, CHIEF COOK AND CHIEF STEWARD REPORT TO THE BRIDGE IMMEDIATELY.'

The lads who work on the Fo'csle moan and groan. I feel relieved as I sling my hammock that night and snuggle down. I haven't seen a cockroach since installing the sticky tape boundary.

The Fo'csle lads sling their hammocks but don't get into them. Tommo organises a couple of games of Uckers to take their minds off things. Uckers is a noisy game when you are trying to go to sleep.

Today I am given the dubious pleasure of cleaning the Port Aft' Cabin Flat for the First Lieutenant to inspect. This involves cleaning everything: and it keeps me gainfully employed for most of the forenoon. It is my responsibility to report that my compartment is ready for inspection, and having completed everything to the very best of my limited capabilities I collect my cap and wait. It is always a worrying time as the Inspecting Officer and his entourage approach, particularly if you know that there are things that you haven't bothered to clean, polish or paint.

I salute smartly. 'Junior Seaman Broadbent reporting the Port Aft' Cabin flat ready for your inspection sir.'

'Very well Broadbent ... let's have a look shall we?' says the First Lieutenant.

I nod.

Every nook and cranny is inspected, a torch is used to

examine dark corners and white-gloved fingers wipe over hidden ledges. Behind the Inspecting Officer is a Chief Petty Officer with a clip-board noting down ... notes.

Then I wait for the decision.

'Good job. Well done.'

That's as much as he ferkin' knows!

At 12:30 the Fo'csle part-of-ship once again connects *Bermuda* to a buoy. At least we are stable for a while and we can eat our dinner with a knife and a fork in each hand. The Fo'csle lads are once again dripping and moaning about all the work they have to do.

'OUT BOOMS AND LADDERS.
CRANE DRIVERS CLOSE UP.
BOATS CREWS AND LAUNCHING PARTIES MUSTER ON THE BOAT DECK.
AWAY ALL BOATS.
THE BOAT DECK IS STRICTLY OUT OF BOUNDS.
I REPEAT, THE BOAT DECK IS STRICTLY OUT OF BOUNDS ...
EXCEPT FOR BOATS CREW AND LAUNCHING PARTIES.
DIVING OFFICER REPORT TO THE BRIDGE ... DIVING OFFICER.'

From the starboard waste, I watch jealously as *Bermuda*'s boats are launched and they skitter around us at full throttle. I spot Tug in the bows of a launch. How I wish I was boats' crew. Instead I am just another one of the dozens of lads holding onto the falls as we lower the lifeboat whaler. I'll have a word with Freckles when the time is right to see how I can get myself into one of the boats.

Water barges are secured alongside after tea. One of the Able Seamen explains to me that *Bermuda* tries to make sufficient fresh water for her own domestic use, but when the Officers have their baths it soon gets used up. Then he burbles on about saving water in the shower. 'Showering Navy style is simple. Get into the shower, switch the water on. Wet yourself all over. Switch the water off, wash your hair, soap yourself all over. Switch the water back on again and rinse yourself off. Switch the water off, then get out of the shower.'

That evening, before I sling my hammock, I stand on a stool and check my taped boundary. There are lots of what I assume are spindly cockroach legs stuck to the tape ... but no ferkin' cockies. Where are the legless bastards? I strip everything out of my hammock and I find three amputees, legless but still very much alive and waving their antennae angrily at me. I scoop them onto a piece of paper, open one of the scuttles and give the legless shits a 'float test'.

We are returning our squeegees to the locker on a chilly, damp, misty morning when we hear the duty Royal Marine Bugler sound reveille earlier than normal at 05:55. The Fo'csle team are fallen in early and *Bermuda* is released from her buoy to commence Naval Gunfire Support exercises.

After dinner, *Bermuda* wallows patiently in the rolling waters of Weymouth Bay, waiting for an Admiral's barge to appear. We know that it's coming because Goosie has us lower the port Accommodation ladder, a contraption constructed from well-stained dark wood, with inlaid chrome tread strips. We carefully winch it outboard and lower it until the bottom platform is about a foot above the oggin. Oggin is a word that everybody appears to use instead of sea. We rig chromed guard-rails and bright white hand-ropes. A couple of Officers, a Petty Officer, a Killick and a couple of lads from the mess dressed in their best suits appear. They just hang around, getting in the way of us workers. An Officer waves for the Admiral's Barge to approach our ladder.

Goosie jumps two feet in the air. 'Clear The Quarter-deck. Quarter-deck Part-of-ship Muster Yourselves on 01 Deck. Behind 'X' Turret! Go On ... Go On! Chop Chop!'

From 01 deck I watch as the blue and gold Admiral's Barge comes alongside the bottom platform of our Accommodation ladder. At the bow and at the stern of the barge stands a ramrod-straight sailor with a boat hook. In a well-practised routine they swing their boat hooks at exactly the same time and the barge comes to a halt. Our official Side Party stands silently to attention for a good few minutes before FOST, followed by a small group of other Officers, make their appearance. The Side Party place their Bosun's calls in their mouths and blow a perfect Pipe-the-Side as our visitors stroll across our deck, down the Accommodation ladder, into the barge and away. Captain Lumby stands and salutes as the Admiral's Barge sweeps away.

We unrig the ladder, stow all the shiny bits and pieces back in their boxes, wind it back inboard and secure it for sea. What I wouldn't give to be a member of an Admiral's Barge crew.

I feel tired after tea. I am looking forward to an evening of Uckers and crawling into my hammock. We manage one uninterrupted game before *Bermuda* needs topping-up again and we are mustered on the upper deck for yet another transfer of fuel from *RFA Black Ranger*. According to an oil-encrusted Stoker we are to take onboard 300 tons of FFO: whatever that is.

The whole fuel transfer process turns out to be quite pleasant. It is a moon-lit evening and *Bermuda* switches her upper-deck lighting off. Once the fuel starts to flow, we Seamen lounge about and wait. Shortly before midnight, everything is released and *Black Ranger* chugs away into the ink-black distance.

As we are putting the final bits of equipment away ...

'AWAY SEA BOATS CREW.

AWAY SEA BOATS CREW!

TOMORROW'S TOMBOLA NUMBERS ARE TWENTY NINER ... SEVEN ... FIVE ... TWENTY SIX ... SEVENTEEN AND ELEVEN.'

The buggers! Now it's going to be ages before I can turn in and I haven't slung my hammock yet.

'We're on our way to Pompey,' says Sugar as we lower the whaler.

'Really?'

'So I've heard. Should be there in the morning.'

'That's good then.'

'I've got a bit of skirt who'll be glad to see me. Well bits of me anyway.'

'Lucky bugger,' someone says.

I hope Sugar is right: it is rumoured that he has a reputation for dishing-out misinformation ... just for a laugh!

After the morning scrub-down, I take advantage of the fresh water in the Juniors' bathroom and have a slow shave. Tug and I are getting ready to ditch the breakfast gash ...

'DO YOU HEAR THERE: NO MORE GASH IS TO BE DITCHED ... NO MORE GASH IS TO BE DITCHED.
DUTY PETTY OFFICER STEWARD REPORT TO THE WARDROOM PANTRY.'

We rush up to the boat deck with our buckets and manage to empty them before a couple of blokes appear and drag the gash chute inboard.

Tug and I take the opportunity to enjoy a cigarette on the Boat deck, leaning illegally on a guard rail with one foot on our respective upturned gash bucket.

'That looks like Ventnor over there. Almost home.' Tug points to the splodge on the misty morning horizon. His eyes always water-up when he sees the Isle of Wight.

On the Quarter-deck we arrange all our berthing ropes and then are sent away to get changed into suits ready for entering harbour. Sugar says that it is best to muster on the starboard side when entering Pompey harbour.

Dressed in our No 2 uniform, with cap chin-stays firmly down, we fall-in as we slowly skim past a deserted Billy Manning's. The Round Tower is deserted as we negotiate the narrow harbour entrance. At 08:00 exactly, *Bermuda* fires a 17-gun salute to the Commander-in-Chief, Portsmouth, before securing alongside *HMS Tyne* moored at the top of the harbour. I bet the inhabitants of Portsmouth are really pleased to know that *HMS Bermuda* is back and has woken them from peaceful slumber ... 17 times.

'DO YOU HEAR THERE! AMMUNITION SHIP.
I SAY AGAIN AMMUNITION SHIP.
NO SMOKING OR NAKED LIGHTS THROUGHOUT THE SHIP.
I SAY AGAIN NO SMOKING OR NAKED LIGHTS THROUGHOUT THE SHIP.'

Bugger! We rig the coir mats, don our anti-flash gear and secure an ammunition lighter alongside. It takes only three hours to replenish our magazines. Thankfully, I carry the more manageable 4-inch shells this time.

The sound of striking matches and flicked lighters signals the end of ammunitioning.

'DO YOU HEAR THERE!
SMOKING IS NOW PERMITTED THROUGHOUT THE SHIP.
I SAY AGAIN SMOKE ...'

We detach our self from *HMS Tyne* and are towed to South Railway jetty. We do an impromptu wash-down and squeegee the Quarter-deck dry. The Side Party are assembled, along with a whole batch of *Bermuda*'s Senior Officers, to welcome Vice Admiral J G Hamilton CB CBE and his staff onboard. Apparently he is Flag Officer Flotillas (Home) ... whatever that means.

Immediately the Admiral's feet touch our freshly scrubbed deck Sugar points to the main mast as a red-and-white flag is hoisted. 'That's the Admiral's flag. St George's cross and one red ball. Now everybody will know that we've got a ferkin' Admiral onboard.'

6

A PINT OF INVERGORDON 'HEAVY'

All ideas of a weekend in harbour are dashed as at 09:00 this morning we depart Pompey, leaving behind a couple of the crew who have not returned from overnight leave. In company with the destroyers *HMS Duchess* and *HMS Diana*, we set off east bound for a place called Invergordon in Scotland.

I have the First Dog Watch in the Ops Room just as we are heading through the narrowest part of the English Channel. I relieve Lash on the PPI. 'Never seen anything like it mate, there are ships every ferkin' where.'

Tansy explains that we are going through what is probably the most congested piece of ocean in the world ... 'So hand over quickly and let's get down to work.'

We learnt about 'clutter' while on course at *Dryad*. It is when the sea is rough and the waves reflect radar beams which show up on the PPI screen as white dots similar to small ships. The skill is to distinguish between clutter and ships: and I don't think it is a skill I've fully mastered yet.

'All those dots aren't clutter,' says Lash. 'They're ferkin' ships.'

We identify each ship and give many a wave an identification letter as we go through the alphabet at least five times. The discussions between Tansy and the Officer of the Watch on the bridge are continual. There is no time for any of Tansy's sea stories. He had said that he'd been to Invergordon before and that it was a desolate place with few pubs and fewer women.

The 'clutter' starts to thin out as *Bermuda* points her bows directly north. I give my relief on the PPI the same information. 'That's not clutter, those are ferkin' Bogeys.'

'No problem, young 'un.' My relief is an RP2 who has done all this before.

'Is the English Channel the most congested piece of ocean in the world do you think?'

'Probably,' he says as he removes his own personal Chinagraph pencil from his breast pocket. 'The Red Sea takes some beating though.'

The Red Sea eh? … and he said it so casually.

I have the morning watch and drape a towel over the foot of my hammock. I whisk a sheet of paper across the FW-H pipe just in case there are any cockies settled there. If there are they'll probably end up at the bottom of mine or my neighbour's hammock, or in the wheelhouse.

There is more than an air of panic about the Juniors' mess as I come off watch the following morning. To prevent us from getting bored during the long, forthcoming hours of the Sabbath, Vice Admiral J G Hamilton CB CBE has ordered Divisions. Freckles is convinced that if the Vice Admiral is to choose one department to inspect, it will be the Juniors.

There are a lot of exchanges and last-minute panics as we extract items of kit that we have stuffed away after the Commissioning ceremony a fortnight ago. Nobody expected this. There is a mess iron somewhere, but no time to find it. Tins of shoe polish are handed around and there is a continuous line of us going to the bathroom to scrub our caps. Thank goodness we have water this morning!

'DO YOU HEAR THERE … FRESH WATER WILL BE AVAILABLE FOR THE NEXT FIFTEEN … ONE FIVE … MINUTES THROUGHOUT THE SHIP.'

'There's no ferkin' water in the ferkin' bathroom,' says one of the lads as he slides down the mess ladder with a grubby cap on his head.

We muster on the Boat Deck with Freckles. This is the first time we have met our Divisional Officer. He calls us to attention and introduces himself as Lieutenant Mackintosh. He's a man of medium height with bushy eyebrows that never stop moving and a sizeable purple wart on his chin. I make sure that I am in the middle rank. Lieutenant Mackintosh inspects us and has something lengthy to say to Tug. Tug is always the one who is picked on: it was the same at *Ganges*. I manage to get inspected without comment. I know that the bow of my cap tally is badly tied and my shoes aren't that clean: they have salt marks on them and they need re-heeling. The crease down the front of my uniform jacket sleeves is dull and I haven't folded the trousers up correctly, consequently they are creased in all the wrong places. We remain at attention as we hear whistles and the occasional bugle from other parts of the ship. Freckles and Lieutenant Mackintosh go into a huddle, out of earshot, and compare notes.

Captain Lumby appears as if from nowhere followed by a line of Officers. He has something to say to everybody on the front rank. Lash is given a good dressing-down as his trousers are a couple of inches short: he must have grown a couple of inches since being measured by the bloke from Bernards of Harwich. As expected, I get 'picked up' for the bow in my cap tally, the state of my shoes and my creased trousers.

Once the Captain and his party are out of earshot Lieutenant Mackintosh lays-in to us, accusing us of being slovenly and untidy. He isn't impressed with our turn-out. Personally, what hurt me most, is when he says that we obviously have no pride in ourselves and that, as members of the Flagship, we obviously have no pride in our ship. That upsets me: I have bags of pride: if only he knew. Anyway, where has he been for the past two weeks?

'COOKS TO THE GALLEY.'

Bermuda slews and bounces. The North Sea is playing with us. From the galley I collect a tray full of burnt roast potatoes complete with long thin carrots in a sticky, unyielding brown-burgundy coloured sauce. My second tray is full of a golden crumble mixture that looks reasonably appetising. The meat and cabbage in Margaret Rutherford's tray doesn't look particularly inviting. *Bermuda* shudders twice as we negotiate the passageway towards the messdeck hatch. We both bounce off the same bulkhead. The fanny smashes into a bulkhead locker that flies open and a large grey asbestos fire- fighting suit falls out onto the deck. We place our food trays on the deck and I stop them from moving while Margaret stuffs the suit back into the locker and slams the door shut.

Down the mess, it is normal to blame the 'Cooks' for the presentation and quality of the food. Today however, the crappy dinner is firmly down to Vice Admiral J G Hamilton himself. I keep it to myself, but I enjoy bits of my dinner, particularly the asbestos-dusted crumble.

After dinner I take a stroll around the upper deck. I have discovered a washdeck locker aft of the boat deck, one deck up and next to the after funnel where the bulkhead is warm.

Surprisingly 'Bogey' Knight has also found it

'Hi Pete.'

'Hi Boges.'

'So you've found this place as well eh?'

'Yeah. Came up to see if I could see Brid.'

'Bridlington?'

'Yeah.'

'How do you know that we're near there?'

He points west. 'These are my home waters. I recognise them.'

'They're just grey waters, mate.'

'They're my grey waters. Just over the horizon there is the best fish and chip shop in the world.'

'I know. It's in Pudsey.'

'It's round the corner from my house ... in Brid.'

'We'll never agree on that, mate.'

'Perhaps not.'

'Ever been to Scotland before?'

'Naah. No need.'

'Reckon it'll be cold?'

'Yeah. You can feel it getting colder now can't ya?'

'Fag?' I offer.

'Yeah … go on then.'

Bogey never has any cigarettes.

I have the forenoon watch on Monday and just after 08:00 we are told that the curving land-mass clear on radar is Kinnaird's Head. It is freezing and for the first time Tansy orders the black heater behind the plotting table to be switched on. The Moray Firth is almost empty of surface contacts, so Tansy tells us what little he knows about the Invergordon Mutiny.

'When was it exactly, this mutiny?' I ask.

'Dunno exactly,' says Tansy as he grabs the microphone. 'I'll ask the bridge.'

'Bridge, Ops Room.'

'Bridge,' comes the metallic reply.

'We are having a discussion about the Invergordon Mutiny, sir. Does anyone on the bridge know when it took place exactly?'

'Wait one.'

Tansy twists his mouth and clicks the microphone off. 'I know what it was all about though. The government had decided to cut the pay of the armed forces by 25 percent. Reluctantly the Navy accepted it …'

'Twenty five ferkin' percent?' the lad sat at the PPI asks.

Twenty five percent … yeah. Anyway the government thought they had got away with it and tried to impose further cuts. It just so happened that the majority of the Home Fleet was in Invergordon when the news of more cuts was announced and the mutiny was started in the Fleet Canteen in Invergordon.

'What happened then?'

'Don't know the details,' replies Tansy. 'But it spread throughout the fleet and some ships didn't make it to sea because the crew refused to go.'

'Ferkin' hell.'

'So it was a real mutiny then?'

'Yeah. Known as the Invergordon ferkin' Mutiny…'

The bridge intercom interrupts. 'Ops Room, Bridge.'

Tansy clicks on the microphone. 'Ops Room.'

'The Invergordon Mutiny took place in September 1931. It was in response to a proposed 10 percent cut in pay.'

'September 1931, Roger. Thank you sir.' Tansy clicks off the microphone and gives it a two-finger salute. '10 ferkin' per cent! It was 25 ferkin' per cent.'

'Is the canteen still there?' I ask.

'Yeah. Last time I was here ... yeah.'

Bermuda anchors a short distance from Invergordon just before dinner.

'CLEAR LOWER DECK. HANDS TO PAINT SHIP!'

Wha ... The whole ferkin' ship?

Goosie explains 'paint ship'. All the ship's stages, about fifty of them, are put over the ship's side each with a crew of two, armed with a pot of grey paint and a brush. All departments are expected to supply men. The section of the ship's side that each stage has to paint, from the gunwale down to the boot-topping (the black bit) is called a 'fleet'. I change into my brand new, stiff overalls. Junior Seamen aren't considered reliable enough to apply ship's-side paint so I am given the job of tending a stage and keeping the paint pots full. At various points on the upper deck, large tins of Pusser's ship's-side grey paint stand on protective sheets, manned by people experienced in the issue of paint without spilling it. There is no paint-issuing station anywhere near the wood of the Quarter-deck.

The stage I am responsible for is manned by an Able Seaman from the Fo'csle who has done this many times before. Partnering him is a Stoker who really doesn't want to be up in the cold, Scottish air dangling over grey, unwelcoming waters on a plank of wood.

Standing on deck, doing nothing more technical than lighting the occasional cigarette, I notice other warships anchoring to seawards of our position: many of them flying Norwegian, Dutch and Danish flags. I know my flags.

As the Scottish sun slowly disappears behind heathered mountains, the Buffer who has spent the afternoon and evening circling us in the motor whaler, decrees that *Bermuda*'s flanks are acceptably painted. During the afternoon the whaler rescues two blokes who fall off their stages into the cold, grey waters of Cromarty Firth. Fortunately, all of them can swim. Now I understand why we underwent the *Ganges* swimming test wearing cold, soggy overalls.

Tuesday's early morning Quarter-deck scrub is supervised by Goosie who has got up particularly early. The number of available 'hands' is diminishing. On reaching the age of 17½ , Juniors are automatically promoted and are no longer required to do the early morning scrub down. Also, there are fewer Men under Punishment as many have figured out a way of avoiding the early morning muster.

The Fo'csle and Top part-of-ship finishes the cutting-in around our pennant numbers (C52) on both sides while we Quarter-deck hands prepare the Quarter-deck for our first *Bermuda* cocktail party. We rig wires and stanchions: one long wire is rigged along our centre line and others down both sides and across the stern. From the awning store, located in the bilges, we snake our way up ladders, through hatches and along passageways with the rolled-up main canvas awning on our shoulders. We lay the awning out along the centre line, unlash it and by a combination of brute force, ignorance and Goosie's know-how we drag it over the dipped central wire. We then secure lines to the eyes on the awning, reeve them through the stanchion tops and pull the wires and awning tight until the awning strops can be secured. It takes us ages. Some of the securing shackles haven't been lubricated and some of the wires are kinked. Once finished, we are under a tent-like structure that stretches from the stern, over 'Y' turret, up to the after screen bulkhead and a little way up the port and starboard sides, stopping where the wooden deck ends.

Have we finished? ... of course we haven't.

Our Quarter-deck and 'Y' turret with the main awning spread

From another locker in the bilges we extract bundles of pink-and-white striped awnings that we suspend from the port and starboard stanchion wires to form a fluttering striped bulkhead down both sides of the Quarter-deck and a deckhead. It looks attractive when we've finished, the sunlight through the cocktail awnings giving everything a nice cosy, glow. After hours of working above head-height, my young arms and shoulders ache.

Have we finished preparing the Quarter-deck? ... of course we haven't.

Then we wash down the deck in special pre-cocktail-party fashion.

'Shoes off. Roll your trousers up!'

The Scottish water that spews out of the fire-hydrants is freezing but Goosie convinces us that it will do us no harm.

We lower and rig the accommodation ladder.

That evening I am on duty while Vice Admiral J G Hamilton holds a dinner party for Senior Officers from all the British, Danish, Dutch and Norwegian ships that have gathered off Invergordon in preparation for the forthcoming Exercise. The Admiral's Barge is busy that evening ferrying Officers to and from the ships that are all swinging at anchor around us.

Next morning Goosie is once again up early and waiting for the Juniors and Men under Punishment to assemble on the Quarter-deck for the morning scrub. The Wardroom Stewards have cleaned away most of the rubbish from last night's party, but we still find cigarette ends all over the place and the deck itself is scuffed in places. Goosie is beside himself: he wanders over his beloved deck identifying places where cigarettes have been ground underfoot by foreign Officers. I am told to arm myself with a scraper and a wire brush to remove any dog-end burns. Whenever I think I have done the last one ... Goosie finds others. Before breakfast, I have become *Bermuda*'s unofficial cigarette-burn removal expert.

According to Daily Orders for today we are located at 57 degrees north – it is the furthest north I have ever been. Boats scurry between the fleet of anchored ships. Only one part of the none-duty-watch are allowed ashore and Stumpy and I decide to give Scotland the benefit of a visit. We both arrange with Tug, who is boat's crew, that he will sling our hammocks for us.

At 19:00 Stumpy and I muster on the Boat deck and leave *Bermuda* via the starboard accommodation ladder into a Norwegian launch that takes us to a small concrete jetty on the shore of a darkening town. On the same boat is Tansy.

As soon as we land I ask Tansy, 'Where's the Invergordon Canteen then Hooky?'

'Up the hill somewhere. It's probably the only place in town you'll get a pint. All the pubs will have been told not to serve anybody they consider too young to shave.'

'I'm seventeen and a quarter,' says Stumpy.

'And me,' I add. 'Almost.'

'It's not too far,' says Tansy, 'and if I remember rightly the beer's good and cheaper than in the pubs.'

The Invergordon Services Canteen is located alongside sports fields at the north end of town: I figure that I am even further north now than I've ever been. The spacious Canteen is not furnished for comfort: plastic tables and chairs, a couple of rugs on the floor in front of a long serviceable bar and low wattage, yellow lighting. The place is full of sailors in strange uniforms wearing peculiar and unnecessary headwear.

'Three pints of Heavy,' Tansy orders.

'Is that the opposite of Light Ale then?' I ask. I've lived in an Off Licence and know all about Light Ale.

'It's what they call Bitter in Scotland,' whispers Tansy out of the corner of his mouth.

We find a spare table between two groups of Norwegians: I recognise the flag.

'Tell Stumpy about the Invergordon Mutiny, Hooky,' I say.

'A ferkin' mutiny!' says a surprised Stumpy.

'I thought you would have told your mess mates all about it?' Tansy replies.

'Forgot most of it.' I admit.

So Tansy relays all the information about the mutiny. At the end he points to the dark football pitch. 'And it all started out there on the footie pitch.'

'Naah?' says Stumpy.

'Right there.'

One of the Norwegian sailors comes over, plonks himself uninvited onto one of our spare chairs and asks Tansy directly. 'You know about British Navy Mutiny?'

'Yes.'

'Tell me.'

'No. It's a state secret.'

'If I buy you more drinks maybe?'

'Listen up then,' says a smirking Tansy.

For no apparent reason, a guy identified by Tansy as the Prof stands on his chair and begins to sing. Almost everybody joins in.

'She's got a face like a messdeck scrubber ...
eyes like a Dogger bank cod.'

Then most people stop: they don't know the rest of it ... but the Prof does. He spreads his arms wide and continues ...

'Teeth like the stumps of a burnt out forest ...
voice like a big bull frog.
She went out with a three badge Stoker ...
and married the silly old sod!'

'Yeah,' says everybody and raises their arms. Then the British Invergordon Canteen choir, conducted by the Prof, gives full voice ...

'She's got a face like a messdeck scrubber ...
eyes like a Dogger bank cod.
Teeth like the stumps of a burnt out forest ...
voice like a big bull frog.
She went out with a three badge Stoker ....
and married the silly old sod!'

Cheers all round and much spilled 'Heavy'. Our foreign guests are looking on in disbelief.

Tansy leans over towards Stumpy and me. 'Prof passed his Eleven Plus with flying colours and has an 'O' level in bawdy songs.'

Stumpy and I nod, feigning understanding.

Prof downs the remainder of his pint in one, takes a deep breath and speaks in a cultured, well-projected voice ...

'I was walking through the Dockyard in a panic,
When I met a Matelot old and grey.
Upon his back he had his kitbag and his hammock,
And this is what I heard him say ...

He waves his arms and the majority of the Royal Navy joins in ...

'I wonder, yes I wonder,
Has the Jossman made a blunder,
When he made this draft chit out for me,
Well I've been a barrack stanchion,
And I've lived in Jago's Mansion.
And I've never, ever been to sea.
I like my Tiddy Oggie ,

And I like my figgy duff,
And I always say good morning to the chief.'

Then the Royal Navy stands up, wave their pints in the air and shout 'GOOD MORNING CHIEF!'

The Prof continues ...

'Oh, I wonder, yes I wonder,
Has the Jossman made a blunder,
When he made this draft chit out for me.'

'I know that a Jossman is the Master-at-Arms, but what's Jago's whatsit?' I ask Tansy as I take a slurp of my pint.
'Jago's Mansions are the barracks in Plymouth. *HMS Drake.'*
'And a Tiddy whatsit?'
'Tiddy Oggie is a Cornish Pasty.'
'I've had one of those,' I admit proudly.
'And is figgy duff the same as ordinary duff?' asks Stumpy.
'Yep.'
Someone over the other side of the room, clouded in dense grey duty-free smoke, yells 'Favourite things. Let's do favourite things.' Prof stands up: waits for the general noise of approval to settle, spreads his arms wide and begins ...

'Transvestites and perverts all dressed in white satin.
Five bob whores, and girls from Prestatyn,
Seedy Hotel rooms, all filled with smoke rings.
These are a few of my favourite things.'

The room is swaying. Everybody who knows the words is singing. Stumpy and I watch open-mouthed. From the back of the room someone takes it up ...

'Big tits and little tits, and ones with pert nipples,
Wrens with fat faces all covered in pimples,

Small tits that stand up, and big ones that swing,
These are a few of my favourite things.'

This earns an enthusiastic round of applause.

'Anything to do with tits always gets a cheer,' explains Tansy.

A bloke on the next table brandishing a half-drunk pint, jumps onto his chair and in a beautiful baritone sings ...

'Wrafs and Welshmen who ...'

There is a roar of disapproval from a table opposite that stops the baritone in his tracks. However, after a large slurp of his beer, he continues ...

'Wrafs and Welshmen, who wear rubber wellies,
Girls in French knickers, and slags from New Delhi ...'

Knowing cheers from all around.

'Bras and suspenders and tassels that swing,
These are a few of my favourite things.'

Roars of approval from all corners of the room. Someone shouts 'Again.' So the baritone pours the remnants of his pint over his head and sings it again.

Three pints later Stumpy and I ask Tansy if he won't mind if we leave: neither of us has developed beer stomachs and we can't keep up with Tansy and his newly acquired Norwegian friend.

'Feel free,' he says with a swing of his arm.

Stumpy and I journey south, stopping occasionally to irrigate some brackish Scottish vegetation. At the jetty there is a partially full boat. We ask if we can cadge a lift to *Bermuda* and a couple of Dutch blokes make room for us on a thwart. We expect nothing less, seeing as we are the Flagship of the forthcoming exercise.

Thank goodness Tug has slung my hammock.

7

A VISIT TO 'LOCH HORRIBLE'

The Junior contingent of the Quarter-deck scrubbing party the following morning are a sorry-looking bunch. A number of us are suffering from last night's visit to the Invergordon Canteen and are finding it difficult to move. I am experiencing my very first serious hangover.

The Fo'csle part-of-ship are also up early as *Bermuda* weighs anchor before breakfast. Once outside the Cromarty Firth, into the relatively wide waters of the Moray Firth, we start a series of manoeuvres and prepare our self for a double jackstay transfer with a Norwegian ship called *Oslo* on one side and the Danish ship *Waldemar Sejr* on the other. We are to prove, beyond reasonable doubt, that ships of different nationalities can efficiently transfer large lumps of concrete back and forth.

Later, we know that something is happening when we see anti-flashed gunners pouring into 'Y' turret. Goosie tells us to go down the mess and make sure everything is secured.

I am midway down the mess ladder as *Bermuda*'s first broadside shocks everything away from under my feet. The poor girl rattles, clatters and throws herself over on her beam-ends. Slowly she rights herself: *Bermuda* is demonstrating her six-inch fire-power.

The bridge tells us what is happening ...

'DO YOU HEAR THERE ... HANDS CLEAR OFF THE UPPER DECK.
WE SHALL SHORTLY BE FIRING 'A', 'B' AND 'Y' TURRETS SIMULTANEOUSLY.
ENSURE THAT ALL LOOSE EQUIPMENT IS SECURED.
GUNNERY OFFICER CONTACT THE BRIDGE.
THERE IS NO FRESH WATER THROUGHOUT THE SHIP.'

In the mess Freckles makes sure that we lash and close everything. When we fire our second broadside *Bermuda* recoils one way and then back again, back again and back again. Light fittings, loosened by the first broadside, crash to the deck along with chunks of deckhead paint. Caps that have been on the top of lockers fly everywhere. My side of the mess loses its electricity supply and all the lights go out. Freckles picks up the telephone in his office and then slams the handset down. 'The ruddy switchboard's down!'

Thankfully, *Bermuda* doesn't fire a third broadside and as the Scottish sun sets on a chilly and windy Thursday we anchor off a place called Buckie.

No cockroaches tonight. Maybe *Bermuda*'s broadsides have taught them to respect our fire-power.

A strong north-north-easterly wind is blowing the next morning: all ships are straining at their anchors with their sterns pointing disrespectfully towards the still-slumbering community of Buckie.

Shortly after the fleet have raised anchor, the Norwegian ship *Oslo* reports that she has lost a Seaman overboard. It isn't an exercise and in the Ops Room we mark the plot. Tansy continually relays the reported 'man-overboard' position to the bridge. Other ships offer to help and for the next three hours we co-ordinate a thorough search of the area. Unfortunately, the lost Seaman isn't found and after dinner it is decided to call off the search. According to Goosie, who has sailed this far north before, these Scottish waters are unforgivingly cold, even at this time of the year. The incident puts a damper on the rest of the day: and is a lesson to all of us who work on the upper deck. Today's fleet is multinational and includes the Danish ships *Flora* and *Waldemar Sejr* (ex *HMS Exmoor*), Dutch ships *Karel Doorman* (ex *HMS Venerable*) and *Groningen* plus the Norwegian ships *Haugesund* (ex *HMS Beaufort*) and *Tromso* (ex *HMS Zetland*). As a fleet we form up in convoy and carry out manoeuvres that are cancelled when one of the Danish ships turns to port when the rest of us turn to starboard. Personally I don't see much of what is going on as I spend most of the afternoon polishing the brass tallies in one of the Officers' cabin flats. At 15:00 I help to wash down the Quarter-deck, which I consider totally unnecessary as windswept 'goffers' are lashing across the deck at regular intervals. At least we don't have to squeegee down when we've finished.

I am in the Ops Room during our return through the Cromarty Firth to Invergordon. As I sling my hammock just after midnight the Fo'csle lads are scrambling up top to anchor us.

On Saturday we have the inevitable mess-cleaning to deal with. The broadsides of a couple of days ago have dislodged a good deal of the paintwork and associated deckhead debris. It has obviously had a shocking effect on our resident tribe of cockroaches as a good sweep-through the mess produces a large pile of traumatised, antennae waving individuals. I think I recognise the one who tried to get into my hammock the other evening. So much for the world's number-one survivors: they are given the ritual 'float test'.

Half a dozen of us spend the afternoon, with Mac and Tommo, learning the intricacies of a card game called Crib, a game-and-a-half that requires a combination of mathematical skills along with the ability to think quickly. By teatime we are playing singles and doubles and refreshingly new phrases like 'And One For His Knob!' and 'Fifteen Two That Bastard!' become part of my messdeck vocabulary.

Those ships that are berthed alongside the jetty open themselves to visitors and some Invergordon residents, wrapped in large coats and wearing woolly headgear, shuffle out of their nice warm homes and queue on a cold windswept jetty to look around some battered, grey warships. *Bermuda* sits sedately at anchor some distance away from the hubbub and excitement that the visiting foreign ships have created. Our boats, however, are in constant use, ferrying ashore those who want to experience the limited delights that Invergordon has to offer.

Tug and I go ashore for a stroll on Sunday afternoon. The Canteen is closed but we do find a small hotel that is open. Inside, we encounter the rules governing the sale of alcohol in Scotland on the Sabbath. The proprietor knows exactly where we are from – it's emblazoned on our caps – but he nevertheless has to comply with the law and makes us sign the travellers' book before we can be served a drink. We sign that we are travelling from Buckie to Invergordon, which in a way is true enough. The beer is good and we limit ourselves to two pints each: Scottish beer is a hangover in a glass.

Although our leave doesn't end until 20:00, we can't fill the early evening hours with anything interesting and we are back onboard for tea.

I've slung my hammock and am busy flicking through section seven of the Admiralty Manual of Seamanship when the Fo'csle lads are sent up top to raise our anchor just before midnight. As I snuggle into my blanket I give a heartfelt thanks to whoever compiled the Watch & Station Bill and put me on the Quarter-deck.

Bermuda heads a multinational flotilla north. We pass between the Orkney island of South Ronaldsay and the small island of Stroma in the middle of the night as we make our way through the notorious Pentland Firth. By the time I come on watch at 03:55 we are steaming west along the topmost coastal ledge of Scotland. I like the morning watch: not only am I able to sneak up-top for a lungful of fresh morning air and a cigarette, I also avoid the morning Quarter-deck scrub.

During the Forenoon the Gunners busy themselves with something called Turret and Quarters drills in preparation for yet another shoot at dinner time.

While we are eating, our six-inch guns open up to knock the shit out of an unassuming, peace-loving, grass-covered place called Hoan Island. I trust that whoever owns the place has given us permission to blow bits of their island to kingdom come. Down the mess, another batch of shell-shocked cockroaches tumble to the deck and play dead.

We have cleared away the mess table and are sitting down to 'duff' and a fag when *Bermuda* takes a sudden and unexpected list to port ...

'DO YOU HEAR THERE ... WE HAVE JUST RECEIVED A REPORT THAT *HMS BARBICAN* IS TAKING IN WATER.

WE ARE HEADING TOWARDS HER AT MAXIMUM SPEED AND WE MAY ENCOUNTER SOME ROUGH WEATHER FOR THE NEXT FEW HOURS.

I REPEAT ...WE MAY ENCOUNTER SOME ROUGH WEATHER FOR THE NEXT FEW HOURS.

CHIEF SHIPWRIGHT AND THE BUFFER REPORT TO THE BRIDGE.'

We run slap bang into roughers. We lose another couple of cups from the rack and a fanny full of custard. Those of us who really need custard on our jam roly-poly go plate in hand over to the other side of the mess to cadge some. Their roly-poly has fallen onto the deck and has picked up some dust and a number of baby cockies from under a locker, so we do a trade.

HMS Barbican is a strange-looking ship. Sugar says it is a Boom Defence vessel, whatever that is. We send over our main Damage Control team and a couple of Shipwrights along with boxes and boxes of equipment. My plan is to lounge around on the upper deck and enjoy the afternoon's watery, yet pleasantly warm sunshine. Goosie however, has other ideas and tells us all to grab metal polish and rags and clean some bright-work. I have already developed an uncanny ability to buff-up brass tallies. I know that the shine won't last for more than an hour: but if I don't think about that, I find the whole process of shining brass tallies to be mind-numbingly relaxing.

We launch the whaler and, with The Buffer and Goosie onboard, it does a couple of circuits to check on the condition of the ship's side paint while we lower the starboard accommodation ladder.

'It's a bit of a mess. It's all a bit of a mess,' Goosie declares as he shuffles his way back onboard. Jumper nods agreement and pulls a face.

We send a second boat full of equipment and Stokers to *HMS Barbican*. Eventually our team of experts manages to fix the problem. *HMS Tenby*, who also responded to *Barbican*'s call for help, is told to remain with *Barbican* to ensure that she is operational. Both *Tenby* and *Barbican* give us a respectful salute as we sweep majestically away.

We battle our way east before turning west again into the weather to carry out torpedo firings at nothing in particular. As the sun sets over what looks like Scottish tundra, we enter the relatively placid, lead-grey waters of Loch Eriboll accompanied by *HM Submarine Sea Scout*. We thought that coming to anchor would be the last operation of the day ... but it isn't. The Fo'csle lads are particularly 'pissed off' to hear ...

'CLEAR LOWER DECK.
ALL NONE-DUTY MEN MUSTER ON THE UPPER DECK FOR EVENING QUARTERS.
CLEAR LOWER DECK.'

I amble up to the Quarter-deck and am immediately told to muster somewhere else by a couple of Officers, both smoking pipes and leaning on the guardrails – something that we lesser mortals aren't allowed to do ... ever.

Once the lower deck is cleared, we are all instructed to muster on the port side where we have a clear run to the starboard side. This means some of the crew going up to the higher decks. I end up on 01 deck. At the sound of a whistle we are told to run over to the starboard side. Then we are whistled to run back over to the port side. We repeat this until we induce a '*Bermuda*' Roll'. It takes us an hour of running from one side to the other to get our armour-plated monster rolling a degree either side of vertical. Whether this is deemed a success or not, I don't know. At 23:00 we are allowed below with the promise that no further exercises will take place today. Monday 12 June 1961 is over ... thankfully.

Sometime during Tuesday morning, Vice Admiral J G Hamilton tells the Captain who tells the Commander, who tells the First Lieutenant, who tells our Divisional Officer, who tells Petty Officer Batten, who tells Leading Seaman Thomas who tells us ... that today the Juniors' Division of *HMS Bermuda* is going to construct a stone jetty. We look at each other over the breakfast tray. Even Freckles can't explain exactly what is in store for us.

At 09:30 all the Juniors are crammed into boats and taken south to a bleak and unforgiving shoreline. It is a cold and wind-whipped morning. All around us, as we step ashore, is silent and soaking wet. There are no trees; only stark, dark brown mountains streaked with hardy, heather-grey vegetation. The boats leave us. We are stranded. Freckles musters us on the seaward side of a hillock. Sometime later the boat reappears and a two-ring Officer disembarks. He doesn't look too pleased as he unfolds a large sheet of paper and addresses us.

'Good morning. Your task today is to lay the foundations for a medium-sized dwy stone jetty. The local authowities have issued us with a plan.' He waves the paper. 'We shall use the local stone for the foundations, so the first task is to collect as much of the local bwickwork as we can and pile it in a position yet to be decided. Cawy on, Petty Officer.'

Freckles looks bemused. He coughs and beckons Mac and Tommo to his side. They agree to divide us into two teams to scour a designated area for building stone which we will deposit at a point yet to be determined. We stand and shiver.

We spend the next hours humping and carrying stones to a slowly growing pile located just inland of a line of high-water seaweed. At midday the whaler reappears and lands a couple of unhappy-looking lads from *HM Submarine Sea Scout* clad in white Chefs' uniforms. They have with them what we hope is a fully operational field kitchen and boxes that we hope contain food. The Submariners set everything up on a plot of level tundra and within a quarter of an hour we can smell something that we hope is good enough to eat.

Dinner is fabulous. A stew that is both hot and full of meat and just the right amount of vegetables. As the Chefs are packing away, it begins to rain. This isn't normal rain, this is saturating, well-muscled Scottish rain and it comes at us with unrelenting force from somewhere overhead. We begin to lay out the jetty foundations. Working in a foot of cold Scottish Loch water with the rain bucketing down and wearing only shirts and trousers is no joke. Both Chefs try to hide under the canopy of their field kitchen but can't, and the Jetty Construction Officer tells them both to join the 'west' of us carrying stones. They don't like that.

Three hours later a boat arrives to take the Chefs and their equipment back to *Sea Scout*. Despite the fact that it is *Bermuda*'s whaler, the boat's crew have orders only to collect the Chefs and their equipment, so the boat leaves us marooned with nothing but our stones to play with. The rain is continual and to say that we are soaked through to the skin is an understatement. Under my shirt is an unseasonable sea jersey that is saturated and hangs like a suit of cold woolly armour over my freezing upper torso. I hope that we will be rescued before nightfall as there is no shelter here ... on the banks of what is now known as Loch Horrible. The foundations of our jetty look reasonably functional by the time we have used up all the available stones and the tide starts to ebb.

The Jetty Construction Officer says it's 'A job weasonably well done' and even a soaking-wet Freckles nods agreement.

We are rescued in time to miss *Bermuda*'s tea.

By the time we muster for the early-morning scrub-down on Wednesday *HM Submarine Sea Scout* has disappeared. We weigh anchor during Stand-easy and without ceremony, slog our way out of Loch Horrible. I wonder how our jetty foundations have survived the night and the high spring tide.

Our first task of the day is something called 'bombardment shooting', which is closely observed by the Staff Gunnery Officer who apparently is one of the many blokes on Vice Admiral J G Hamilton's staff. I'm glad I didn't join the gunnery branch: they seem to spend an awful long time each day at 'Action Stations' and wearing that horrible anti-flash gear.

Outside the Loch, the fleet forms itself into a convoy around *Bermuda* while the Anti-Submarine Frigates flit around the edges trying to detect and destroy *HM Submarine Sea Scout*. We are an impressive armada of sea power pounding our way east and west along the top ledge of Scotland. We must be scaring the living daylights out of the numerous fishing vessels that we arrogantly expect to get out of our way. Whether we are responsible for any hurriedly abandoned nets, damaged equipment or loss of a lucrative catch, I don't know. This convoy stuff must be important because we are at it all day, proving to our Vice Admiral that an international group of ships can manoeuvre themselves as one unit. Our convoy changes course and direction by wireless-transmitted orders, then by signal lantern and then by semaphore. Then we do it all over again in a slightly different formation. I spend some time that afternoon greasing guardrails on the Quarter-deck: seeing the whole convoy suddenly change direction without warning is an impressive sight. It is cold – we are above 58.5º north according to my information and the wind cuts right through whatever I am wearing.

After tea the Fo'csle party are assembled once again to anchor us in Spey Bay, surrounded by our protective, international convoy.

After sunset all ships illuminate their upper decks. Maybe it is to impress the occupants of the two small crofts that we can see on the mainland. More than likely it is on the whim of Vice Admiral J G Hamilton. For a quiet hour I sit on my favourite washdeck locker, out of the wind, and enjoy the sight of the illuminated fleet while smoking cigarette after cigarette.

The Fo'csle lads are up early and the convoy bids a silent and unobserved farewell to Spey Bay.

Lower deck is cleared for the reading of another punishment warrant. I am at the back alongside a noisy exhaust fan and don't hear any details of the charge. Later in the day Tommo explains that the Leading Steward who has been sentenced to 90 days' imprisonment and dismissal from the service has committed an unlawful sexual offence against an unnamed younger member of his branch.

During the forenoon ...

'HANDS TO ACTION STATIONS.

HANDS TO ACTION STATIONS.

ASSUME DAMAGE CONTROL STATE 1 CONDITION ZULU ALPHA.

CHIEF STEWARD REPORT TO THE BRIDGE. ERR WATER ... WATER IS ...'

My 'Action Station' is HQ1. Along with an army of others I assemble outside Damage Control Headquarters. As a relatively inexperienced Junior, I am allocated to the forward fire-fighting team where I am partially responsible for ensuring that the hoses are pulled from the bulkhead-mounted cradles in a smooth and un-kinked manner. Apart from having to wear full anti-flash gear and a life jacket with my gas mask slung over my shoulder, it doesn't inconvenience me much.

Eventually ...

'ASSUME DAMAGE CONTROL STATE 1 RELAXED CONDITION ZULU ALPHA.

ACTION MESS VICTUALS CAN NOW BE COLLECTED FROM THE MAIN GALLEY.

THE WATER SITUATION WILL BE BROADCAST SHORTLY.'

This enables us all to relax, and along with a Junior Chef I am sent to the galley to fill a battered old fanny with some galley-made tea. Fortunately, because I have a young Chef with me, it is a bother-free exercise. We lounge around, drinking what is awful tea until ...

'ASSUME DAMAGE CONTROL STATE 2 CONDITION YANKEE BRAVO.'

This signals the end of Action Stations. The 'enemy' has been vanquished. Down the mess we relax after dinner and get the cards out.

'DO YOU HEAR THERE ... FRESH WATER WILL BE RATIONED AS FOLLOWS.

BATHROOMS FORWARD OF SECTION CHARLIE AND AFT OF SECTION SIERRA ONLY WILL HAVE FRESH WATER UNTIL 14:15. SECTIONS DELTA TO ROMEO WILL HAVE LOW PRESSURE FRESH WATER BETWEEN 20:00 AND 21:30 THIS EVENING.

SHOWERS MAY NOT OPERATE NORMALLY.

CHIEF SHIPWRIGHT REPORT TO THE BRIDGE.

THE SHIP'S COMPANY ARE REMINDED THAT THE JUNIORS' BATHROOM IS STRICTLY OUT OF BOUNDS.

WILL THE PADRE MAKE HIS WHEREABOUTS KNOWN TO THE OFFICER OF THE WATCH ON THE BRIDGE.'

In the afternoon we lower all our guardrails before being cleared off the Quarter-deck. A large blue helicopter appears from somewhere, hovers above us, lowers a wire and hoists someone up and away.

Sugar points to the mainmast as the red and white Admiral's flag is lowered. 'Life should be a bit less hectic now he's ferkin' gone,' he says as he gives the departing helicopter a formal Churchillian salute.

We both ignore the fact that all the Admiral's staff are still onboard.

The Gunnery branch are once again closed-up to fire our four-inch guns. They sound quite different from the six-inch ones: they are sharper but not as loud. They appear to shoot into the distance and I wonder what would happen if a fishing boat or any other unsuspecting vessel were to get in the way. I suppose the powers-to-be have thought of that.

'CLEAR LOWER DECK OF SEAMEN.

PREPARE FOR JACKSTAY TRANSFER.

CLOSE ALL UPPER DECK SCREEN DOORS AND STARBOARD SIDE SCUTTLES.

THE UPPER DECK IS OUT OF BOUNDS TO ALL MEMBERS OF THE CREW NOT INVOLVED IN THE TRANSFER.

THERE WILL BE NO FRESH WATER THROUGHOUT THE SHIP UNTIL FURTHER NOTICE.

CANTEEN MANAGER AND THE PADRE REPORT TO THE BRIDGE.'

As we pound west into a head wind *Karel Doorman* takes up position on our starboard side. I have a particular interest in heaving-line throwing and I am surprised to see that the Dutch employ a machine to launch a line towards us. Is this the future I ask myself: are heaving-line throwers like me to be made redundant by a machine? The jackstay is rigged and a bloke that looks very much like Vice Admiral J G blasted Hamilton is returned to us.

My Friday starts at 03:45 with the morning watch. At 09:10 exactly, in accordance with our Daily Orders, *HMS Puma* joins us from astern while I help to arrange all the jackstay transfer equipment that we have only stowed away the previous evening. As far as I can see the only thing transferred between *HMS Puma* and ourselves is the well-travelled concrete block that goes back and forth a few times. The high point of the jackstay transfer is my heaving-line throw which is spot-on perfect.

Down the mess, we are all looking forward to tucking in to a tray of beautifully scorched rice pudding when there is a loud wooshing sound through our partially opened scuttle.

'ACTION STATIONS.

ASSUME DAMAGE CONTROL STATE 1 CONDITION ZULU ALPHA.

WE ARE UNDER ATTACK FROM UNIDENTIFIED ENEMY AIRCRAFT ... FROM THE ROYAL AIR FORCE.'

Oh shit!

Bermuda apparently didn't notice *HM Submarine Truncheon* suddenly appear in the centre of the convoy and fire a couple of 'for exercise' torpedoes at us. Apparently a combined air and submarine attack has caught us well and truly with ours pants down. I am seconded to a small team who are responsible for collecting the necessary Damage Control equipment required to shore up our 'damaged' hull and pump out any water. I spend a long time sitting on my backside outside HQ1 waiting for somebody to tell me what to do.

It is almost tea time before ...

'ASSUME DAMAGE CONTROL STATE 2 CONDITION YANKEE BRAVO.'

I stow my gas mask in my locker and am halfway up the mess ladder with my towel wrapped around my waist and my washing gear in hand when ...

'DO YOU HEAR THERE ... THERE WILL BE NO FRESH WATER THROUGHOUT THE SHIP UNTIL FURTHER NOTICE.

THE MAIN GALLEY WILL NOT BE ISSUING HOT FOOD UNTIL FURTHER NOTICE.

CHIEF SHIPWRIGHT REPORT TO THE BRIDGE.

MAIL IS NOW READY FOR COLLECTION AT THE REGULATING OFFICE.

WILL THE PADRE MAKE HIS WHEREABOUTS KNOWN TO THE OFFICER OF THE WATCH ON THE BRIDGE.'

'I bet the Admiral has enough hot water for his ferkin' bath,' someone says.

I struggle back into my stinking number 8s. I don't respond when Tommo asks, 'Anyone fancy a game of crib?'

I can't avoid Blacky: he comes at me on the blind side.

'Us Gunners are having a hard time of it you know, mate.'

'I know,' I say.

'I'm thinking of putting in a request form to change branches.'

'To what?'

'Your branch doesn't seem to do much.'

'Course we do.' I don't mention Blacky's black eye: I suppose it is a gunnery injury.

'I'm thinking of joining the Royal Marines.'

'What, as a bandsman?'

He squashes a runaway cockroach under his shoe. 'Naah. I'm from a musical family. I can play a good saxophone and the piano, but I'm thinking of applying to be a full-time paratrooper type Marine. I've been reading up about it.'

'I've been invited for a game of crib. See you later,' I lie.

The 'squashed' cockroach flexes itself, waves its antennae and scuttles away into a shoe locker.

We anchor off Invergordon just before teatime. Fortunately we are far enough away from prying eyes that our two 'for exercise' torpedo holes just below the waterline on our port side can't be seen.

Just as we are about to stow everything away and head down the mess for a smoke ...

'FO'CSLE AND QUARTER-DECK SEAMEN TO MUSTER.

HM SUBMARINES SEA SCOUT **AND** *TRUNCHEON* **WILL BE BERTHING ALONGSIDE IN THE NEXT TEN MINUTES.**

THE MAIN FORWARD AND AFTER CREWS BATHROOMS AND THE JUNIORS' BATHROOM ARE STRICTLY OUT OF BOUNDS UNTIL FURTHER NOTICE.'

'It's so the Submariners can get a shower,' Tommo explains. 'They only get a cup full of water every other day to drink, wash, brush their teeth, shower and wipe their arses with.'

The powerful smell of diesel oil the Submariners bring with them is surprising. They are a slovenly, unshaven lot. Looking wide-eyed at everything as though seeing things for the very first time and speaking in whispered tones.

I get a nice letter from Wakefield in the second batch of mail, but I do notice that the number of kisses on the bottom has decreased significantly and I am now addressed as 'Dear Pete' instead of 'My Darling Pete'.

I must look taken aback as I read Wilco's single-page letter that is packed full of sexually explicit stuff.

Tommo asks: 'Bad news young Peter? You've got a bit of a glow on.'

'Err ... no, nothing like that.'

'It's either bad news or filth judging from your colour.'

'A little bit of filth, Hooky.'

'Need anything explained to you?'

'Not really ... no.'

It is 23:45 before it is broadcast ...

'DO YOU HEAR THERE ... LIMITED FRESH WATER WILL BE AVAILABLE FOR THE NEXT THIRTY MINUTES IN ALL BATHROOMS'.

I say 'Sod it' to my pillow. It takes ages before I fall asleep: I keep going over Wilco's letter.

8

OUT OF BOUNDS IN AARHUS

The Quarter-deck scrubbing party un-berths *HM Submarines Sea Scout* and *Truncheon* at the crack of dawn on Saturday and they slink out of Cromarty Firth.

We are promised a weekend of relaxation and recreation according to Daily Orders. We are also told that things could change at short notice ... or no notice at all. Before dinner the lower deck is once again cleared for the reading of another punishment warrant. This time it is for 'aggravated insubordination' and 'striking a senior officer'. Apparently the Able Seaman from the Fo'csle part-of-ship has stuck-one-on the Assistant Fo'csle Officer, the Fo'csle Petty Officer and a Midshipman who was in the wrong place at the wrong time.

Stumpy and I take advantage of a couple of hours' shore leave to stretch our legs on Sunday. The two hours allocated to the Juniors' department are outside the hours during which alcoholic beverages can be purchased on the Sabbath by registered travellers.

We each buy a different Sunday newspaper and find a sheltered bench in a park. It is nice to watch the swaying trees: a pleasant change from rolling grey seas. The newspapers are full of Scottish news: a waste of a good English four pence!

'I see that Surrey beat Yorkshire by an innings and 43 runs,' says Stumpy.

'Piss off.'

We don't stay ashore long as the strengthening wind is coming from somewhere bitterly cold.

Bermuda's first task of the new week is to fend off more attacking aircraft. We effectively fight them off before joining the protective screen around the Aircraft Carrier *HMS Hermes*. We are no longer the largest ship of the fleet, despite being the most senior. We refuel from *RFA Tidesurge* later in the day. In the afternoon I help one of the Damage Control parties who are in constant demand, plugging imaginary leaks, pumping out non-existent flood-water and fighting a number of make-believe fires.

It appears that at no time have we managed more than three hours' continual sleep. It would be convenient for us to keep our hammocks slung, so that we can flop into them whenever we're not doing something, but of course, we can't do that.

I have to pass the Sick Bay on my way back from the Quarter-deck each morning. There is always a group waiting for it to open for business at 08:00.

This morning I am surprised to see a morose-looking Lash in the queue. 'You OK, Lash?' It is a stupid question I suppose.

'Not too bad.'

'Never had you down as a Sick Bay Ranger.' A few of the other queue members glare at me. I offer Lash a fag.

Lash, who rarely has cigarettes of his own, accepts one gladly. 'I've got a wind problem.'

I tap his shoulder. 'I've noticed mate.'

'Serious Pete, it's almost continual. This farting business is becoming embarrassing.'

'I've noticed.'

'Have ya?'

'Yep: everyone has.'

'Everyone?'

'Fraid so mate.'

'I think it's something I'm eating.'

By the time breakfast is over, everybody in the mess knows all about Lash's problem.

On Thursday afternoon the fleet disperses. *Bermuda*, along with her escorts *HMS Puma* and *HMS Undaunted*, sets a course for a place in Denmark called Aarhus.

A Pay Officer sets up a desk in the forward capstan flat and exchanges our Bank of England money for some Danish stuff. Not wanting to miss a Danish trick, I change all my money.

'CLOSE UP SPECIAL SEA DUTYMEN.

HANDS FALL IN FOR ENTERING HARBOUR PROCEDURE ALPHA.

HANDS OUT OF THE RIG OF THE DAY CLEAR OFF THE UPPER DECK.

CLOSE ALL UPPER DECK SCREEN DOORS AND SCUTTLES.'

I rarely read a newspaper so I don't realise that Denmark and the United Kingdom are currently embroiled in a fishing dispute. Along with most of my messmates, I don't understand why our dignified approach, with all the appropriate flags flying, is thwarted by a Danish fishing vessel that has purposefully streamed its nets across the main approach channel. *Bermuda* is therefore denied free legitimate passage until the obstruction is cleared. Lined up for entering harbour it is difficult to see if the gesticulating crowds that line our approach are glad to see us or not. I am excited: I am about to experience my very first 'proper' foreign Naval visit. From what I can see, Denmark looks to be a nice tidy place.

Sugar is unfolding the brow dodgers, so I have the privilege of throwing the first heaving-line to Aarhus's No. 1 Jetty. It arcs perfectly but lands a few yards away from the dockyard-mateys who are all dressed in smart blue shirts and trousers. One of them manages to grab the 'fist' before it bounces its way back into the water and we efficiently feed out our very best berthing ropes and wires. I notice that one of the blokes dressed in blue on the jetty isn't a real bloke: she has the unmistakeable shape of a woman. I am impressed – Danish women can apparently pull just as efficiently as any of the blokes. A mobile dockside crane is available to hoist out our two brows, one on the Quarter-deck for the exclusive use of the Wardroom and official guests and one on the boat deck for the rest of us. Both our brows have gleaming white canvas dodgers on which is painted our ship's name and the ship's crest. At the bottom of the after brow we position a couple of polished wooden stands on which are lifebelts emblazoned with our name and lots of 'tiddly' white ropes.

HMS Puma and *HMS Undaunted* berth some distance away and around a corner. We reckon that we have the best berth, as befits the Flagship.

One additional piece of Naval bullshit that I, nor the rest of the Quarter-deck team, don't expect is the covering of all the outboard berthing ropes and wires with white canvas. None of us know exactly how to do it but Goosie and one of our Killicks sort everything out and we soon have our berthing ropes looking white and pristine.

The Commander-in-Chief of the Home Fleet has slipped aboard without me noticing him. If we think that we have finished once we have lashed our canvas covers onto the berthing ropes and wires, we are mistaken. We have to change into clean Number 8s and rig awnings. It takes ages for us to rig both the main canvas awning and the pink-and-white decorative ones in preparation for the first serious Wardroom Cock & Arse Party (Sugar's words) of the trip. Officers flit around pointing and criticising things. Goosie calmly organises everything.

Down the mess, one of the lads, a Junior Stores Assistant not involved in any of the serious working stuff, explains to us that the Padre has been on the Tannoy to tell us something about Aarhus and the parts of town that are out-of-bounds to us. He has made notes of the places the Padre has said we should avoid. Tommo confirms that they are probably the best places to visit.

Freckles explains what Procedure Alpha is all about. Apparently it is a historic procedure when a Royal Naval ship is entering a foreign port – a demonstration that the ship comes in peace with the majority of the crew visible on the upper deck and not manning guns. It is still a ferkin' nuisance, no matter what it signifies.

The pomp and ceremony of the first night's cocktail party is well under way on the Quarter-deck as Stumpy and I hand in our station cards, wander over the brow and set foot, for the first time, on Danish soil. The Royal Marine band is playing something uplifting on the jetty and a stream of well-heeled civilian visitors are arriving onboard through a gap in the side awning.

Aarhus doesn't have a great deal to offer in the form of entertainment. Before we hit the town proper, we meet up with some of *Bermuda*'s crew on the way back to the ship who complain about having to fork-out a complete day's pay for a pint of weak Danish beer.

Stumpy and I just wander. The bars that we come across are empty – a clear indication that members of Her Majesty's Royal Navy aren't that impressed with what the watering holes of Aarhus have to offer – but we are satisfied with the simple pleasures of life, sitting on a bench or lounging against an available wall, smoking and admiring the Danish girls ... all of whom ignore us.

By the time we walk back up *Bermuda*'s brow, the cocktail party is in full swing. The Royal Marine band has gone, replaced by the giggles and laughter from those silhouetted on the inside of the pink-and-white striped side screens.

Blacky comes back onboard feigning drunkenness and telling everybody in the mess how accommodating the Danish girls are. We ignore him.

On Saturday *Bermuda* is officially 'open to visitors' and Tug I are duty. We spend a long morning clearing up the mess that the Wardroom Stewards have left after the party. I am amazed at how many cigarette burns are on *Bermuda*'s wooden deck and Goosie can't relax until he gets us all on our hands and knees to remove them before we wash down. A couple of lads are put onto a floating pontoon with mops on the end of long poles to clean the ship's side. Another pair polish 'Y' turret and I, along with a small team of others, am given the technical job of scrubbing the wooden gratings that cover the bollards and fairleads.

Throughout the ship, notices and rope barriers are hung, passageways cleaned and doors clipped and locked in preparation for our first invasion of foreign visitors. Along with compartments that contain top-secret Royal Naval equipment, the messdecks and bathrooms are out of bounds. Two of the Officers' Heads are given a special clean and designated as the visitors' facilities. As Duty Watch we are stationed at various places to help and offer advice to our Danish visitors. Unfortunately, there aren't many of them and the afternoon turns out to be a bit of an open-to-visitors malfunction. Maybe it has something to do with our fishing dispute: maybe it is just because the good people of Aarhus have better things to do on a pleasantly warm Saturday afternoon.

Tug and I spend the afternoon 'hanging around' at the bottom of the ladder leading from 01 deck to the Quarter-deck. We have noticed that some of our female visitors wear high-heeled shoes and skirts and find it difficult to negotiate the steep ladders gracefully.

On Sunday, unbeknown to us in the Juniors' mess, Vice Admiral J G Hamilton transfers himself to *HMS Undaunted* and the pennant flying from the top of our mast is lowered.

At 20:00 we 'single up' and have tugs ready to un-berth us as the *Danish Royal Yacht Dannebrog* passes us on her way to sea. Salutes are exchanged and *Bermuda* follows at a respectful distance. Lower-deck rumour has it that we are on our way to Copenhagen. Aarhus has been a disappointing run ashore and the information given to us by the Padre was inaccurate and misleading. We hope the Danish capital will have more interesting stuff to offer.

'The beer won't be any cheaper,' says Mac. 'If anything it'll be more expensive.'

We all have our paper and pencils at the ready when the Padre gets on the Tannoy to tell us all about the places that are out-of-bounds in Copenhagen. I have the Danish equivalent of four British pounds to splash out on whatever the capital city has to offer me.

9

COPENHAGEN:
FRIENDLY OLD GIRL OF A TOWN

We arrive in Copenhagen in the early morning. Once again all the accoutrements of a ceremonial visit are wheeled out: brows, dodgers, lifebelts on polished wooden stands, white canvas covers on our berthing ropes and wires and of course the Quarter-deck awnings are rigged. The decks are scrubbed to within an inch of their life and every splash of Kattegat water removed.

By the time we have finishing rigging the Quarter-deck, the first batch of those going ashore are streaming over the brow towards the delights of Denmark's capital city. Down the mess Tommo gives us the rundown on what he remembers from his last visit. If he remembers correctly, the famous Mermaid statue is on the waterside not far away from where we are berthed. However, running alongside the Mermaid statue are the notorious Whispering Gardens where gentlemen of a certain type try and entice young, and sometimes not so young, sailors into the bushes.

Stumpy, Tug, Streaky and I skip across the brow in our best suits that evening. The cocktail party guests are arriving on the Quarter-deck and the Band of the Royal Marines is standing silently to attention on the jetty waiting for sunset. Between the four of us we are confident that we have enough money in our pockets to afford a couple of expensive Copenhagen drinks.

I am disappointed at the size of the Mermaid: she is tiny. I expected her to be life-size at the very least. She is covered in bird shit and not very well endowed in the chest department. All four of us keep a wary eye out for anything untoward from the Whispering Gardens but there is nothing. One of the first places we come across is a tattoo parlour. Stumpy has an inbuilt attraction to tattooists and before we know what is happening we are all sitting in a beautifully clean parlour with the sound of a well-oiled needle machine buzzing away in the background. Streaky and Tug are made of sterner stuff than I am, and when asked by Stumpy if they are 'Going to get one?' they refuse. I end up with a bunch of Danish flowers surrounding my name on a piece of ribbon located just under the outstretched claws of my green-winged eagle. Once again my starboard forearm is swathed in lint and adhesive tape.

Streaky has written down the list of places identified by the Padre and the taxi driver understands completely. The first is a large open bar full of noisy Danes and a good sprinkling of lads from *Bermuda*, *Puma* and *Undaunted*. The first round of drinks costs me a small fortune. None of us are real beer experts. I suppose because I lived in an Off Licence I am considered best-qualified to pass judgement – in my humble opinion, the pale urine-coloured beer is tasteless. I'm annoyed with both the cost and the fact that about a third of my glass is froth. When I complain about the amount of froth the barman slices it away with a large lollipop stick. We find a table in the corner and watch the well-endowed Danish girls gyrating nicely to the music from the jukebox. We all sing along to 'Blue Moon' by the Marcels and 'Warpaint' by The Brook Brothers: confident that we know all the English words. Nearly every female in the place is wearing a blue denim skirt: maybe it is a uniform of some kind. By the time Streaky buys our fourth round my head is starting to buzz. The music is getting louder, the place more crowded and my bunch of Danish flowers is itching.

A gang of four denim-skirted women, each carrying their own chair, plonk themselves down at our table and introduce themselves with firm handshakes and smiles all round. One, who speaks perfect English, explains what they are selling and at exactly what price. The price is outrageous. A dribbling Streaky slowly counts his change and shrugs his shoulders apologetically at the largest of the four. 'Sorry.'

One of the women leans over to check Streaky's money, purses her lips, exhales noiselessly and shakes her head.

Streaky looks her straight in the cleavage. 'Sorry.' He turns to look inquiringly at Tug, Stumpy and I. 'Don't suppose any of you have …?'

We all shake our heads. Even if we wanted to, we can't muster the required amount.

The magnificently sculptured woman gives Streaky an understanding tap on his shoulder and sashays away.

The English speaker explains to us how ridiculously expensive cigarettes are in Denmark and wants to know what price we can buy them for onboard our ship. Once the vast price difference is established, she asks if we could bring some cigarettes for them the next time we are in town and they will buy them from us at twice the price. We know that in Portsmouth we are only allowed to take 25 duty-free cigarettes a day out of the dockyard. However, there is no dockyard gate in Copenhagen and after four beers, we are all tempted, particularly Streaky who doesn't smoke .

'Do you think I could trade cigarettes for … err you know … thingie?'

'Positive thinking, Streaks,' I say. I am impressed.

We hand our cigarettes around and are surprised that only one of our female guests smokes.

The bar is a writhing, noisy mass of drunken singing Danes and sailors by the time we have to leave. Juniors' leave ends at 23:00.

We all rummage for change to pay the taxi and Stumpy is sick behind a large wooden crate somewhere between the taxi and the shit-encrusted mermaid.

Down the mess all is dark and all four of us have forgotten to ask someone to sling our hammocks for us. Stumpy manfully tries to get his up, but gives up in the end and spreads it out under the mess table and goes to sleep. I don't know what Streaky or Tug are doing: I am busy getting to grips with mine. The lad who has the next slinging point to mine gives me a hand.

'What's Copenhagen like, then?'

'OK.'

'Lots to do?'

'Yep.'

'Loads of girls?'

'Loads.'

'Did you talk to any?'

'Yep.'

'Do anything else?'

'Got a tattoo.'

'Want any help?'

'Naah. Think I'll crash on the mess stool.'

'See you in the morning then.'

'OK.'

I wake on Thursday morning, still dressed in my trousers and white front, curled around the wheelhouse hatch combing with my hat used as a pillow. I have a stonking headache that jabs at the inside of my skull whenever I move, and my arm itches. A wodge of lint and sticky tape prevents me from scratching my itch. I vaguely remember getting a tattoo.

As I throw my unused and badly lashed-up hammock into the hammock stowage a smiling Tommo asks me if I enjoyed myself. I say that I can't remember much about it.

It is much later in the day when I have re-learned how to string a reasonably coherent number of words together, that the subject of last night's 'proposal' is raised. Both Mac and Tommo overhear the exchange.

'That's normal in the Scandinavian countries because their smokes are so expensive,' says Mac.

'But they were such nice girls ... er women.'

'Not worth the risk.'

'They offered double what we pay.'

'Not enough.'

'But there's no Dockyard Gate here.'

'Did you notice that the Leading Regulator on the brow when you went ashore last night?'

'No.'

'He is looking for uncommonly large bulges in your uniform.'

'I had a predominantly large bulge!' Streaky jokes.

'So did I,' I say.

'You know what I mean. You can still get charged with smuggling if you take more than your allowance of fags ashore. Take some advice from me ... don't do it!'

HMS Blackwood arrives the following morning and berths around the corner.

Another Punishment Warrant is read and an elderly bloke, who should have known better, is sentenced to 90 days at the Royal Naval Detention Quarters in Gosport for smuggling fags when we were in Invergordon.

The level of bullshit is racked-up a couple of notches this morning. The Quarter-deck, surrounding areas and fittings, are spit and polished. We are dismissed before the King and Queen of Denmark arrive onboard for dinner.

Do Royalty do dinner?

In the afternoon we host a children's party. I have an amble up to the Boat deck after dinner, just to see how things are going and to have a look at the teachers, who all turn out to be men with beards. On the Boat deck there is a slide, swings, roundabout and even a large tray full of sand. I don't know where these things have come from, but they obviously belong to *Bermuda*: maybe they are Admiralty Pattern items: 'children, for the use of'. The Duty Part of the Watch have dressed themselves up as pirates, cowboys or Red Indians.

Later the Commander-in-Chief escorts the Minister of Defence ashore. Even the schoolchildren on the Boat deck fall silent as *Bermuda* ceremonially welcomes Vice Admiral J G Hamilton back onboard.

Next day, Tug and I cobble together enough money for an early evening wander about town. We buy a single postcard each and write a short message to our mums while enjoying an extremely expensive cup of coffee in the centre of town. I would have sent a postcard to the girl in Wakefield and to Wilco but that would have trebled my costs, so I don't. We stroll past a few bars where groups of Her Majesty's finest are doing what they do best – drinking to excess!

Copenhagen is not an enjoyable place for two inexperienced Junior Seamen with empty pockets and we gradually make our way back through the Whispering Gardens, past the Mermaid and back onboard. We've done Copenhagen.

Sitting round the mess table that evening, Lash explains to us about his flatulence problem. 'It's definitely something I'm consuming regularly.'

'Is it?'

'According to the SBA, it could be anything ... even what I'm drinking. What I've got to do is cut something out for a week and see if there is any improvement or change.'

'And what are you cutting out this week?' I ask.

'Spam. Don't ferkin' like it much anyway.'

'It's not the ferkin' Spam then is it?' Tug asks.

'Obviously not,' replies Lash.

'What's the next thing to stop then?'

'Coffee. Don't ferkin' like it anyway.' He farts.

'Bloody hell, Lash, that's awful,' says Tug, waving his arms around. 'Your insides must be rotten.'

'Sorry lads. It's a medical mystery. I do try and control 'em.'

'Well try harder!'

Saturday. We know that we are sailing because this morning we remove and stow away all our bullshit items. Immediately after dinner, the canvas covers on our mooring lines are removed and in the afternoon a couple of harbour tugs pull us away from the jetty. We fire a gun salute as we leave, but we don't receive one in return.

10

NINETEEN SHILLINGS FOR
AN ENGLISH POUND

Blacky is stuffing his kit into his kit bag in preparation for his move to the For'd Seamen's Mess. Tomorrow, at the age of seventeen and a half, he will automatically be promoted to Ordinary Seaman.

'Thought any more about the Marines, Blacky?' I ask.

'Definitely going for it. I've got myself a contact down the Marines' mess. Once I've established myself in the For'd Mess, I'll see what I can arrange.'

'Right then.'

'I've already organised myself a tot.'

'You can't have: you're not old enough.'

He strokes the side of his nose, 'It's not how old you are, mate, it's how many friends you have.'

I recognise the symptoms. This is how Blacky's stories begin, with a claim to have friends. 'Blacky, you're full of shit.'

'What makes you say that?'

'You do.'

'You haven't seen my best cap have you?'

'No.' I decide that I'd rather be on the Quarter-deck than talking to Blacky, so I make myself a sausage sarnie from what is left in the breakfast tray and leave.

On the Quarter-deck Jumper points out three fishing boats: one on our starboard beam and two off our port quarter. 'Problem is young 'un, they're not really fishing boats.'

'What are they, then?'

'Russians.'

'Russians?' I peer closer and I spot my very first Russian on the bridge wings of the nearest boat.

'Look at all those aerials, they're not fishing – they're listening to every word we say and taking pictures. Right now both of us could be in the centre of someone's long-range lens.'

'Naah.'

At Stand-easy I plonk myself on my favourite wash-deck locker, light a cigarette and stare at the nearest of these strangely rigged vessels and wonder what life onboard a Russian boat is like.

During the Last Dog watch in the Ops Room Tansy explains that the three 'Intelligence Gatherers' are not unusual and they will probably stay with us for the foreseeable future. We give them special identification letters: Bogeys 'X-ray, Yankee and Zulu'.

Our three Russian escorts stop as we enter the Firth of Forth. We pass under the Forth Rail Bridge and berth our self in Rosyth dockyard. My first impression of Rosyth isn't good: it is wind-lashed, rain-swept and grey.

In the cold light of morning, Rosyth looks slightly more appealing. Blacky makes a big deal out of the fact that this will be the last time he will be scrubbing the Quarter-deck. To celebrate the fact that we won't have to put up with him anymore, a couple of the Men under Punishment arrange to give him a good hosing down.

A soaking wet Blacky doesn't quite get the point of it. 'Mates eh?' he says … to himself.

'DO YOU HEAR THERE … AMMUNITION SHIP.

NO SMOKING OR NAKED LIGHTS THROUGHOUT THE SHIP.

I SAY AGAIN … NO SMOKING OR NAKED LIGHTS THROUGHOUT THE SHIP.

CLOSE ALL UPPER DECK SCREEN DOORS, SCUTTLES AND DEADLIGHTS.'

From amid the early-morning Rosyth haze an ammunition lighter appears and is berthed alongside. We spend the forenoon passing a combination of four-inch and six-inch shells along a human chain. Thankfully it isn't a full day's job and by dinner time we have re-stocked our magazines.

Fag!

The mess is somehow different now that Blacky has gone.

Celebratory fag!

Lower deck is cleared the following morning for what we expect to be the reading of yet another Punishment Warrant, but we are wrong, Mrs Lumby's husband wants to talk to us. It takes him 10 minutes or so to congratulate us on what we have achieved so far, emphasising the success of our partial destruction of Hoan Island and relaying words of gratitude from the elders of Copenhagen. Apparently, we conducted ourselves in a manner expected of those representing the Royal Navy. He finishes by saying that we still have a lot of hard work to do and that we should be proud to be serving onboard the Flagship of the Home Fleet. We are all waiting to hear what our next overseas visit will be, but he finishes by telling us to enjoy the next seven days in Rosyth.

Wednesday's visitors include the Captain of *HMS Duncansby Head*, the Chief of Staff to Flag Officer Scotland and the Captain of the Fishery Protection Squadron.

Down the mess Tommo gives us the lowdown on Rosyth, Dunfermline and Edinburgh: they all have very different attractions. Rosyth is a town built around the dockyard. It has numerous pubs, and when a large ship like *Bermuda* comes in, it attracts the professional women from miles around. Dunfermline is a short bus ride away and is a town built on a slope with a plentiful array of good pubs and a dance-hall. Edinburgh is over the bridge and has all that is expected of a capital city. I am beginning to realise that pubs are considered to be the main attractions of any Scottish village, town or city.

'Shall we hit the town then?' asks Tug.

'Which one?'

'Rosyth, I suppose.'

'Maybe tomorrow, after we've been paid.'

'Good thinking.'

The following morning we scrub down the Quarter-deck on an insipidly damp and dreary Scottish summer's day. Thankfully, it is also pay-day and Tug, Stumpy, Streaky and I spend some time discussing tactics for our first foray to Rosyth.

That evening we stroll down the brow and into Rosyth dockyard – a quiet and empty place on a grey, overcast evening. Instinctively we know our way to the Dockyard gate. On the way we pass the Rosyth Dockyard Canteen which, with its invitingly lit yellowed windows, looks an ideal place to start a run ashore. Rosyth Dockyard Canteen dispenses excellent Heavy: I am developing a taste for the stuff. We find empty snooker tables. Those that have played before take the time to explain the Scottish rules of the game to me.

Three pints later and with the rules of snooker buzzing around my head, we venture out of the Dockyard Gates and into Rosyth proper. The pubs closest to the gate are heaving with *Bermuda*'s drinkers. We aren't confident enough yet to slink into these crowded places where, no doubt, the professional women that Tommo has told us about will be plying their trade. So we look for a side street and somewhere quieter. We find a pub that is full of local men who stare at us strangely as we occupy a small table in a dark corner. It is my turn to get the drinks, and I manage it OK. 'Four pints of err ... Heavy, please.'

I pay with a pound note that the bloke behind the bar scrutinises. 'English money?'

'Yes.'

'Only worth nineteen of your English shillings here in Scotland, yae ken.'

'Pardon?'

'Only worth nineteen shillings this side of the border.'

A couple of blokes sitting near the end of the bar snigger and I immediately become suspicious.

I hold my hand out for my change. 'There are twenty shillings in a British pound.'

There is an audible intake of breath from the end of the bar. One of the blokes slams his pint glass on the bar top.

I carry two pints to our table and come back to the bar for the remaining two. There is a ten-shilling note topped by coins sitting in a puddle of beer on the bar top. The barman is wiping something at the back of the bar, his back towards me. I pocket the money without counting it, pick up the two remaining pints and make my way back to the table.

'Have you heard that a British pound is only worth nineteen bob here in Scotland?'

'It isn't is it?' asks Tug.

'Blimey,' says Streaky.

'Ferkin' hell!' exclaims Stumpy through a mouthful of Heavy.

The beer isn't as nice as the stuff in the Canteen. By the time we've all bought a round, we decide that we've had enough of Rosyth and stagger back onboard like real sailors.

We tell Tommo about the unexpected devaluation of the British pound.

'You tell the bastards to 'stick it' if they ever try that one on you again. What pub was it?'

'Can't remember.'

Once I have slung my hammock I count my money, but I can't work out if I have been 'seen-off' or not. The King of all

Cockroaches is eying me up from around the curved corner of a fan trunking ... but I've had four pints of Heavy and am not the least bit intimidated. If he wants a confrontation then I am up for it.

Next day, we have another go at snooker in the Dockyard Canteen: I've definitely added snooker to my compendium of games. Tug in particular is becoming quite good at 'pocketing' his balls. Tug and I appreciate the funny side of anything that is remotely connected with Tug's 'tackle'. We both remember the Foreskin Manipulation Day that took place a few weeks after we joined *HMS Ganges*. With a grimace we both recall his failure that day, his subsequent circumcision and how he earned his nickname.

After a couple of pints, we decide that Dunfermline has survived long enough without the benefit of our company, so we catch a bus. We end up in a pub called St Margaret's where we learn that Scottish pubs close at 22:00 and there is no official 'drinking up' time.

On Sunday Goosie is Duty Petty Officer, so once again the Quarter-deck is scrubbed properly.

'Have you seen Daily Orders?' asks Tug.

'Course.'

'We've got a children's party this afternoon.'

'Have we?'

'And we're duty.'

'I know that.'

At 13:30, we muster outside the door of the compartment that contains the slide, roundabout, swings, bags of sand and lots of dressing-up clothes.

A busload of morose-looking children assemble on the jetty as Tug and I are putting the final securing bolt in place on a ship-side grey see-saw. Tug has opted to dress as a pirate and I am dressed as a cowboy with a large Stetson. I am looking forward to seeing what the teachers are like. Who could resist a man of the wild and woolly west? As they troop onboard I am disappointed to see that all the teachers have beards – again.

The kids are wonderful. Despite the language barrier, we manage to get them playing in our Boat deck playground: the tyres suspended on ropes from the main crane gantry prove particularly popular. There is no communication with the teachers, who stand in a 'wee bunch' on the starboard side, smoking their pipes and stroking their leather elbow patches.

Blacky appears and asks Tug where all the teachers are.

Tug points to the 'wee bunch'.

'Is that them?'

'No, they're Scotland's latest rock and roll group,' I say.

'Are they? What are they called?' asks a wide-eyed Blacky.

'He's taking the piss,' explains Tug.

'I ferkin' knew that ... really. Nothing very attractive here then?'

'Well spotted, Blacky.'

'May as well piss off ashore then. Pity you two are duty. I found a great pub the other night: packed solid with young Scottish lasses all gagging for it.'

'Where's that then?' I ask.

Blacky taps the side of his nose. 'State secret, mate ... state secret.'

'You're full of shit!' Tug and I say together.

I scoot over to where a young boy has fallen off the roundabout. All he wants is a friendly arm around his shoulder. By the time he has recovered and is back among his mates, Blacky has gone.

'He never fails to come out with a load of bollocks does he?' says Tug.

'A pub with loads of girls all gagging for it indeed.' I scan the playground.

'What if he's right, though? What if he's telling the truth for once?'

'Don't. You know what Blacky's like.'

'You're right, but wha ...'

'Don't.' I point towards the swings. 'We've got another casualty, your turn.'

Tug is quickly down on his knees wiping away little tears from the rosy cheeks of a little girl who has been a little slow in getting off one of the tyres.

As the afternoon light is failing, the kids line up to say a combined 'Thank You' and skip across the brow. The teachers corral their charges back onto the buses without a backward glance.

It starts to rain as we begin the dismantling of our playground.

11

THE BATTLE OF BEN SHEILDAIG

We are looking forward to a relaxing dinner when ...

'EMERGENCY LEAVING HARBOUR ROUTINE.
SPECIAL SEA DUTYMEN CLOSE UP.
UPPER DECK SEAMAN MUSTER AT YOUR PART-OF-SHIP.
CLOSE ALL UPPER DECK SCREEN DOORS AND SCUTTLES.
HANDS OUT OF THE RIG OF THE DAY CLEAR OFF THE
UPPER DECK.'

Within 15 minutes we are trundling under the Forth Railway Bridge.

Sugar says: 'The ferkin' Stokers must have known all about this. Our main engines can't be flashed up in 15 minutes.'

As we exit the Firth of Forth two of the Russian 'Intelligence Gatherers' appear from nowhere and take station on our port and starboard quarter.

We grab dinner as the Anti-Aircraft guns crew close up and we spend the first part of the afternoon tracking and firing at invisible aircraft. The Damage Control state is continually changed and we are warned that Action Messing will be exercised for tea.

And it is ...

'ACTION STATIONS FOR ACTION MESSING.
ASSUME DAMAGE CONTROL STATE 1 CONDITION ZULU
ALPHA RELAXED.
ALL PERSONNEL ARE TO REMAIN CLOSED UP FOR TEA
WHICH WILL BE PROVIDED AT THEIR STATION.'

The object of this exercise is to test the galley's ability to feed us while we remain at Action Stations. I sit on the deck outside HQ1 with all the others and examine the inside of my butter-free corned beef sandwich. Two hours later the exercise is over. Down the mess we exchange culinary information: the Ops Room crew had white bread sandwiches with jam ... and butter.

'Must have run out of ferkin' butter before they got round to us then!' I say.

That evening we bounce along the northern ledge of Scotland once again. Our Russian escorts remain with us. We have Spam for nine-o-clockers. Lash turns his nose up at it.

I have the Forenoon watch in the Ops Room on Tuesday, and I know exactly where we are as the Scottish sun tries its best to shed light upon us and warm us. We are not far from Loch Horrible on our way still further west to another remote Scottish Loch called Torridon that is somewhere in the Western Highlands. It sounds uninviting.

We round Cape Wrath a little after 09:30. Tansy grants me a quick 'fag break' so that I can have a look at this strangely named place. From a sun-washed distance it looks as bleak as its name.

'CLOSE UP SPECIAL SEA DUTYMEN.

PREPARE FOR ENTERING ... ERR ... A LOCH.

COOKS TO THE GALLEY.

NAVIGATOR'S YEOMAN REPORT TO THE BRIDGE.

WILL THE PADRE MAKE HIS WHEREABOUTS KNOWN TO THE OFFICER OF THE WATCH ON THE BRIDGE.'

We lose our Russian escorts as *Bermuda* negotiates her way between grey-brown Scottish mountains well into the bowels of Loch Torridon where we drop anchor into its deep, iron-grey waters ...

'DO YOU HEAR THERE ... FRESH WATER WILL BE RATIONED AS FOLLOWS.

BATHROOMS FORWARD OF SECTION DELTA AND AFT OF SECTION TANGO ONLY WILL HAVE FRESH WATER UNTIL 21:45 APPROXIMATELY.

THE SHIP'S COMPANY ARE REMINDED THAT THE JUNIORS' BATHROOM IS STRICTLY OUT OF BOUNDS.

CHIEF SHIPWRIGHT AND THE CHIEF SAILMAKER REPORT TO THE BRIDGE.'

The Fo'csle Juniors stagger back down the mess, damp and cold. They haven't heard the 'water rationing' pipe and are more than a little pissed off when they have to sit down the mess in the hope that our bathroom will have water sometime after 21:45.

We don't of course.

On Wednesday *HMS Troubridge* anchors behind us.

'She was a Destroyer ... now she's a Frigate,' say Sugar.

'How did that happen, then?'

'Paper work, young 'un ... paper work.'

That evening we all sit around the mess table for the very first *Bermuda* mess quiz. Tommo writes down the answers to questions broadcast over the ship's Tannoy. The questions are mainly Navy-related and we Juniors don't have the background knowledge to answer many of them. Tommo knows a few. We have a quarter of an hour after the last of the 50 questions to get our completed answer sheet to the bridge. We know that we haven't done well and we finish at the very bottom of the *Bermuda* Quiz League. The winner is one of the Senior Rates' messes.

Just before dinner on Thursday...

'FOR EXERCISE, FOR EXERCISE, FIRE IN THE MAIN GALLEY. FIRE IN THE MAIN GALLEY.'

Sod's law: I am queuing to collect the mess trays. Along

with everyone else in the queue I am swept aside by men wearing Fearnought suits. Hoses are snaked everywhere, men in breathing equipment stagger around. Smoke bombs are set off, people are shouting at each other. Dinner is definitely buggered up. Once again we collect a couple of white loaves and half-a-dozen tins of something pink and processed.

The following day the Juniors division are ferried ashore to construct a dry-stone cairn in the rain. We stand on the windswept banks of the Loch expecting someone to appear who knows how to construct a dry-stone cairn: but nobody arrives. After three drenched hours our boat arrives to take us back onboard. We squelch back onboard, cold and wet, to be greeted by the news that the Juniors' bathroom has hot, running fresh water ... for now.

'DETAILS OF TODAY'S WATER RATIONING WILL BE BROADCAST SHORTLY.
ENGINEERING OFFICER, AND CHIEF SHIPWRIGHT REPORT TO THE BRIDGE.'

I enjoy a wonderfully hot and powerful shower: interrupted by ...

'CLEAR LOWER DECK IN FIFTEEN MINUTES. HANDS MUSTER AT THEIR ABANDON SHIP STATIONS.'

Shit! We're ferkin' sinking.

On 01 deck we are told that the Admiral wants us to get *Bermuda* rolling again. This time it takes us an hour to get the old lady rolling one-and-a-quarter degrees either side of vertical.

It has been a different day. As I snuggle down, the King of Cockroaches reappears. He makes sure that I am OK, turns his back and, with antenna waving, scurries away into the darkness. I have finally removed the last of the clogging paint from around the edges of my Punkah Louvre and I am able to move it.

It is decided to change to Harbour Routine for the weekend and I am duty as from Saturday dinnertime.

At 09:00 Vice Admiral J G Hamilton and his staff leave to construct headquarters at the base of a mountain called Ben Something-or-other. The Daily Orders say that we are to be prepared for Exercise Battle Day. What we don't know, until it is explained to us, is that Exercise Battle Day is a Seamen-versus-Stokers Divisional punch-up.

'AWAY ALL BOATS.

DUTY WATCH OF SEAMEN MUSTER ON THE BOAT DECK.

ANYONE WHO HAS SEEN THE PADRE RECENTLY CONTACT THE BRIDGE.'

I work on the Boat deck putting all our boats in the water. Then I am one of the Launch crew that ferries the Seamen and Stokers ashore. Despite many being clad in fancy dress and armed with a variety of 'soft' weapons, there is an aggressive atmosphere in the air.

The Seamen, under the Command of the Buffer, are assembled on the north side of Ben Something-or-other. The Stokers, under the command of the Chief Stoker, are mustered on the south side. Once both Divisions are assembled, *Bermuda* sounds her horn and both sides start to scale the 1,360 feet to the top of Ben Something-or-other. All forms of disruptive behaviour are encouraged and the first Division to plant their banner on the summit will be adjudged the winner. It is rumoured to be a meaningful re-enactment of a historic battle between two Scottish clans ... or is it a long forgotten Scottish-English battle, or is it something dreamt up yesterday by Admiral J G Hamilton over a few pink gins?

At tea-time we begin to ferry the victorious Seamen's Division back onboard. Stories are told of altitude sickness, of

The Seamen's Base Camp below Ben Something-Or-Other

the day's battles, skirmishes and how the Stokers were outfoxed by the Seamen's strategists. The vanquished Stokers have a different story of course: they have been subjected to a series of ambushes in contravention of the Geneva code of conduct. Our final few trips are reserved for the injured. About 30 individuals are helped onboard by *Bermuda*'s Sick Bay assistants: many with twisted ankles and some who have bloody wounds. 'Blacky' is among those who has suffered a series of injuries to his head and upper body. He is kept in Sick Bay overnight.

The husband of Mrs Lumby relays a 'Very Well Done' from Vice Admiral J G Hamilton over the Tannoy. It makes me proud to be English. As I've never scaled a mountain of any kind in my life, I am disappointed to have missed today's skirmish.

Sunday 16 July: I start to panic. I suddenly realise that one month from today I will be automatically promoted to Ordinary Seaman. I will be transferred from the cosseted Juniors' mess

to the For'd Seamen's Mess where I will have to live with blokes much older than me, blokes who I don't know and who don't know me. On the plus side, I will no longer have to scrub the Quarter-deck every morning.

For some unexplained reason, Sunday is a relaxed day and the Daily Orders are devoid of scheduled tasks. The Duty watch runs boats for those who want to revisit the site of yesterday's battle. For those less adventurous there is a fishing competition and by dinnertime *Bermuda*'s upper deck bristles with hastily constructed fishing rods.

I need only two numbers for a full house on one of my three Tombola tickets.

This evening we have another ship's quiz. This time the subject is football and Tommo is the person to write down the answers. We do OK and jealously guard our answer paper from the port side who send copy-scouts over. There are no Leeds United questions so I contribute little. In the end we come third behind the main Stokers' mess and the For'd Seamen's mess, each of which are home to a couple of the ship's PTIs – so what chance did we have?

As we are congratulating ourselves with a slice of yesterday's unyielding sponge cake, a smiling Lash sits himself down. 'I think I've cracked it.'

'What?' I ask.

'The farting problem.' He gives his backside a tap.

'That's good.'

'I think I've isolated the culprits.'

'Culprits?'

'It's sardines.'

'Not the Spam, then?'

'No it's those ferkin' sardines … I'm convinced it's them.'

'That's you buggered for nine-o-clockers then.'

'Never liked 'em much anyway.'

The anchor is hoisted early on Monday and we head west out of Loch Torridon. There is a sharp, early morning chill in the air and, according to those who are meteorologically trained, it is 'blowing a bit of a bastard'. We do a seemingly unnecessary circuit of the Isle of Skye, collect our two Russian escorts from somewhere and then pummel our way south down the Irish Sea. The weather slowly improves the further south we travel. It is nice to know that we are heading back into English Territorial Waters.

'Have you heard about Blacky?' asks Tug.

I shake my head as I offer him a cigarette.

'He's in Sick Bay. Got 'filled-in' by a Royal Marine.'

'Filled in? I know he got a bit of a battering on Ben what's-its-name ... the mountain, but ...'

'This is different. Apparently Blacky went down their mess yesterday evening to ask them about joining the Marines.'

'Oh yeah, he told me he wanted to do that.' I light our cigarettes.

Tug inhales a long, satisfying lungful. 'According to my mate things were going OK until Blacky said that he isn't interested in being a bandsman – he wanted to be a real Marine.'

'Yeah, he told me that as well.'

'What he doesn't know is that all the bandsmen are actually trained Marines. They've all earned their green berets.'

'I didn't know that.'

'Neither did I until today. Anyway, you know what Blacky's like – he goes on and bloody on. All of a sudden becoming the world's expert on everything to do with the Royal Marines.'

'Yeah.'

'Apparently he called one of them 'just a trombonist' and he was decked.'

I smile. It is wonderful news.

'He's in Sick bay with a broken nose and a dislocated jaw.'

'Serious then?'

'Sounds like it.'

'Anybody charged?'

'Don't know.'

'Great news then?'

'Yeah.'

An unsmiling Lash barges past us.

'Careful, mate,' I say.

'Sorry, Pete. Thought I had the farting problem cracked but it's started up again.'

'So it's not the sardines then?' says Tug.

'Apparently not.'

On Wednesday morning, as we are approaching Plymouth and a much-awaited civilised 'run ashore', our Russian escorts depart when a Canberra aircraft appears.

'ACTION STATIONS.

ASSUME DAMAGE CONTROL STATE 1 CONDITION ZULU ALPHA.

WE ARE UNDER ATTACK BY ENEMY AIRCRAFT FROM THE ROYAL AIR FO ...'

I scuttle off down to HQ1 with my anti-flash gear on and my gas mask slung over my shoulder. Normally, uninvited aircraft means trouble. The RAF could have had the decency to drop our mail off before they started attacking us. According to Sugar it is our job to defend Queen and Country and the job of the RAF to deliver our mail.

For the remainder of the day we carry out something called 'Sleeve Target Firings' with close range weapons. The gunners apparently enjoy shooting at a target towed behind an RAF aircraft.

Nobody will be going ashore in Plymouth tonight – *Bermuda* continues her way east, past Portland Bill, the Isle of Wight, through the Dover Straits and into the Thames Estuary.

Bermuda comes to anchor a little way off Southend-on-Sea's pier at exactly 08:30. I am mess sweeper this morning so I manage to grab a quarter of an hour on my washdeck locker. I have competed in the pool on that pier when a member of the *Ganges* swimming team, but I don't recognise it from this angle.

We rig the accommodation ladder and all the associated bullshit items early and we are cleared off the Quarter-deck. I am given a rag and a tin of metal polish and told to polish some brightwork on 01 deck. By now, I know each individual brass tally by name.

During Stand-easy His Worship the Mayor is received onboard.

After dinner, a whole load of Officers, dressed in their finest, are ferried ashore. Then we rig all the awnings, including the pink-and-white striped ones, in preparation for yet another of *HMS Bermuda*'s cocktail parties.

'DO YOU HEAR THERE … THE STARBOARD SIDE OF THE UPPER DECK IS OUT OF BOUNDS UNTIL FURTHER NOTICE.

THE SHIP'S COMPANY ARE REMINDED THAT WATER RESTRICTIONS ARE STILL IN FORCE.

CHIEF STOKER REPORT TO THE MAIN GALLEY.'

Many of us make our way to the upper deck as the Royal Yacht *Britannia*, with Her Majesty the Queen onboard, passes us on the starboard side. It is dark and well after sunset so no salutes are exchanged. Officers stand rigidly to attention. Junior Seamen peer furtively around the corners of upper deck screen doors.

Lash has decided that white bread is the culprit and turns in happy.

Once again our Saturday starts with rigging *Bermuda* for visitors who are ferried onboard by our boats. There are plenty of girls: some pretend to be disappointed when we tell them that we are sailing on Monday. Boatloads of trippers taking 'a cruise around the warship' whistle, cheer and wave at us: and we respond in typical Naval fashion. Girls, girls, Southend girls!

Overnight leave is granted to those who live within a 10-mile radius of Southend. It doesn't include anybody in the Juniors' mess.

Sunday's Daily Orders has nothing specific on it and we look forward to a second day of 'ogling' those girls who have paid good money to 'cruise around the warship'. But we don't reckon on Vice Admiral J G Hamilton getting out the wrong side of his hammock this morning.

'DO YOU HEAR THERE.

DIVISIONS WILL BE HELD ON THE UPPER DECK AT 10:45.

CHIEF SHIPWRIGHT REPORT TO THE QUARTER-DECK.

SENIOR ENGINEERING OFFICER REPORT TO THE WARDROOM.

WATER WILL BE AVAILABLE THROUGHOUT THE SHIP UNTIL APPROXIMATELY 10:15.'

Breakfast becomes a rushed affair with everybody wanting to avoid the cleaning of the galley trays. Stumpy gets roped-in for that.

Not having touched my kit since the last Divisions, I have some last minute adjustments to make: thank goodness we have Mac and Tommo to help us.

It is a pleasantly warm day as we fall-in on the port side of the Boat Deck. The starboard side of the ship is still out of bounds for some unknown reason.

'DO YOU HEAR THERE ... THE STARBOARD SIDE OF THE SHIP IS NO LONGER OUT OF BOUNDS.'

Our Divisional Officer is reportedly unavailable and one of the Admirals staff inspects us. He stops in front of me. 'Where are you from?'

'Pudsey sir.'

He blinks. 'That's in Lancashire isn't it, home of cricket?'

'Yorkshire sir.'

'Your cap tally could do with some adjustment ... and your shoes could do with a serious polish.' He turns to Freckles who is scribbling something on his clipboard. He waits until Freckles has finished writing and moves on to Lash.

'Keeping well lad?'

'Well sir, I have a prob...'

'Very good.' And he walks on.

Down the mess is a letter from Wilco. She is really annoyed that NAAFI has sent her to the Royal Naval Air Station Yeovilton just as she was looking forward to seeing me when we get back into Portsmouth. There is a large red pair of lips on the bottom of the page. She's kissed my letter. Wilco can't spell orgasum ... as far as I am aware.

In the afternoon I bump into Blacky on my way to the upper deck for some 'wash-deck locker' time and an ogle at the 'Fanny Boats' (Sugar's description).

I can't ignore the fact that he has a patch over one eye, a bent ear and a purple bruise covering one of his cheeks. 'How are you?' I ask.

'Not bad.'

'You look as though you had a rough time on that Scottish mountain.'

'I tripped on the way down ... a couple of times. I was wearing the wrong footwear: If I'd had my mountaineering footwear on I'd have been OK.

'What's under the patch, then?'

'An eye with something in it.'

'Hear that you had a bit of a problem down the Marines' mess.'

'Naah.'

'How's life in the forward mess then?'

'Not bad. There's some right thicko's up there.'

'Is there really?'

'I don't think the Killick of the mess likes me very much.'

'Why's that then?'

'Don't know. He's a Yorkshireman. That's probably got something to do with it.'

'DO YOU HEAR THERE ... THE STARBOARD SIDE OF THE UPPER DECK IS OUT OF BOUNDS UNTIL FURTHER NOTICE.'

Despite that, I enjoy an hour in the pleasant Southend-on-Sea sun. I take the trouble to wave nonchalantly at some of the tourist boats as they pass.

'DO YOU HEAR THERE ... THE STARBOARD SIDE OF THE UPPER DECK REMAINS OUT OF BOUNDS UNTIL FURTHER NOTICE.

GESTURING AT BOATS CONTAINING HOLIDAY MAKERS IS NOT PERMITTED.'

The Fo'csle Seaman are turfed out of their hammocks at 04:30 on Sunday and while the Essex sun is arising we slip quietly away from Southend-on-Sea.

From somewhere in the mess someone shouts, 'Lash has started farting again!'

We are on our way to Portsmouth. The Pompey residents, including Goosie, have uncharacteristic smiles on their faces. We have left a Junior Writer from Blackpool behind in Southend. He said that he had an auntie in Southend and wangled himself afternoon leave yesterday.

We do a few more Damage Control exercises as we scuttle along the south coast at a reasonable rate of knots.

12

BEWARE ... POMPEY LIL

'PREPARE FOR ENTERING HARBOUR.
CLOSE UP SPECIAL SEA DUTYMEN.
CLOSE ALL SCUTTLES AND UPPER DECK SCREEN DOORS.
HANDS OUT OF THE RIG OF THE DAY CLEAR OFF THE UPPER DECK.'

Dressed in our best suits we enter Portsmouth, salute anybody who requires a salute and berth on North Corner Jetty after tea. I throw my heaving-line at a particularly obnoxious looking dockyard-matey, but miss him. My monkey's fist hits a bollard and bounces into the uninviting waters of Portsmouth harbour. The heaving-line thrown by someone else arcs beautifully over the heads of the waiting berthing party, one of whom nonchalantly catches it. According to the messdeck grapevine we are scheduled to be in Pompey for the next two months.

The main engines are shut down and a tired *Bermuda* wheezes and relaxes.

There is a significant change in my letters from Wakefield. No longer are my envelopes Sealed With A Loving Kiss (SWALK) and the triangle of kisses on the bottom of my letters is getting smaller: the last letter only had three little kisses.

Another letter from Wilco explains that she is only going to be at *RNAS Yeovilton* for three months while one of the permanent NAAFI girls has a baby. Then she will return to *HMS Dryad*. She has once again kissed the bottom of the page. As I re-read her sexually explicit letter I am disappointed she's not here.

Tommo and Mac offer us all plenty of practical advice on runs-ashore in Pompey. Portsmouth is unique: it has played host to the Royal Navy for hundreds of years: consequently it knows all there is to know about 'runs-ashore' and has developed its own character. Tommo rolls off a list of Commercial Road pubs that we should avoid until we are confident to tackle the town's most peculiar and colourful characters. Consequently, my first tentative forays to licensed premises beyond the Dockyard Gate are short, unimaginative affairs. Stumpy occasionally makes a beeline to the tattooist by *HMS Vernon's* main gate. I decide that I've decorated myself enough.

Pompey Dockyard is full of ships during late July as it is approaching the main summer leave period. Disregarding those crewmembers who live locally, thousands of sailors are ashore each night. As a Junior rate I have to go ashore in uniform.

The licensed premises on The Hard are awash with hardened drinkers: not the places for Junior Seamen. Tug and I stroll the short distance down Queen's Street to the Home Club – a place where those who have all-night leave can rent a room for the night. As Juniors' leave expires at 23:59 in Pompey it isn't an option for us, so we just have a pint.

Tug and I decide on Monday afternoon that it is about time that we tackled a bar or two down Commercial Road. We tell Tommo what we are planning.

'Which ones?'

'Probably the Sussex.' It is a guess based on what I have overheard.

'Not recommended. Not even on a Monday. Six days a week the Pompey girls ... you know what I mean by Pompey girls?'

'Err.' I am thinking on my feet here. 'Pompey girls err. Are they prossies?'

'You could call them that.'

'Right.'

'Well, six days a week the Pompey girls operate out of the Immoral, but on a Monday they congregate in the Sussex.

'So where would you recommend then, Hooky?' asks Tug.

'The Mucky Duck ... the White Swan or The Golden Fleece. Stay well clear of the Lennox, there's a dust-up most nights in there – and avoid The Criterion, that's not a Seamen's pub.'

'We'll try the White Swan then.' I say.

'Careful though. Pompey Lil has been known to visit the Mucky Duck occasionally.'

'Pompey Lil?'

'If you see the barmen cower and the conversation stop, it's probably because Lil has entered.'

'Right then.'

'She's rumoured to devour young Seamen for breakfast.'

'Good job we've only got leave until midnight then.'

'Good one, young Peter ... good one.'

Tug and I have a couple of pints in the Home Club. We roll down Queen's Street as though we know where we are going. The White Swan is only half-full and we order our pints and find a table in a far corner facing the main entrance door. The only scary woman in the place is the one with masses of red hair who serves us.

'What would you do if you woke up next to that in the morning?' asks Tug.

'God knows.'

'I think I'd leg it.'

Two pints later, as we both reckon we are being 'eyed-up' by a couple of blokes standing at the end of the bar, we decide it is time to leave.

We make it back onboard safely enough and decide that Commercial Road is best tackled in a large, organised group.

Muddy has slung my hammock for me.

Tommo is still up. 'Good run?' he asks.

'Good yeah, Hooky, thanks.'

'The lads slung your hammocks for you.'

'Thanks,' says Tug.

'Did you get to The Mucky Duck then?'

'Yeah.'

'Good was it?'

'OK until a couple of strange blokes started eying us up.'

'From The Sussex over the road probably,' Tommo explains. 'No Pompey Lil then?'

'Don't think so, no.'

'Was Wilf behind the bar?'

'No, it was a woman.' I say.

'Lots of red hair ... big tits?'

'Yep.'

'That's Wilf.'

'A bloke?'

'Naah. She just likes being called Wilf.'

'Right then.'

'You won't have tried The Ponderosa then?'

'No. What's that?'

'Turn in. I'll tell you tomorrow.'

The one good thing about being in the Dockyard is that there is no early morning scrub down. Wooden sheets are laid all over the Quarter-deck. Goosie, who lives in Portsmouth Married Quarters, is a much more relaxed person when he is able to go home each night.

Stumpy is causing us some concern. He's found a small tattoo parlour off Queen's Street and every couple of days he scuttles off there to get another tattoo. We realise eventually that the attraction is a female tattooist called Brenda who wears revealing blouses and contrasting lace underwear.

My first visit to Southsea is a result of my first lesson in Naval solidarity. A crewmember from a visiting South American Frigate has reportedly stabbed a lad from one of our ships. The 'buzz' goes around the Dockyard and almost everybody who is not duty goes down to Billy Manning's the following evening looking for any South Americans. Diplomatically, the visiting Frigate sailed early and has spent the night anchored off Nab Tower. Despite that, because Southsea is awash with men from all the ships in the Dockyard, it is a memorable night. I get more than a little drunk and am happy that my radius of activity has been increased.

Before our first summer leave period starts, on the first Friday in August, we have to get *Bermuda* settled down into one of Portsmouth's dry-docks. It is a 'cold move', without engines, so a variety of tugs moved us away from the jetty and into our dock. Our hull support cradles were placed in the dock bottom before the dock was flooded and a team of divers from the Dockyard, along with our ship's divers, are now in the water to ensure that *Bermuda* settles accurately on her cradles as the water is pumped out. Docking takes most of the day but by early evening *Bermuda* is sitting high and dry in the bottom of her dry-dock with only feet to spare at either end. A single, specially lengthened dockyard brow is rigged with a large green safety net underneath: it is a seriously long drop to the dock bottom. The Wardroom will have to use the same gangway as the rest of us. The onboard toilets, bathrooms and galleys are closed. All our facilities are now on the dockside. It is a strange feeling to know that *Bermuda* is now sitting on wooden supports. I have an unexpected attack of vertigo as I look over the ship's side into the dock bottom.

Taking into account the amount of 'liquid refreshment' that is consumed by crew members each night it is impractical to expect everybody who wants a midnight 'slash' to stagger over the brow to the shore-side facilities. The Navy's answer to this problem is to place large piss-buckets in selected onboard heads. On Wednesday I am duty and my first job, along with the other Juniors, is to collect the piss-buckets from the shore-side facilities before lights-out and distribute them throughout *Bermuda*'s heads in accordance with the official Pee-Pee (Piss-bucket Plan). The buckets are heavy and thigh-high, sized to accept gallon upon gallon of recycled Brickwood's best.

Later in the day Stumpy falls ill and is taken to Sick Bay. He isn't allowed visitors as all his scabby tattoos indicate that he may have contracted something called Hepatitis B. The following day he is transferred to a place called Haslar, seriously ill. I am a little upset about it: he borrowed three quid from me a couple of days ago.

I get a letter from Wilco. She is enjoying herself at *RNAS Yeovilton* but is missing me terribly. In her opinion the Naval Air Service types aren't as much fun as Radar Plotters. She has spelled orgazum with a 'z'.

Lash has gone 34-hours-and-a-bit without an eruption. He still can't identify the culprit, but has an idea it is a combination of the white bread and something processed. Someone suggests it could be the 'tinned cow' that he consumes liberally.

'Hope not,' says Lash. 'I love my condensed milk, I do.'

Thursday morning is one to remember. I am part of the team detailed to empty last night's piss-buckets. What the designer of these receptacles didn't take into account is how heavy they are when full to overflowing. Transporting each of them up ladders along passageways and across a bouncing brow is a job for two. Before breakfast, Margaret and I stagger down passageways and up ladders trying unsuccessfully not to spill anything. Soaking our shoes and the bottom of our trousers with everybody else's waste isn't the best start to a busy day.

I am given the solitary job of shining the brass tallies on the port forward side of the Quarter-deck screen this morning. During the morning Stand-easy I hear that a two-badge Able Seaman from the For'd Seamen's mess called Digby has been found dead in the bottom of the dry-dock this morning.

According to Tommo, it isn't uncommon for drunks to be found dead in the bottom of Portsmouth's dry-docks: the main pontoon walkways only have flimsy, knee-high wire guardrails.

On the dockside are a couple of blue Naval Patrol vehicles and an ambulance. I personally don't want to see a dead body this morning so I take my rag and bluebell around to the opposite side and find some grimy starboard side tallies to buff-up.

Daily Orders the following day confirm that Able Seaman Digby Wigmore has been found dead in the dock bottom and that investigations as to the cause of his death are taking place. The thoughts and commiserations of the entire ship's company have been sent to his family along with a bunch of NAAFI flowers purchased from the ship's Tombola fund.

13

KICKED INTO TOUCH BY THE BLONDE

With a spring in my step, my leave pay in my pocket and my little brown case in my hand I am on two weeks' leave. I stand in line while the Dockyard Police on the main gate search the bags of everyone wearing a *Bermuda* cap tally. By the time I have my little brown case searched there are already a few of *Bermuda's* crew detained and obviously going nowhere. We are allowed to take 200 duty-free cigarettes for main leave and anybody caught with more is taken to one of the holding cells behind the Gatehouse for the weekend to await the Naval disciplinary process to 'kick-in' on Monday morning.

One advantage of being in the Dockyard is that we are the first to board the London train from Portsmouth Harbour station. Today I manoeuvre myself well and manage to get myself a seat.

Winkle-picker shoes, drainpipe trousers and the Wakefield girl's scarf

I make the Waterloo taxi rank in good time and share a cab with a Royal Marine Bandsman called Dave, also from *Bermuda*, who is on his way to see his parents in Bradford. We arrive in Kings Cross in plenty of time for our train to Leeds, and find ourselves an empty compartment where I can enjoy a cigarette. Dave doesn't smoke: he is a professional trumpet player. By the time the train pulls out of Kings Cross we still have the compartment to ourselves and we both remove our shoes and make ourselves comfortable. He tells me that *Bermuda*'s band practises in a compartment located between the main Engine Room and the after ammunition magazine: a warm and potentially explosive place. Apparently they play jazz too, not just military marching music.

'Do you remember Blacky – a Seaman who went down your mess to ask about joining the Marines?' I ask.

'Clearly.'

'Apparently he fell up the ladder when he left.'

'Absolutely correct,' says Dave.

Just after Northampton, we get thirsty and Dave volunteers to go the dining car as he is 19 and can't be refused – particularly wearing his green beret.

We finish our beers just before the train stops at Sheffield. I light a cigarette as the new passengers stroll up and down the passageway looking for a seat. To my surprise a couple of young girls join us.

No sooner have they sat down, than I offer them cigarettes from my packet of Export Woodbines.

'Thanks,' says the prettier of the two. 'That's a long 'un. Never seen Woodies that big before.'

'Specially made for the Navy. Duty-free,' I explain.

'What's duty-free then when it's at 'ome?'

'Special fags for the Royal Navy. We get 'em for nothing ... almost.'

Dave isn't impressed with the girl sitting opposite him, who has her hair piled up on the top of her head. The girl opposite me, enjoying her first duty-free Woodbine, looks like Helen

Shapiro and has beautiful green eyes. Both girls are returning to Doncaster after a night out at the Mecca in Sheffield. The girl with the green eyes is impressed when I tell her where we have been during the last three months. The name Invergordon makes her giggle. The girl opposite Dave has nodded off.

'You must cum down to Donny while yuwer at 'ome then,' the green-eyed girl says. Then she hiccoughs and giggles.

'I might do that.'

'Good.'

'Have you got a telephone number?'

'We 'aven't gorra telephone.'

'I have,' and I give her the number of the shop.

The girl with the green eyes jabs her friend awake as the train pulls into Doncaster. I help her to her feet and politely hold the compartment door open for them as they leave. I watch them wobble their way down the platform.

'I might have got myself a date,' I proudly explain to Dave.

'Good for you. I'm not into girls myself.'

That is a bit of a shock: I wouldn't have guessed.

At Leeds, I take a taxi to Pudsey. Mum has shut the shop by the time I arrive home and my brother Tony is in bed.

'When do you go back?' asks Mum.

'Two weeks today ... well yesterday, exactly. Got to be back onboard by the Friday morning.'

'Not three weeks then?'

'Now I'm on a ship ... no.'

'Do you like being on a ship?'

'Oh yeah, it's great.'

I am tempted to show Mum my tattoos but decide it is better to wait until the morning.

'What's that then?' Mum asks the following morning, pointing to my arm.

'It's an eagle.'

'It's got green feathers.'

'It's only a tattoo.'

'Suppose you've got to have them if you're in the Navy.' She looks closely at the group of Danish flowers. 'What are they? Are they flowers?'

'Yeah. Got that one in Copenhagen ... in Denmark.'

'That's nice.'

Tony says that they are both bloody brill. He has started to swear a little, I notice.

I have a stroll around Pudsey in my uniform to show off the Radar Plotter's badge and my *Bermuda* cap tally, but I don't impress anybody. I get a few 'Touch your collar for luck, sailor?' requests, but not from anyone interesting.

Letters to and from the Wakefield girl have been getting shorter and less meaningful during the last few weeks and I am half-expecting things not to be the same as before. I suppose at our age, relationships are built on the length of time spent together. A three-month separation is a difficult one to handle at seventeen. For me it is nice to have contact with a girl again, but within a few days of my being home we have agreed that our relationship is going nowhere fast and we should 'kick it inta touch' – which is a rugby saying, apparently. She gives me back the photograph of *Bermuda* that I sent her and that she has kept by the side of her bed for a few weeks. It is a bit creased where she has kissed it before going to sleep ... some months ago.

Mum, Tony and the lady who lives next door are interested in my sea stories. Tales of building jetties in the highlands of Scotland, playing my part in the bombardment of an innocent Scottish island and having taken a drink or two in the place where a Naval mutiny had taken place have them spellbound ... I think.

By the beginning of the second week, the prospect of going back starts to loom large. I read in the *Daily Mirror* that a Soviet cosmonaut called Titov has become the second human being to orbit the Earth, and the first to be in outer space for more than a day. What is the world coming to?

During my last week I buy myself a Ronson Varaflame cigarette lighter with tortoiseshell sides and a small protective leather wallet. It costs me twelve shillings and sixpence. A cylinder of butane gas fuel costs me one and four pence. The bloke in the shop shows me how to fill it and adjust the height of the flame. I spend hours getting the hang of it. Mum thinks it is an extravagant purchase but I reckon it is money well spent. What better way to impress the girls than with an oversized, duty-free Woodbine and a Ronson Varaflame lighter with tortoiseshell sides?

I regularly ask Mum if anyone has telephoned for me while I was out, but nobody has. I am a little disappointed that the girl with the green eyes hasn't rung – maybe she's lost my number.

All too quickly it is my last full day at home. I kiss Mum goodbye and catch the bus into Leeds.

The train leaves at 22:00. I watch a bloke, with a Gunners badge on his arm, kissing his girlfriend goodbye: she is trying hard not to cry. I don't know if I am jealous or thankful: I remember how much of a wrench it was leaving the girl from Wakefield after my last leave.

At Waterloo I see Dave the bandsman in the distance talking to a young Steward.

14

MULTIPLE MARILYNS

On Wednesday 16 August 1961 I am exactly 17½ years old and officially no longer a Junior Seaman. No longer will I be cocooned within the relative safety of the Juniors' mess with a Petty Officer and a couple of strong-arm Killicks to look after me. Now I will be transferred forward to the notorious For'd Seamen's Mess where my naval education will begin in earnest.

I have to fill out a formal request form to be rated Ordinary Seaman. Once my request is signed I join a whole gang of defaulters, leave breakers, smugglers and men of strange and illegal habits, waiting to be seen by the ship's Commander. As I am not a defaulter, I am near the front of the queue and after listening to a short but half-expected lecture on the significance of my first step up the Royal Naval promotional ladder, I am officially promoted to Ordinary Seaman. Along with the increase in rank comes a 40 percent increase in pay: I am now earning four pounds and eleven shillings per week before deductions. I am on my way!

I ask Goosie if I can have the forenoon off as I am moving mess. He looks at me in a strangely sympathetic fashion and says, 'Up until Stand-easy'.

It takes me half an hour to track down the Killick who is responsible for the allocation of locker space in the Forward Mess. He works on the Fo'csle and his name is Leading Seaman Bilton, known to everybody as 'Yorky'. Within minutes, he identifies me as a fellow Yorkshireman and allocates me a place in the port after section of the mess.

The entire messdeck area consists of about eight distinct sections, four on each side. Each section is divided from its neighbour by a two-tier bank of lockers and contains a long athwartships table and a pair of cushioned benches. On the ship's side of each section are a couple of bunks that fold down to make a long comfortable seat. The entire length of the mess is partially divided down the ship's centre line by massive circular structures that support 'A' and 'B' turrets and the various trunkings and chutes that supply ammunition. Allegedly it is the roughest, toughest and most misunderstood part of *Bermuda*: even the cockroaches only visit mob-handed.

I learn that 'Yorky' comes from York and whenever York City Football Club aren't doing well, he supports Leeds United. What a stroke of luck that is.

I ask him what mess Blacky is in.

He pulls a strange expression. 'He's over the other side. But for how much longer, I don't know.'

'Why's that then?'

'He was given his nickname at *Ganges*, is that right?'

'Yes.'

'Because he was a black catter?'

'Yes.'

'He still is. He's a prime bullshit artist ... an habitual liar ... and messdecks don't like those kind of people. We deal with smugglers, thieves, crabs and arse-bandits in our own way ... but anyone who bullshits his messmates is in real trouble.'

'So he's on the starboard side, then?'

'Yep. By the way you're down for 'Cook-of-the-mess' today. It's the best way of getting to know everybody.'

The For'd Seamen's mess has a much lower deckhead than the Juniors' mess. There is a mature atmosphere to the place: a combination of elderly bodies, tobacco, ingrained gash buckets, stale food, cigarettes and stale alcohol. There is a permanent pulsating rumble – the whole For'd Seamen's mess structure appeared to be alive and throbbing.

Suddenly I am sharing a mess with people who are twice my age. Yorky introduces me to those who are slumped over the mess table. 'The ugly looking bugger here is Wiggy Bennet. Next to him is Soapy Watson whose ambition is to become Captain of the forward heads. The bloke you think may be looking at you ... but isn't ... is 'Squinty' – so called for obvious reasons.'

I nod as each is introduced. There is no formal handshake or any other form of greeting offered. I had marched down Queen's Street next to Soapy on the day we joined *Bermuda*.

Yorky continues: 'The bloke almost asleep on Squinty's shoulder is Languid – he's part Welsh. Prof, next to him, is our songster. Missing are Deeps, one of the ship's divers, Joe and Sugar, who you already know.' He swings his arm. 'This is Ordinary Seaman Peter Broadbent, a fellow Yorkshireman from Pudsey.'

There is a series of uncoordinated grunts and unintelligible words of welcome.

'Peter has volunteered to help Sugar as 'Cook-of-the-mess' today.'

Sugar accompanies me to the shore-side galley to collect the dinner trays. It is a much longer journey than it is from the Juniors' mess. There are many more ladders to negotiate.

By the time we make it back to the mess everybody is sitting on benches either side of the table. There is a strange smell that I later learn is the Navy tot.

Cooks-of-the-mess clean and return the trays to the galley as well as ditch the gash. Today a big ugly Chef sends me back to clean one of my trays properly: bastard. I watch in amazement as more than one of my messmates wash their hands and faces in the dish-washing fanny instead of trudging over the brow to the shore-side bathroom.

After dinner I listen to a series of stories, jokes and discussions, which I don't completely understand. I watch a couple in the adjacent mess secreting duty-free cigarettes in the strangest of places in order to smuggle them ashore later that afternoon.

I ask Yorky where I can sling my hammock and am told that there isn't enough room in the mess for everybody and that I will have to find my own slinging point outside the mess.

According to Sugar, although Yorky is officially in charge of the mess, he isn't actually. The 'Father' of the mess is a bloke called Joe who has been demoted from Petty Officer, then down to Killick, and then down to Able Seaman because of his fondness for young boys. He is the ship's painter, the bloke who dishes out paint to whoever wants it, and has a propensity for wearing bright red lipstick and a dangly earring when he is ashore. It is rumoured that his best friend is an alcoholic Steward who spends the evenings with Joe in the paint store sipping the clear alcohol from the top of the tins of metal polish. Nobody argues with Joe.

Another elderly member of the mess is Alf who, despite his 35 years, has never progressed beyond his present rank of Able Seaman because he has difficulty with reading and writing. He is convinced that everybody senior in rank or rate is an idiot.

My first evening is spent watching the professionals playing Uckers. The game attracts an unusually large, spellbound audience. I hear language ... serious grown-up language ... that I've never heard before. In the starboard forward corner is an animated group playing a card game called Euchre: I can't figure it out and when I ask someone how it is played he is unable to explain. Officially, gambling for money is not allowed in the Royal Navy ... with one notable exception ... the starboard forward corner of *Bermuda*'s For'd Seamen's mess. I realise that my language has to deteriorate fast – surrounded by people swearing as only sailors can is an ear-opener. I am determined to learn the way of the For'd Seamen's mess quickly.

For the first time since I joined the Royal Navy, there is nobody to tell me to turn in, so at about 22:30 I grab my hammock, shoulder it up a ladder and along to the capstan flat where Sugar tells me there are a few spare slinging points. There are already lots of swinging hammocks and the lights are out by the time I arrive. Crouching low, I scour the darkened deckhead looking for a black-painted hammock bar. Eventually I find a great space just above a warm, oil-stained motor of some kind which will make it easy for me get into my hammock. There is a smell of well-oiled machinery about the capstan flat.

I sleep OK until I feel something hard and unyielding in the small of my back. In the gloom I can see a frothing individual wearing an earring and holding the free end of my hammock lanyard in one hand. Slowly I figure out that he has undone the bottom end of my hammock and lowered it so that I am sitting on the motor.'

'Who told you to ferkin' sling here then, young 'un?'

'Nobody ... I just ...'

'This is my ferkin' place.'

'Sorry.'

'There's a spare place over by the Paint Store and another above the hatch to the cable locker.'

'Where's the last one you said?'

'Hatch to the cable locker... over there.' He smells of beer.

'Thanks.' I swiftly roll out of my hammock, lash it up and drag it over to where I think the cable locker hatch is. I can't find a spare hanging point in the dark so I open my hammock, lay it out on the deck, curl up and go to sleep.

In the morning I see the spare hanging point directly above me. I sling my hammock, lash it up properly, drag it back down the mess and begin my day. A real shock is the For'd Seamen's mess bathroom. It is massive and more than a little intimidating. I am now sharing washing and showering facilities with real men. Ensuring that my towel is firmly secured around my waist suddenly becomes extremely important. I wish I'd paid more attention to Whacker's 'towel-wrapping' lesson in the Annexe of *HMS Ganges* all that time ago. My initial visit is brief.

'Give Sugar a hand collecting the breakfast trays, young 'un,' says Yorky.

Another new arrival in the mess is a bloke called 'Donk' – welcomed by everybody like a returning hero.

'Just completed 83 days in Colchester,' Sugar explains to me in a whisper.

'Colchester?'

'Military prison.'

'Really?'

'Stuck one on an Officer.'

'No!'

'Yeah. Put him in Sick Bay for a few days. The Officer departed the ship after … and has never returned.'

'What's his name?'

'Donk.'

'Why Donk?'

'You'll see if you bump in to him in the bathroom.'

Over the following days I settle myself into my new mess. I appear to be 'Cook-of-the-mess' more often than anyone else, but I accept that in good grace. I watch, and slowly learn the basic rules of games such as Uckers, Cribbage, Chase the Pisser and Knockout Whist … but not Euchre.

Everybody over 20 years old is entitled to a daily measure of rum which is issued at exactly 11:45 each day in a passage aft of the main galley. Yorky explains the simple 'tot time' rules applicable to those who are 'under age'. We are not allowed anywhere near the starboard forward part of the mess that is the designated 'tot' zone.

A few days later I am in the passageway aft of the main galley when …

'UP SPIRITS.'

The daily rum issue is about to take place. I hide behind a stanchion some distance away and observe the sacred ceremony. A group of Regulators form a boundary at either end of the passage and at the top and bottom of the access ladders.

A pair of Officers, accompanied by a number of Petty Officers from the Supply Branch and a member of the Regulating branch, appear with all the ceremonial equipment. Central to the whole business is a large wooden barrel with brass straps and the words 'THE QUEEN GOD BLESS HER' in brass letters riveted to the side. Rum and water is measured in the prescribed ratio of two parts water to one part neat rum, and stirred with a large wooden paddle. The mess 'Rum Bosuns' queue patiently with their rum fanny at the ready. As each reaches the front of the queue, he states his mess and holds the base of his fanny over the edge of the large wooden cask. The Supply Branch Petty Officer consults a clipboard and states how much rum is to be issued and by means of a series of different-sized brass rum measures, the rum and water mixture is poured carefully into the mess fanny.

It is the closest I have ever been to the tot. The smell of the rum and water mixture is intoxicating. I only have two-and-a-half years to wait.

Later that evening Yorky explains to me why Navy rum is mixed with water. It is to prevent storage: apparently the mixture quickly goes flat and is undrinkable after a few hours. Senior Rates like Petty Officers and Chief Petty Officers are issued with neat rum. They are trusted not to store it as they are deemed responsible. According to Yorky every Senior Rate has a small bottle of rum stored in his locker for that 'special occasion'.

I don't feel inclined to ask any of my new messmates to go ashore with me, instead I turn to Tug and Streaky who are still in the Juniors' mess. I have, however, picked up a lot of information about what is available in Pompey. Languid remained awake long enough one evening to confirm that the Commercial Road bars such as Lennox, Albany, Sussex, The Golden Fleece and Criterion are most definitely out of bounds. He says that the main problem with the Sussex is that the local queers congregate around the adjacent statue of Queen Victoria. Then Languid falls asleep.

Sugar gives me the low-down on the Ponderosa, officially known as The NAAFI Club. He has grown out of it himself, but thinks it is a place that my mates and I would enjoy. It is rumoured down the mess that Sugar has ravished a fair proportion of the female residents of Portsea Island in his younger, more profligate days. I don't know what the female population of Portsea Island is exactly ... but it is probably a lot. I don't know what profligate means, exactly.

'Ignore the bars outside of the Dockyard gate – they're full of piss heads,' says Sugar.

'Right then.'

'Left up Queen's Street. Have a pint in the Home Club if you're thirsty. Cheapest pint in town, but be careful of any of the blokes in raincoats who are hanging around.'

'OK.'

'Continue up Queen's Street, Vicky barracks on your left. Carry on past Aggies and the Traf' Club on the left. If The Standard isn't too full that's a good place for another pint.'

'Right then.'

'Give my love to Barbara behind the bar in The Standard. She's the owner.'

'Will do.'

'Turn right at the top. On your right you'll see the 'Mucky Duck', The White Swan. Depending upon how busy it is it's a good place to grab a 'quick one'.

'I've been in there.'

'Now you're approaching the grown-up part of town.'

'OK.'

On the opposite side of the road you will see the Lennox, Sussex, Albany and Criterion.'

'Languid has told me about them.'

'Avoid 'em. Avoid 'em all until you're a little older.'

'How much older?'

'About five years.'

'OK then.'

'Continue up Commercial Road, under the railway bridge, bear round to your left and pay a quick visit to The Balmoral ... but be careful, the ladies of the night converge on 'The Immoral': it's their HQ you might say.'

'HQ?'

'Headquarters.'

'Right then.'

'Frightening bunch they are. Continue up the road ... Oh! In the Balmoral give my love to Ange: she's an old Pompey scrubber who collects the empties, has done for donkeys' years ever since she retired professionally.'

'What does she look like?'

'Defies description: just ask for Ange. Continue up the road, turn right by the large pub on the corner, The Three Horseshoes, and walk down to the end. On your right you will find the NAAFI Club set back a little. You'll recognise it because there will be loads of young girls outside waiting for you to sign them in.'

'Sign them in?'

'They can't get in by themselves. They need someone with a Naval Identity card to sign them in.'

'Sounds good.'

'Don't expect them to stay with you once inside, though. Buy them a drink and try to hang on to one if you like: but they're NAAFI Club regulars, as were their mothers before them ... and probably their grandmothers too.

'Naah.'

'True. Anyway the NAAFI Club is great for lads of your age. Plenty of music, somewhere to dance and plenty of young, unattached girls. Get down there and spread it about a bit.'

Later, I tell Tug and Streaky all about the NAAFI Club.

'What are we ferkin' waiting for then?' says Tug.

'18:00 on the brow tonight then?'

'Yep.'

'Yep.'

'Lash is still farting for England,' says Streaky. 'It isn't the bread.'

At 18:00 all three of us are standing by the brow, Tug and Streaky are resplendent in their best uniform suits. I am wearing a pair of dark-grey drainpipe trousers, a shirt, a tie, a light grey windcheater jacket and my Pusser's shoes. My chin and armpits are saturated in 4711 Eau de Cologne.

'Careful where you go, smelling like that,' says the Quartermaster.

We've had three pints by the time we stroll down the drive to the NAAFI Club main entrance. Sugar wasn't exaggerating: there are at least a dozen girls hanging about outside.

'Sign us in please,' they say as we pass.

We all three nod OK and three girls from the front row attach themselves to us.

Once inside we have to present ourselves to a lady behind a desk and sign the girls in the visitors' book.

'First time here, boys?' asks the woman behind the desk.

We nod as we ask the girls their names so that we can sign them in. Strangely, all three are called Marilyn.

'*Bermuda* eh?' says the woman behind the desk as she takes the caps that Tug and Streaky hand over and places them on a shelf in a small room behind her. 'Tell Able Seaman Kayne that Nora misses him.'

'He's in the same mess as me – I'll tell him.' I say.

'Nora's my daughter.'

'OK.'

We head for the nearest bar, by which time the three Marilyns have skipped away upstairs without so much as a farewell wave.

Sugar is right. The NAAFI Club is brilliant. Two large bars downstairs and a dance hall above, each with its own jukebox. The beer is subsidised slightly, the music is contemporary and loud. It is definitely the place for those of our age.

For the next few weeks Tug, Streaky and I make the NAAFI Club our local. We recognise the girls waiting to be signed in and beckon to those of our choice. Nora's mum remembers me, as I tell her that I've passed on her daughter's message to Sugar.

We are used to the fact that there are always plenty of girls to dance with, but they rarely agree to a second dance. The procedure appears to be that if a girl dances with you more than once and then allows you to buy her a drink without her mates ... you are well on the way to the next step in the process – that is, a 'necking' session in the garden outside followed by a promise to meet up the following evening. In reality, few relationships ever develop. The Pompey girls who frequent the NAAFI Club are a fun-loving crowd who are out for a couple of free drinks, a dance and not much else. Almost opposite the NAAFI club is the entrance to the Wrens' Barracks. However, at our tender age, we tend to ignore the occupants, not knowing exactly how to deal with Wrens, who generally arrive in the NAAFI Club in an intimidating, black-stockinged flock.

As the holiday season is upon us, Southsea becomes an alternative to the NAAFI Club. The Festival Bar, opposite the pier, is always a popular place with girls who are on holiday. From there, it is only a short walk along the promenade to Billy Manning's fairground, a permanent Southsea feature. It has all the standard attractions including a Waltzer, but the surrounding bars – such as The Seahorse – have more appeal by the time we have staggered that far. Visiting girls certainly come a close second to getting drunk. We are still legally under age, and knowing that we are breaking the law and getting away with it is a bonus.

In Naval Ports, as an Ordinary Seaman, I no longer have to be back onboard by midnight. I can stay out all night if I want to ... but I don't.

15

THREE HOURS AND 32 MINUTES ADRIFT

I am slowly settling into the For'd Seamen's mess. At my age, it is easy to adapt. Despite all the potential problems associated with living in such an environment, I am working hard to fit in. I have little influence, but generally my messmates are an understanding lot. They tolerate me and offer advice, not all of it good. I know that if I get into trouble they will help, and that is important. I feel that I am growing up at last. Yorky keeps me pointed in the right direction. 'Never go ashore with anyone from the mess ... not yet. Never take anything ashore for anyone else. Never make promises you can't keep and never, ever do what your mate Blacky does – try to impress your messmates by bullshitting.'

I organise with Yorky that Tug can be in our mess when he is transferred up for'd.

Tug is officially promoted to Ordinary Seaman towards the end of August and I spend Friday helping him move his kit into the locker below mine. I know of a recently vacated slinging point in the capstan flat and show him where it is. He isn't impressed with our sleeping arrangements.

The next day Tug and I decide to take advantage of the fact that we now have all-night leave. Tug wants to go home for the day and invites me to join him.

As we turn out of the Dockyard, Tug points south to the smudge on the horizon. 'That's Ryde,' he says, pointing directly ahead, 'and somewhere over there is Cowes,' moving his pointing finger to the west.

Lounging on an upper-deck seat onboard the Portsmouth-to-Ryde ferry, I watch *Bermuda*, berthed on South Railway Jetty, dwindle into the distance.

We berth at the end of Ryde's long wooden pier. As soon as we are ashore Tug telephones home to tell them he is on his way and has a friend with him. It is the first time I'd ever been on a populated small island and the pier doesn't feel that stable to me. We catch a little train that transports us down the pier, then we wait for a lime-green bus to take us to a place called Newport, which until today I thought was in Wales.

In Newport we walk through a maze of small streets before eventually catching another lime-green bus that takes us directly to Cowes. As far as I can tell, there is nothing direct about the Isle of Wight. West Cowes is a maze of narrow streets, crowded with holiday-makers and the remnants of Cowes Week Sailing Regatta that, according to Tug, finished a few weeks earlier.

Tug lives in a flat in a large white building overlooking the River Medina. His parents welcome him home with lots of hugs and kisses: they shake hands with me. Tug's twin sister Helen is a revelation, nothing like Tug at all. She is strikingly beautiful with a sinuous, willowy figure and a face that could launch ships. I am transfixed, but she pays me little attention.

That evening we decide against going back onboard and instead go to Tug's local sailing club for a couple of pints. We decide to catch the first ferry back in the morning.

Sunday morning dawns with a blur and a blinding headache. It is gone seven.

Helen pokes her head around the door. 'What time do you have to be back onboard your ship?'

Tug unsticks his eyes and glares at the wall-clock. 'Oh shit!'

We get dressed while Helen makes us each a cup of strong, Island tea. Neither of us finishes the drink. I still retain a forlorn hope that there is some magic method by which we can get back onboard in the next twenty minutes.

Hurriedly dressed, we scuttle down a deserted Cowes High Street to where the buses to Newport depart. We have just missed one: we watch its back-end turning a distant corner. It is half an hour until the next one so we sit on a pavement and discuss what punishment we will receive for being adrift.

'What do you think we'll get?' I ask.

'Dunno. Depends on what time we get back I suppose.'

'Suppose so.'

'Isn't there a quicker way of getting to Ryde?'

'This is the quickest way.'

'Isn't there a taxi or anything?'

'Don't think so. Not at this time on a Sunday morning.'

'Does your head hurt?'

'Yeah, does yours?'

'Yeah.'

'We're definitely in deep shit aren't we?'

'Definitely... yeah.'

It is almost 11:00 by the time we shuffle back onboard. The Duty Petty Officer is waiting for us at the top of the brow. 'And where have you two Ordinary Seamen been?'

'Isle of Wight, PO,' explains Tug. 'We went home last night and didn't check up on the times of the buses from Cowes to Ryde this morning and ...'

'Your station cards are in the Regulating Office. I suggest you go down there and tell your sob-story to Master-at-Arms Foggo.'

The Regulating staff are sorting out the day's mail as we sheepishly arrive outside the Office. Master-at-Arms Foggo, who is sitting behind a small desk, smiles at us as we arrive and puts his cap on. 'Ah-ha! My two young escapees have returned to the mother ship have they?'

We both nod.

'Go back down the mess, get changed into Number 8s and report back here with your caps in five minutes when the Officer of the Day would like to have a word with you both.'

So that's exactly what we do and we are subsequently charged with returning back from shore leave three hours and 32 minutes adrift.

The Officer of the Day reminds us that 'leave is a privilege' and that we have broken 'the bond of trust'.

As expected we are placed on Commander's Report which will take place the following day. In the meantime we are confined onboard: we can't legally set foot on the jetty ... for anything.

Goosie isn't very pleased with me. 'Where have you been?'

'Isle of Wight.'

'Isle of ferkin' Wight! What you doing over there, then?'

'Went home with my mate.'

'And didn't work out how to get back on time?'

'Yeah ... PO. I mean no ... PO.'

'When do you see the Commander?'

'Tomorrow ... PO.'

Down the mess Yorky also has an opinion. 'Where the ferk have you been?'

'Went over to the Isle of Wight. Tug lives over there.'

'And?'

'We slept in and missed the bus.'

'Seen the Officer of the Day yet?'

'Yep.'

'And what did he say?'

'Leave is a privilege and Commander's report.'

'Both of you,' he points to us both in turn. 'Will receive seven or 10 days number 9s and a period of stopped leave.' He grins. 'Welcome to the club.'

Monday morning's Commander's report is a long-winded affair. Dressed in our second-best suits a long line of us are corralled down to one of the after cabin flats and form a queue outside the Commander's cabin. Master-at-Arms Foggo struts up and down with a clipboard under his arm, ensuring that we know exactly what to do once we enter the great man's cabin. 'Smartly march up the table and come to a halt. Then follow my instructions ... exactly!'

Tug and I are about halfway down the queue. Ahead of us are a bunch of Chefs who have apparently been caught misappropriating Naval nosh. A couple of three-badge Able Seamen, who I recognise from the mess, are directly ahead of us. One is charged with aggravated insubordination, the other with striking a Petty Officer Stoker.

I stand in front of the Commander, a sophisticated-looking gentleman an inch or two taller than me with a deep suntan and unfriendly brown eyes. He informs me that 'Leave is a privilege'. An Officer who I have never seen before tells the Commander that I am a useful Seaman who works diligently on the Quarter-deck: that I have been in the For'd Seamen's mess for a relatively short time, keep myself clean and tidy, and this is the first time I have been in trouble onboard *HMS Bermuda*.

Master-at-Arms Foggo sums up everything the Commander has to say in very few words. 'Seven Days Number Nines. On Caps. Righta Tin. Quicka March.'

That is me dealt with. I wait for Tug, who receives exactly the same.

In the Regulating Office one of the Regulating Petty Officers gives us the run-down on *Bermuda*'s harbour punishment routine. We will be mustered an hour before Reveille to work for an hour and help empty the piss-buckets. We will have half an hour for dinner and muster again for work. Half an hour after tea we will be mustered again and work for an hour. The final muster of the day will be at 22:00 when we will be checked. If we miss any of the musters, we will automatically be placed on Commander's report.

While the rest of the crew enjoy what Portsmouth has to offer, Tug and I spend the next seven days onboard. For an extra three hours during the day we scrub toilets, polish decks, clean bedpans from the sickbay, empty piss-buckets ... and scrub toilets again ... whether they need cleaning or not.

In Wilco's latest letter, she hopes that I am enjoying my time in Portsmouth. I don't tell her about my stoppage of leave.

Sugar stands at the head of the mess table with his arms outstretched. On his head is draped a pair of women's knickers, mainly white with small, royal blue spots. He has a stupid grin on his face. 'Morning gentlemen. Yet another intimate item of female apparel freely given.'

'Put them with the others,' says Yorky as he tosses him a locker key.

'If I'm correct, this is my seventh contribution,' says Sugar as he slowly removes his head covering, sniffs the knickers, smiles, and turns away swinging them from his index finger and whistling.

I have a slice of sausage on the end of a fork hovering betwixt plate and mouth and I must look confused.

'We have a spare locker where we keep items of interest,' says Squinty.

'Knickers mainly,' adds Deeps.

I almost ask why, but stop myself.

On the first day of September, the second leave party returns onboard. The dry dock is filled and with a barely noticeable shudder, *Bermuda* is once again afloat. The dock gates are opened and we are towed around to South Railway Jetty. Our toilets and bathrooms are immediately back in working order: no more piss-buckets to empty!

A variety of trucks appear on the jetty. Lower deck is cleared to form a human chain that stretches from the back of the trucks, up and over the brow and along decks, down ladders and along passageways to the appropriate storeroom. It is getting dark before the last of the trucks is emptied.

Monday is my last day of punishment. It has been a long week. Tomorrow my daily routine will return to something like normal.

I write letters to Mum and Wilco. I try my very best to keep my Wilco letter clean and rational ... but fail.

A few days later Sugar and I are working almost shoulder to shoulder, polishing brightwork.

'Is there really a locker full of women's knickers in the mess?' I ask.

'Locker number sixty-six over the starboard side in the corner. Locker sixty-six ... full of knicks.'

'Are they all clean?'

'Doubt it, some of 'em have been there a while.'

I breathe on a large brass tally to make it 'mist up' before I give it a final buff. 'So it's not just this trip's collection. then?'

'There's some Second World War stuff in there.'

'You're having me on ... you're taking the piss.'

'No. I'm not.'

'Crikey.'

'There are some strange and exotic pieces in locker sixty-six believe me, young Pete. My favourite pair are a ...' He waved an arm. 'Doesn't matter. Yorky's got the only key. I suppose if you ask him nicely he'll let you have a quick rummage.'

'Err ... no, that's OK thanks.'

'The Stokers' mess have something similar. They have a locker number twenty-two: all the two's, full of shoes. Stokers are strange ... Stokers are.'

The following day we have a mess auction of Digby Wigmore's kit. We don't need cash: successful bids are recorded and the money taken out of our pay over the next few months or so. Traditionally, it is a way of raising money for his dependants and is an official method of obtaining a piece of someone else's kit. I don't have much of an income to compete with the extraordinarily high prices bid by other members of the mess. Towards the end, I successfully bid a couple of quid for his scissors – I think that is a reasonable contribution. The Regulating Petty Officer who is conducting the auction tells us that the total raised could be well over 170 pounds. Digby's underwear and bed linen will apparently be used as polishing rags, as they don't attract any sensible bids.

Friday 8 September. Daily Orders for today have the bold title 'AMMUNITION SHIP'. Coir mats are rigged and *Bermuda* is towed up the harbour to the ammunitioning area. We smokers find somewhere where we can enjoy our last intake of nicotine ...

'DO YOU HERE THERE ... OUT PIPES.

NO SMOKING OR NAKED LIGHTS THROUGHOUT THE SHIP UNTIL FURTHER NOTICE.'

I know, from my limited experience, that ammunitioning *Bermuda* is never easy. The four-inch shells are lighter than the six-inch ones but they come at us faster. I am employed in the bowels of a lighter surrounded by mountainous crates of live ammunition. With the sleeves of my shirt rolled down, my trouser bottoms tucked into my socks and wearing my anti-flash gear, I am told that I am fully protected against anything explosive.

Eventually we are fully re-stocked. The clatter of cigarette lighters and the striking of matches is heard throughout the ship as we are towed back to our berth on South Railway Jetty just after tea.

Instead of Saturday morning messdeck rounds, the lower deck is cleared of Seamen, and anyone else who can be spared, to spend time over the ship's side perched on a plank of wood and wielding a paintbrush dripping with Pusser's ship's-side grey paint. It is unexpectedly pleasant: suspended over the side where there is a continual stream of boats taking waving holiday-makers on a 'See the Warships' tour of the Dockyard. I am a picture in my paint-splattered Navy-blue overalls.

The second most influential lower-deck position onboard, after the 'Ship's Painter', is Captain-of-the-forward-heads, the largest toilet complex onboard with dozens of individual cubicles and a battery of bulkhead-mounted 'pistols'. *Bermuda* was built at a time when exposed copper pipes were popular but a bugger for whoever had to keep them clean. In early July the Able Seaman in charge of the Forward Heads was awarded a sabbatical in Colchester for a serious misdemeanour involving a young Stores Assistant. Soapy, who is the permanent Capstan flat cleaner and who has apparently coveted the Captain-of-the-forward-heads job for yonks, is promoted after a short but poignant inaugural ceremony involving a curved Admiralty Pattern toilet brush and a couple of rolls of toilet paper. According to messdeck rumour, Soapy is so overwhelmed by his promotion that he can't work for the next few days.

16

FIFTEEN TWO THAT BASTARD

On Sunday 10 September, the protective wooden sheets are removed from the Quarter-deck and I help to give it a good scrub. Then I am detailed-off to be bowman of the ship's whaler while the Duty Petty Officer inspects the ship's side for any marks left by our ammunitioning lighters. *Bermuda* glitters and shines: there isn't a speck of rust that hasn't been covered with paint.

After dinner on Monday, men in brown overalls shuffle over the forward brow.

'SINGLE UP.

CLOSE UP SPECIAL SEA DUTYMEN.

CLOSE ALL SCUTTLES AND UPPER DECK SCREEN DOORS.

HANDS OUT OF THE RIG OF THE DAY CLEAR OFF THE UPPER DECK.

CHIEF SHIPWRIGHT REPORT TO THE BRIDGE.'

I am surprised to see that we still have a number of dockyard-mateys onboard as we hoist our two brows. We secure a couple of tugs and are slowly pulled out into the centre of the harbour. We disconnect the tugs before negotiating the narrow harbour entrance.

We anchor not far from Nab Tower and the Engineers and Mechanics set to work alongside our brown-overalled guests to test whatever has been repaired or added to *Bermuda* while she has been in dry-dock. It takes two days for them to sort out and rubber-stamp everything.

We edge closer to Portsmouth after tea on Wednesday and launch our boats to take our brown-overalled guests back to the dockyard and to shuttle those crew members who live in Portsmouth home for a last night with their families. Half of our mess live in Portsmouth, or pretend to, and it is nice to have some elbow-room this evening. I have a game of cribbage with Yorky and I beat him. He flings the crib board at me, calls me a lucky bastard and says he will never play crib with me again. I think I've found a flaw in Leading Seaman Bilton's character.

Next morning, as the liner *Queen Elizabeth 2*, followed by *HM Submarines Tireless* and *Plover* pass us, *Bermuda* ups anchor and trundles her way west...

'ACTION STATIONS.

ASSUME DAMAGE CONTROL STATE 1 CONDITION ZULU ALPHA.

DRESS OF THE DAY IS ANTI-FLASH GEAR WITH RESPIRATORS.'

It is Spam sarnies for dinner. We spend the afternoon on the degaussing range. I don't know what degaussing is, even after reading about it in the Admiralty Manual of Seamanship ... but we do it anyway.

I settle down to a quiet evening in the mess until ...

'DARKEN SHIP.

CLOSE ALL SCUTTLES AND SCREEN DOORS.

ENSURE THAT ALL DEADLIGHTS ARE CORRECTLY SECURED.

RIG BLACKOUT SCREENS ON ALL UPPER DECK SCREEN DOORS.

THE SHIP WILL REMAIN DARKENED FOR THE REST OF THE NIGHT.'

Bermuda stops while the Darken Ship Officer is taken around the ship on one of our boats to inspect our 'blacked-out' standard. For an hour or so *Bermuda* is a wallowing, completely dark, armour-plated hazard to shipping in the approaches to the English channel. Later, still blacked out, we replenish our self from *RFA Black Ranger* as we steam west towards Land's End on our way to Milford Haven in Wales. I've never been to Wales before.

I've always been a great listener. Sitting on one end of the mess table, its surface festooned with ashtrays overflowing with duty-free cigarette ends, the screwed up ends of thin, hand-rolled 'ticklers' and active beer cans, I learn about the major seaports of the world and more about the moral character of the opposite sex than I ever expected. For instance I learn that the ugliest women in the world are to be found in the bars down The Gut in Malta. That Lockhart Road in Hong Kong has more bars along its relatively short length than the entire town of Northampton: and that they are full of 'desirable' and available Oriental women. Bugis street in Singapore is full of transvestites, called Kie-ties, the majority of whom are allegedly ex-RAF servicemen. Sea stories abound – each one more exaggerated than the last. I learn that our American cousins, who are allegedly punished for contracting VD, rarely report it. Consequently the main American Naval base in the Philippines is the Venereal Disease capital of the world. Helsinki and Wellington New Zealand are the places where the most compliant women are to be found. I learn that nowhere in the British Commonwealth will we encounter more frightening and intimidating women than those who frequent some of the bars down Portsmouth's Commercial Road or Plymouth's Union Street. Where else could I gain such an insight into the cultural low-spots of yet-to-be-visited places?

'Why do they call roll-ups 'ticklers'?' I ask when there is a lull in the conversation.

Prof puts his hand up. 'I know the answer to that one.'

'You're not going to ferkin' sing, are ya?' asks Lanquid.

'Course not. Young 'un has asked a sensible question and I'm going to give him a sensible answer.'

'That'll make a change then,' adds Soapy.

Prof silences everybody by holding up his hands. 'In days gone by ... before Yorky joined ...'

Yorky throws a perfectly aimed shoe that hits Prof on his shoulder.

'... a company called Tickler were the first to issue jam and marmalade to the Navy in air-tight jars ...'

'The Navy were issued with jam?'

'Only the Wardroom probably,' explains Yorky.

'Anyway,' continues Prof. 'Those that rolled their own cigarettes quickly realised that the air-tight tins kept their tobacco nice and moist ... and ever since, rolling tobacco in the Royal Navy has been referred to as Tickler.'

'Thanks Prof,' I say. I believe him.

Apparently when the stories start to become suspiciously exaggerated, listeners pretend to swing an imaginary lamp: this is when the arguments invariably begin. Sea-story evenings teach me how to be a good and polite listener.

Uckers, Chess and Cribbage are regularly played in ship's competitions but games such as 'Shit On Yer Oppo' and 'Chase The Pisser' are not officially recognised because the Wardroom can't understand the rules.

Friday. The pubs and delights of Milford Haven are to remain an unobtainable smudge on the horizon as the bridge changes its mind and we do an about-turn bound for the exotic delights of Plymouth: or so the For'd messdeck rumour has it. The 'natives' of Plymouth raise a can or two in celebration. Out comes the best West Country foo-foo and 'Janner' aftershave lotion.

I overhear the following exchange of information.

'What's the first thing you're going to do when you get home, Jan?'

'Give the Old Lady one.'

'Yeah, I know that, but after that ... after that what?'

'Then I'll put mi case down, take mi coat off, kiss the kids and go down the pub for a decent pint.'

Our Plymouth visit is cancelled. Instead we spend Saturday around Land's End doing more 'darken ship' exercises and some four-inch firings. Our Russian 'Intelligence Gatherers' re-appear. The Plymouth natives are pissed-off: some of them have had a 'going home' shower.

I am spooning the last of what I assume to be gravy when Squinty leans over my shoulder and plonks a brown paper bag in the centre of the mess table. 'Now then.' He points a ramrod-straight index finger at the bag. 'Fifteen two that bastard.'

We cribbage players know exactly what he means.

Yorky looks up from his book and smiles knowingly. 'It's not what I think is it?'

'Take a look,' says Squinty as he purposefully folds his arms and waits.

Yorky opens the top of the bag and looks in.

'Is that a ferkin' winner or what?' asks a puffed-up Squinty.

Yorky turns the bag around so that he can view the contents from a number of different angles. 'Looks good to me.'

'Good enough for a race?'

'Maybe.'

Squinty grabs the bag and tips the contents onto the table.

A large antenna-waving cockroach glares at us all in turn, flexes his back muscles and settles himself.

'Just look at that upper leg development,' says Squinty. 'He's a ferkin' athlete if ever I saw one, if ever I saw one.'

'Where did you find him?'

'Outside the Main Galley door.'

Squinty's specimen starts to move towards the table edge: Yorky picks it up, looks directly into its eyes and tosses it back into the bag. 'If you can find someone to race we'll rig everything up after 'nine-o-clockers'. Have a word with the Stokers' mess.'

I lick my spoon and watch as Squinty secures the top of the bag and tosses it into his locker.

I have the Last Dog Watch. By the time I've had a shower and got changed I am sent to the galley for 'nine-o-clockers', which tonight is bread and a monstrous block of bright yellowish cheddar cheese.

'Caterer's getting rid of his out-of-date cheese, by the smell of it,' says Prof. He is the mess cheese expert: he ate something called Stilton once.

Yorky carves the block into hand-sized chunks with his Seamen's knife – the same knife that he uses for cleaning the soles of his boots and the insides of his fingernails. Those who don't want a block of contaminated cheese organise the table top. A couple of six-foot-long electrical cable trays appear and are laid upside-down along the length of the table.

A black-bearded individual, who smells of fuel oil and is introduced as 'Clinker' from the main Stokers' mess, appears carrying a circular duty-free tickler tin in the centre of a wooden mess tray. 'Within this tin is the three-times inter-mess champion. He has digested a high-protein supper of spaghetti-in, and is ready to take on any challenger.'

Prof, waving a couple of sheets of paper, muscles his way to the centre spot. 'I shall accept any bets: I'll discuss odds for either of the runners, twenty-five to one for a dead heat.'

'Up the ladder, young 'un.' Yorky waves at me. 'Keep an eye out for any unwanted visitors.'

'OK.' I perch myself at the top of the ladder where I can see down the passage while enjoying a bird's-eye view of our mess table.

Members from the other mess areas congregate around our section. To a voiced fanfare Squinty appears with his brown paper bag clutched to his chest. Squinty and Clinker glare at each other until Yorky steps between the two of them. 'By mutual agreement the referee for this evening's competition is Leading Seaman Collins. All bets are to be placed within the next five minutes.

The competition will take place over a single six-foot course within the confines of approved Admiralty Pattern cable trays. Physical encouragement is not allowed. Verbal encouragement is permitted. With the agreement of both trainers a small piece of this evening's mature cheddar will be placed at the finishing line of each tray.'

The cable trays, perforated sheet-metal plates formed into a 'U' shape, are placed upside-down, side by side. The paper bag and the tickler tin are placed on the table and both managers throw a dice. Clinker throws a five and Squinty a three.

Jumper takes over. 'The choice of tray is yours, Clinker.'

Clinker ponders for a while, checks on the table surface, walks to the end and inspects both small nuggets of cheese.

'For ferk's sake, Stokes ... get on with it,' someone shouts.

'Piss off,' replies Clinker.

'Language ... we don't tolerate bad language in the Seamen's messdeck,' someone from the back shouts.

'Yeah ... wash yer ferkin' mouth out,' shouts someone else.

'This one!' says Clinker, pointing to one of the trays.

'Time to release the runners.' says Jumper.

Squinty is the first to release his runner into the small starting zone at the head of his tray.

Clinker looks at Squinty's cocky and sniffs. He places his champion in the starting zone of his chosen tray. 'Gentlemen ... sorry ... thought I was in my Stokers' mess for a minute there ... let me introduce Flash.'

'You call him Flash?'

'Yep.'

Jumper waits until both runners are facing the same way and, with a nod of agreement from both trainers, declares the race underway and the starting barrier inside both trays is tripped.

I check the passageway: it is empty. Our runner takes an early lead and has travelled a couple of feet before something interesting catches its eye and it stops. As though it is a signal, Flash flexes its legs and strolls nonchalantly down the course. As it passes ours, Flash waves a dismissive antenna, turns 180 degrees and stomps back towards the starting gate.

Clinker waves his arms and questions his champion's parentage. 'There's ferkin' cheese at the far end you stupid ferkin' animal ... err insect ... err ... whatever you are.'

'Language, Clinker ... language,' warns Jumper. 'Remember where you are. You're not in the Stokers' mess now, you know.'

Laughter all round. Even Clinker smiles.

'Come on then, Bannister!' yells Squinty, clapping enthusiastically. 'Come on.'

'You call him Bannister?'

'Why not? It's a reasonable name.'

'Bannister?'

'Roger Bannister,' replies Squinty.

There are mumbles of agreement all round.

Flash does another about-turn and scuttles past Bannister, who has stopped and is staring at Tug who is sitting to one side.

'Move, young 'un. Go and sit by the finishing line,' whispers Squinty.

Tug does as instructed, Yorky makes room for him and Bannister scampers down to the finishing line, over the lump of cheddar and into Squinty's welcoming brown paper bag.

Flash is a good two feet behind. Clinker nods acceptance, turns his cable tray over, picks up Flash and fixes it with a Stoker's stare. 'What the ferk were you doing, Flash? After everything I've taught you. Now I've got to return to the mess and try to explain to everybody that you've lost the championship for us. It will take ages for us to train a replacement.'

A sorrowful Flash cocks his head on one side and looks despondently at Clinker.

'Float test, Clinker?' someone asks.

'Those are the rules, I suppose. Bye-bye Flash.' Clinker places the beaten champion into Languid's outstretched hand. Jumper opens a scuttle, there is a rush of cold, damp air and Languid tosses Flash into the cold, dark waters of the Western Approaches.

'Rest in peace, Gordon,' mumbles a morose-looking Clinker.

'I thought you said his name is Flash?'

'Flash Gordon.'

'That makes sense,' says Prof.

'Don't know what I'm going to tell the blokes in the mess. We've been training him for a couple of months now.'

'Did you teach him to swim?'

'Piss off,' replies Clinker. 'Have some ferkin' consideration.'

'Time to pay out,' says Prof. 'Form an orderly queue.'

'Where are you going to keep Bannister then, Squints?' asks somebody.

'In the knicker locker.'

Nobody voices any dissent.

'Three cheers for Bannister,' says Prof. 'Hip hip...'

'Hooray!'

'Hip hip ...'

'Hooray.'

'Hip hip ...'

'Hooray.'

Clinker quietly slinks away.

Prof takes up position at the head of the table and spreads his arms ...

He was an oil drenched Stoker,
Up from town upon a whim,
And she, a poor man's daughter,
Took a fancy unto him.

Well he courted her most cruelly,
Filled her head with hopes and dreams.
Told her she would be a lady,
But nothing was what it seemed.

They stood on the bridge at midnight,
His heart was all a quiver,
As he groped for her suspenders,
Her leg fell in the river.

Able Seaman 'Skid' Marks bet all his money on Bannister and has won three pounds two shillings and sixpence.

Get up there, lad, and stow those oars correctly!

17

AMSTERDAM MAKES A BLOKE OF ME

We anchor in Plymouth Sound at 09:00 on a warm and clear Sunday morning. Natives of Plymouth and surrounding areas are really pissed off to learn that, once again, there will be no overnight shore leave while we are here. One of our unhappy Janners in the mess kicks the front of his locker. 'I've had two ferkin' showers in two ferkin' days.'

The ship is awash with unhappy Janners for the remainder of the day.

We receive mail. I get the news from Pudsey. The weather has been lousy all through summer, the next-door neighbours have bought themselves a couple of yappy Pomeranian dogs and Mrs Butterworth on the corner has moved her toilet indoors.

At first light on Monday morning the Fo'csle team have the anchor 'straight up and down'. The Plymouth natives aren't pulling their weight.

Once out and into clear water we are again targeted by a squadron of 'enemy' aircraft. The Russians are waiting for us. All our gun crews are closed up and it is interesting to watch the turrets silently swerve to track the aircraft as they approach, fly over us and then disappear into the West Country morning mist. A number of jackstay transfers keep us busy for most of the day. We exercise a major fire in the Wardroom galley just before tea, which upsets all the Commissioned ranks. The Quarter-deck is full of frustrated and hungry Officers kicking their heels and smoking until all the fire-fighting equipment is stowed away and the fire officially declared 'extinguished'.

I learn to be careful what questions I ask and to whom. One night I am at the mess table with Yorky and Squinty.

'What does CDA on the toilet door mean?' I ask.

Yorky looks at Squinty. Squinty blinks. 'You tell him, Squints – you're the expert on such matters.'

'Ya wha?' says Squinty.

'You're the expert,' say Yorky. 'You've 'caught the boat-up' more times than I've had hot dinners.'

'Probably,' says Squinty, smirking. He takes a long, noisy slurp from his can.

'Tell young 'un, then.'

Squinty takes another mouthful of beer, wipes his mouth on his sleeve and turns to face me. 'CDA means Caught Disease Ashore.'

'Disease?'

'VD, young 'un. You know what the ferk that is, don't you?'

'Yeah – I've seen the film ... three times.'

Yorky laughs.

Squinty empties his can and tosses it in the general direction of the mess gash bucket ... and misses. 'Diseases of a carnal nature ... particularly those contracted in the Far East ... can be seriously infectious, ... seriously infectious.'

I nod. I've seen the VD film in technicolour and I have a graphic flashback.

'While it cannot be enforced one hundred percent, those who've been certified by the Sick Bay as having officially 'caught-the-boat-up' are required to use the CDA traps to avoid contamination.'

'So I shouldn't use that trap, then?'

'Not unless you have a chit from the Sick Bay.'

'I did though ... I used it the other day. All the others were occupied.'

'Keep a close eye on your tackle for the next week or so then, young 'un. It can take between ten to 14 days before things start dropping off.'

'Wha!'

'He's having you on,' explains Yorky. 'It can take years with some strains.'

'No?' I am getting worried now. I have a sudden urge for a long hot shower and a groin scrub.

'Just keep an eye open for anything strange in your knickers, young 'un.'

I imagine all sorts of itches and tickles during the following days. It is a while before I accept the fact that if everything remains the same in the underpants region in the next couple of years ... I will probably be OK.

After dark we carry out a series of Starshell illumination firings which are quite attractive in a strange way, lighting up the Western Approaches as they do.

I have a reasonably good scratch as I turn-in tonight.

On Friday morning we re-enter Portsmouth and berth on our reserved slot on South Railway Jetty with our bows pointing south. Lower Deck is cleared for the reading of another Punishment Warrant for a Leading Cook who has been working a catering fraud involving meat.

Weekend leave is granted and more than half my mess disappear with lecherous grins on their faces and extra DFs secreted about their person.

Tug and I are told that if we want to find out about Stumpy we should ask someone in the Sick Bay.

'Excuse me, PO. Do you know where Ordinary Seaman Borrowdale is?'

'Who?' replies a rather harassed-looking Petty Officer Sick

Berth Attendant.

'Ordinary Seaman Borrowdale: he was admitted to hospital recently with some kind of illness.'

'Ahah ... the idiot who covered himself in tattoos?'

'Yes, that's him.'

'Yes, that's him WHAT!'

'Yes, that's him, PO.'

'Ordinary Seaman Borrowdale is no longer my problem. As soon as he was on the other end of the brow he became someone else's responsibility.'

'Do you know where he might be?' asks Tug.

'Haslar hospital probably. Now piss off – I've got work to do.'

'Thanks, PO.'

A snort and a grunt.

Down the mess Sugar tells us to catch a HLD that does regular runs across the harbour to Haslar Hospital – only a short walk from the jetty on the other side.

Royal Naval Hospital Haslar is a monster of a place and it takes ages for Tug and I to find anyone who will help us. Battalions of men in white coats and nurses in starched blue-and-white uniforms scuttle around apparently far too busy to talk to us. Eventually, we find someone who has the authority to tell us officially that Stumpy is infectious and we can't see him. We leave feeling deflated and find a pub that is full of Submariners. We have a quick pint before eventually finding our way back onboard.

Every night for the rest of the week Tug and I grace the NAAFI Club with our presence. Nothing has changed: the Marilyns are grouped around the main door wanting to be signed in. Nora's mother, the lady behind the desk, remembers me.

'How are you, boys? Enjoy your trip?'

'It was OK, thanks.'

'Pity you didn't manage to get ashore in Guzz.'

'Guzz?' I asks.

'Sorry, Plymouth.' She smiles understandingly. 'And you missed out on Milford Haven as well.'

'We did, yeah.'

'Not much of a run ashore though ... Milford Haven,' she says.

'Do you know where we're going next?' I ask.

'Rosyth, Invergordon, Greenock, Newcastle, Amsterdam, Antwerp, Scapa Flow and Belfast ... but not necessarily in that order.'

Tug and I smirk at each other. 'Can you write that down for us?'

'More than my life's worth, darling. You'll have to remember it all.'

'Tell us again, then.'

'Greenock, Rosyth, Invergordon, Newcastle, Amsterdam, Antwerp, Belfast and Scapa Flow ... but not in that order ... necessarily.'

'Belfast?'

'Fraid so, darling. Look after yourselves there, won't you? ... and give my love to Able Seaman Kayne. Tell him that my daughter and I are always thinking of him and would love to see him again. Individually or together.'

'Err, what's your name then?' I ask nervously.

'Just tell him Nora's mother. He'll understand.'

'Will do.'

'And give my regards to Ralph if you find yourselves in Danny's Bar in Antwerp: he's the owner ... big, well-built gentleman. Tell him that Nora's mother from Copnor still remembers his last visit with ...' she puckers her lips and smiles, 'with complete satisfaction.'

I nod. 'With complete satisfaction. OK I'll do that.'

A queue is forming behind us. 'Thanks ... err Nora's mum,' says Tug. 'Time for us to get a beer.'

Back onboard I tell Sugar what Nora's mum has said.

'She's a woman and a half, she is. Makes a great pot-mess.'

'Pot Mess?'

'Stew. Problem is she's an insatiable piece of work.'

'Insatiable?'

'Nymphomaniac.'

'A what?'

'A Nympho. A forty-five-year-old Nympho.'

'Oh, I've heard of them.'

'Not much to look at, but a very entertaining lady.'

'So you'll be seeing her again then?' I ask. 'She said that she's always available.'

'No bloody fear. She's too much of a handful for me. Beware, young 'un: be very careful.

'Of what?'

'I was about your age when I first succumbed to her charms ... or rather when she succumbed to mine.'

I wink. 'Gotcha. Thanks Sugar, I'll be careful.' I am still a little confused but don't want to admit it.

We put to sea at exactly 14:30 on 27 September escorted by the destroyers *HMS Trafalgar, Scorpion, Jutland* and *Broadsword*.

In convoy formation, we make our way through the English channel and north east towards Ijmuiden, the North Sea Canal and Amsterdam. Judging from the expressions of expectation on the faces of many of the mess members, Amsterdam has something special to offer us.

Bermuda shackles herself to a couple of buoys off Amsterdam's Central Station. It takes the Quarter-deck team a long time to get the back end secured to its buoy, as it is the first time we've done it.

We spend the latter end of the afternoon and early evening rigging the awnings. According to those in the mess who have been to Amsterdam before, the city is something special, particularly a place called Canal Street. I am invited to accompany a few of the guys for a quick run-ashore, but I remember Yorky's warning about going ashore with older members of the mess.

Friday 29 September 1961 is a day that should be written large in my diary … and underlined! After being asked a second time, and ignoring Yorky's advice, I agree to go ashore with Languid and Squinty who, unbeknown to me, have formulated a plan.

Canal Street and its surrounding area is an eye-opener. In window after window after window provocatively dressed ladies display themselves with beckoning smiles, perched suggestively on chairs or lounging on settees. The placid waters of the canals stand motionless and quiet while the many canal-side bars are overflowing with customers. As the sun is setting, more ladies of Canal Street switch their lights on: in some windows there are pairs of women! Languid suggests a wander. Squinty agrees and I gulp. Things happens so quickly. I have a double-take at a particularly striking dark-haired lady in a window who smiles invitingly at me, strokes her shimmering dark stockings and snaps seductively at the crutch area of her red-and-black underwear. I am heading towards the next bar when Squinty disappears. Languid calls me over and bundles me through a bright red door that clangs shut behind me.

A well-proportioned, perfumed arm guides me towards a black-sheeted bed. The lady in red-and-black underwear removes my cap and places it on a bedside cabinet. She turns it so that 'HMS Bermuda' is facing the bed. She drapes my trousers carefully over the back of an upholstered chair, being careful of the creases, and removes my shoes and socks for me while I stare at the ceiling and panic!

To be perfectly honest, the following eight-and-a-quarter minutes are something of a blur. While the 1812 Overture is playing, I am encapsulated and manipulated within a confusing arrangement of sweet-smelling limbs and tensioned elastic.

The lady knows all about the complexities of a teenage, English boy's body.

Tchaikovsky's cannons roar ... and it's all over.

As I zip myself back up and check that I still have my identity card and wallet, she hands me a number of business cards. 'What is your name?'

'Peter.'

'That was free, Peter – thank you.'

'Thank you,' I splurt and discreetly adjust myself.

She points at the cards. 'Those are for messmates – 10 percent discount on presentation of card.'

'Thanks.'

I must have done something right because she shakes my hand as she opens the door.

'Lost your cherry then, boyo?' asks Languid as I join them sitting in a darkened corner of the nearest bar. They have a large, cold beer waiting for me. How did they know how long it would take me?

'Twice.'

'Bollocks. You were only in there ten minutes.'

'I don't hang about, me ... and she thanked me.' I don't mention the business cards in my pocket.

Squinty snorts.

'Magnificent tits as well,' I say.

Languid nudges Squinty in the ribs. 'He's a ferkin' expert already.'

The end of my special day is brought to an abrupt end when I have to manipulate my hammock from the mess to the Capstan flat. How I manage to sling it correctly I don't know: but somehow I do.

I awake the following morning a fully-paid-up heterosexual member of the crew: I feel as though I have really achieved something significant.

I receive a scattered round of applause as soon as I enter the mess with my hammock.

'Heard you did it twice, young 'un,' says Yorky.

'That may have been the beer talking,' I admit as I toss my hammock nonchalantly into the stowage rack.

'Was it everything you imagined?'

'Can't remember.'

'Can't remember anything?'

'No. Not really.'

'What a waste.'

'I know.'

'What a ferkin' waste.'

'I remember the 1812 Overture was playing ... in the corner.'

'With cannons?'

'Oh yes. Definitely with ferkin' cannons.'

Joe comes at me from behind, drapes an arm over my shoulder and whispers, 'I hear that you've been batting for the other side, darlin'.'

'Yes.' I cough.

'Shame.' He blows me a kiss and minces away to his paint store.

I give Yorky the business cards. 'Ten percent discount apparently, if anyone takes a card.'

He tosses the cards onto the mess table and addresses the mess. 'Pete's latest conquest has given us some discount cards, if anyone is interested.'

'Not after he's been there,' exclaims Squinty.

18

OVER THE BROW INTO ANTWERP

Wednesday 4 October dawns cold and foggy. Fog sentries are placed and a bell is rigged on the Fo'csle. All the Seamen take turns at lookout. I spend a chilly half hour on 01 deck while the rest of the Quarter-deck crew single up on the after buoy so that we can slip ourselves at a moment's notice.

By mid morning the fog is finally clear enough for the bell-ringing to cease and our accompanying Destroyers to sail. *Bermuda* unhitches herself from her buoys at 15:00, gently negotiates the Canal and enters the North Sea three hours later.

Early next morning we pass a lighthouse to starboard and enter the River Scheldt. Slowly we meander our way down-river and at dinnertime berth alongside No 22 Jetty at Antwerp for what is officially termed a five-day ceremonial visit.

The first full day in Antwerp is spent getting ready for what we are told will be a large number of visitors on Saturday. Once again, I am duty. Unofficially, the backs of some ladders are removed. The For'd Seamen's mess is unofficially responsible for the removal and storage of the back of the ladder that runs down from the upper deck to the Canteen flat. This is the busiest ladder for visitors and is the responsibility of our mess because it is rumoured that we have the largest number of perverts. Prof states that the females of Antwerp are inclined to wear trousers at this time of year.

On Saturday morning, instead of cleaning the mess, we fall in to clean the visitors' route. The Wardroom Stewards have overlooked all the dog ends in the scuppers and those stuffed inside the gratings by last night's Wardroom guests.

After dinner the queue of people waiting to come onboard stretches way down the jetty. There is a good sprinkling of women which promises to give the day some sparkle. My job is to assist all the visitors to safely negotiate the wooden steps from the inboard end of our brow to the boat deck. All I have to do is offer a supporting arm to everybody. I manage to hold the hand of almost every young woman who comes onboard as I help them negotiate the steps. Prof is right: disappointingly, almost all the women are wearing trousers and boots. There is a chill in the air, but it isn't too cold to wear a skirt ... in my humble opinion.

Unfortunately I don't get the chance to mingle. Once the last visitor is onboard I am moved to the other brow to help those leaving to climb a more rickety set of wooden steps. Loads of women smile at me – absolutely loads. Surprisingly, most of them say 'Thank you' in English. The people of Antwerp are a polite lot.

After tea, Yorky announces that Wiggy has taken over from Squinty as Bannister's trainer. Wiggy has been an apprentice model maker for 11 months after leaving school and is good with his hands. It was decided a few days ago that Bannister needs more fresh air and exercise. Being cooped up in the putrid atmosphere of locker 66 isn't good for his health: he needs to stretch his legs. Wiggy has promised to make Bannister a harness and take him for regular training walks on the upper deck.

Tug and I get dressed in our best suits and skip over the brow into Antwerp on Sunday. Those who have already been ashore confirm that both Danny's Bar and the Texas Bar are still in operation and conveniently located on opposite sides of the same street.

Sailors have an inbuilt ability to find their way through a foreign dockyard into an unknown town. They instinctively know where to buy a postcard so that they can write a brief message to those at home before getting down to real serious sightseeing stuff: finding a good bar.

Our taxi driver knows where we want to go before we even ask.

Now, Pudsey West Yorkshire in the 1950-60s, is not known for its sexual diversity. I am totally unprepared therefore, to face the clientele of Danny's Bar: a collection of the most overdressed and extraordinarily attractive men... all dressed as pantomime dames. Tug and I sit with our chins on the table watching the jostling and cavorting clientele. They all ignore us – this is their bar, they are the attraction and we are the silent audience. I am hesitant and very careful when I go to the toilet. The beer at Danny's Bar is good but it comes at a price. I eventually pluck up courage to identify Ralph.

Thankfully, Ralph is as heterosexual as it is possible to be. A muscular, crop-haired bloke wearing a Portsmouth Football Club shirt.

'Nora's mother from Copnor asked me to pass on her best regards to you.'

'Best regards?' he asks, as he swipes the froth from the top of a couple of beers.

'Yep.'

He narrows his eyes and looks directly at me. 'You haven't been involved with Nora's mother, have you?'

'No, not really. I only know her because she works at the NAAFI Club. She said ...'

'She works in the ferkin' NAAFI Club?'

'Yeah, The Ponderosa.'

'Want a word of advice, my young friend?'

'What?'

'Never accept an invitation home from Nora's mother. I doubt very much that you would escape unscathed. She has a habit of first inviting you for Sunday dinner ... that is the way she snared me.'

'Crikey.'

'Came all the way to Antwerp to escape her ... 12 years ago.'

'Blimey.'

'These fellers are far easier to deal with than women dressed as women ... if you get my drift.'

I nod but I don't really understand. 'Nice place you've got here.'

'Thanks, young 'un. Have a couple of beers on the house. Keep an eye on the guy with the bulky moustache wearing the thigh-high silver boots – he's getting a bit too close to your mate over there.'

'What do I do if he gets too close?'

'Panic! ... then run for it.'

'What's Nora's mother's name then?' Tug asks.

'Don't know,' says Ralph. 'She was always just Nora's mum to me.'

We finish our free drinks and stroll over the road to the Texas Bar where we come face to face with Antwerp's squad of female professionals.

Fortunately, a couple of wide-eyed young sailors who have to divvy-up their combined change before buying a couple of small beers, don't impress them and we are totally ignored. While sipping our extremely expensive beer we play a game between ourselves, each of us picking our ugliest 'lady' who we reckon will be the last to be whisked away. We run out of beer and money long before the last of the 'ladies' is whisked away. Perched on a stool with curling armrests at the end of the bar, near to the door, is a well-rounded woman with bright red hair. As each of the ladies is escorted to the door she stuffs an amount of cash into her ever-expanding cleavage before giving the departing couple, or threesome, a blessing in the form of the wobbly cross.

Rumour has it that there is a friendly relationship between the Texas Bar and Danny's Bar. It is even said that they get together twice a year for a combined drug-buying jolly to Amsterdam.

Tug and I return onboard, having witnessed another stitch on life's rich tapestry.

Monday is designated recovery day. Antwerp's beer is difficult to shake off. I spend the day polishing bright work that doesn't need polishing.

Tuesday is taken up with humping stores onboard and making sure that the various lighters that come alongside don't scuff our sparkling paintwork. I spend a pleasant few hours on a floating pontoon positioned between *Bermuda*'s side and the jetty, with a long-handled paint brush called a Long-Tom, and a bucket full of ship's-side grey paint. I am Admiral of my own pontoon.

On a damp Wednesday morning we 'single up' and with the help of a couple of Antwerp's orange tugs we are towed out into the middle of the Scheldt and bid a dignified farewell to Antwerp. There is only a small bunch of people to see us off. I identify a couple of individuals who could be Danny's Bar regulars, standing astride their bicycles energetically waving frilly white handkerchiefs. One has a bulky moustache.

Later in the day as we steam north, we meet up with the Dutch warships *Karel Doorman* & *Groningen*... and like *Bermuda* does when meeting another warship ...

'ACTION STATIONS.

ASSUME DAMAGE CONTROL STATE 1 CONDITION ZULU ALPHA.'

We close and clip everything before exercising manoeuvres and pretending to transfer things between us.

We battle north, our ultimate destination being the Monte Carlo of the North: Invergordon.

19

SURVIVING THE STORM

There's nothing more relaxing than lounging on a wash-deck locker, out of the prevailing wind with a full packet of cigarettes, a Ronson Varaflame lighter, the afternoon off, a full stomach and the prospect of 'Last Dog and all-night-in'.

This Thursday evening the sea is flat, the sun is setting vermilion red and *Bermuda* is at peace with herself for a change. Everything is just perfect ... just perfect!

Wiggy breaks the peace and quiet. He waves a hand at Bannister who, dressed in a black cotton harness attached to a short length of stick, is loping alongside his starboard foot. 'If I keep pace with him he can go for ferkin' miles.'

'Miles?'

'No, not miles exactly, but you know what I mean. However,' he taps the side of his nose, 'if I put the stick on the deck ...' He bends down and places his stick on the deck. 'It's too heavy for him to pull so he just goes round in circles. So I don't have to walk around with him – I can just stand and watch him when I get tired.'

'That's brilliant.'

'The Marines are training up a challenger. They've got him on a special 'Bootneck' diet of Spam and sardines apparently. They'll have him ready for early September, they say. They call him 'Mad Mike' after that mercenary bloke in Africa.'

We sit smoking cigarettes and watching Bannister do his circuits. It is a strange way to end the day.

Our exercises with *Karel Doorman* & *Groningen* take us to every corner of the North Sea, and it isn't until Friday breakfast time that we carefully berth *Bermuda* alongside Invergordon's Admiralty Pier. It is Friday the 13th.

During the weekend we are joined by destroyers *HMS Lynx, Murray, Keppel, Blackwood* and *Trafalgar*. Late on Sunday *HMS Rhyl* and *HM Submarine Sea Scout* arrive ready to start a Monday-morning confrontation.

Now that our finances have been replenished, Tug and I once again trek up to the Invergordon Canteen which is the only place we can get a drink on a Sunday without having to sign the travellers' book.

There is something about the Invergordon Canteen that makes people perform – particularly Prof. He takes centre floor, holds his arms wide and asks 'What's it to be, lads?'

Someone from the back shouts 'The Oggie song!'

From some other part of the room there is a chorus of 'Oggie, Oggie, Oggie – Oink, Oink, Oink!'

A Royal Marine stands to attention and asks the room, 'Where you be going to, Janner?'

'Oiy be goin' to Looe,' replies Prof before taking a long swig of his beer.

'Cor Bugger Janner, I be goin' there too.'

Then the whole canteen gives voice in a surprisingly well-practised response. 'Oggie, Oggie, Oggie – Oink, Oink, Oink!'

Prof starts and those who know the words join in ...

'Oh how happy us will be,
When we gets to the West Countreeee,
Where the Oggies grow on trees,
Cor! Bugger Janner!

Half a pound of flour and marge,
Makes a lovely clacker,
Just enough for you and me.
Cor! Bugger Janner.

You make fast, I'll make fast,
Make fast the dinghy.
You make fast, kiss my arse,
Make fast the dinghy.'

And then with real enthusiasm and much waving of pint glasses everybody joins in ...

'And we'll all go back to Oggie land,
To Oggie Land, to Oggie Land,
And we'll all go back to Oggie land,
Where they can't tell sugar from tissue paper,
tissue paper ... marmalade and jam.

The everybody yells...

'Oggie, Oggie, Oggie!'

There is the sound of a dropped glass. An instant cheer fills the room. Everybody appears to know exactly what to do.

The same Royal Marine once again gets to his feet and asked, 'Where you be going to, Janner?'. And it all kicks off again. I join in – there is a good ring to the tune and the chorus is easy to remember.

There is a lull. The rivalry between a large contingent of Royal Marine bandsmen, who are sitting around a closely grouped set of tables in the far corner and the Fo'csle Seamen, is getting a bit serious. The Stokers are getting more than a little fractious with the Blue Card watch-keepers who are on an adjacent table.

A bloke stands on his table and raises his glass ...

'In the deepest part of Africa,
Where the Yanks have never been.
Lies the body of a dead Gorilla,

Shagged to death by a Royal Marine.
With a can of Pepsi Cola,
And a ferkin' great tub of ice cream,
We will all march past in a column of threes,
To the band of the Royal Marines.'

Then the rest join in ...

'To the band of the Royal Marines.'
THE ROYALS!
To the band of the Royal Marines.'

Then, as they say in the For'd Seamen's mess, 'the shit really hits the fan'. The Royals dump their pints on the table and are on their feet in seconds. Closely followed by the Fo'csle part-of-ship. Fists, beer and glasses fly in all directions. A guy behind the bar blows loudly on a whistle while his mate makes a grab for the telephone.

The police arrive within minutes, just as the first set of chairs are being launched. Both duty constables of the Invergordon Constabulary survey the scene and, deciding that retreat is the best part of valour, bugger off.

Someone yells 'Free beer' which calms things down a bit. Tug and I decide that it is time to leave and manage to sneak out of a small door to the right of the bar. The guy on the telephone behind the bar is asking the person on the other end to get in touch with *HMS Bermuda* urgently. A full pint glass hits him on the shoulder as Tug and I disappear.

'That came out of nowhere,' says Tug as we stand on the jetty before climbing *Bermuda*'s forward brow.

'Frightening.'

'Hope someone's slung our micks.'

'So do I.'

The Officer of the Watch at the top of the brow asks us where we have been.

'I say 'Church, sir,' at the same time that Tug says 'Just walking around, sir.'

'Get turned in ... quietly now.'

A couple of naval Tillies scream to a halt at the bottom of the brow as we disappear through a screen door.

Thankfully someone has slung our hammocks and I sleep the sleep of the partially inebriated.

The For'd Seamen's mess is a severely hung-over collection of bruised and battered individuals on Monday morning. Despite there being little lower-deck enthusiasm for the task, we disconnect our vessel from Invergordon's Admiralty Pier and slink away with our metaphorical tail between our legs early on a cold, misty, autumnal morning. I don't know exactly what piece of Scotland we have selected to take our frustrations out on, but by mid morning, *Bermuda* is 'knocking-ten-bells-of-shit' out of a small section of innocent real estate with her six-inch guns. We are showing off, firing all three turrets at the same time that heel us back on our beam-ends. Everything shudders: light covers clatter to the deck, unlocked doors clash open and large sections of deckhead paint, that have sat undisturbed for 20 years or more, come crashing down. Mystified cockroaches fall to the deck or stagger out from underneath lockers.

'DO YOU HEAR THERE ... ENSURE THAT ALL LOOSE GEAR AND EQUIPMENT IS SECURED.

WE SHALL SHORTLY BE FIRING A BROADSIDE.'

'Where would we be without our superiors on the bridge?' someone asks.

Yorky points at me, Tug and Streaky. 'Grab yourself a dustpan and brush each and sweep up all that broken glass.'

It takes us about an hour to clear the deck of rubbish. We have to remove all the hammocks from the main stowage as both the light-shades overhead have been blasted to smithereens. All the lights suddenly go out and some of the small red emergency lights come on.

'DO YOU HEAR THERE.

AREAS FORWARD OF SECTION DELTA MAY SUFFER SOME ELECTRICAL DISRUPTION IN THE NEXT THIRTY MINUTES.'

'Arseholes.'

'You'll be saying bollocks to the Chief next.'

A couple of our Destroyers manage to get towing wires onboard us but the weather is deteriorating and, despite their combined efforts, they can't move us: maybe we have our brake on. We do some high-speed manoeuvres in the evening which make *Bermuda* creak and groan like the elderly lady she is. Safety lines are rigged on all the upper deck ...

'RIG UPPER DECK SAFETY LINES.

THE UPPER DECKS ARE STRICTLY OUT OF BOUNDS.

DO YOU HEAR THERE THE UPPER DECKS ARE STRICTLY OUT OF BOUNDS ... ERR, EXCEPT FOR SEAMEN OF COURSE.'

Brilliant! Those on the bridge have finally figured out who actually rigs and unrigs the ferkin' safety lines.

During Tuesday afternoon, while *Bermuda* is being tossed all over the place by the most violent seas that some of the crew can remember, their Lords at the Admiralty officially inform us to expect bad weather. The pressure drops and a north-westerly wind increases steadily through the Dog Watches, reaching severe gale force shortly before midnight when I drag myself up to the Ops Room for the Middle Watch. The weather worsens throughout the Middle Watch. Through the Ops Room scuttle I can see sheets of water at our level, only a deck lower than the bridge. *Bermuda's* elderly bones are being battered: everything moves, groans or creaks. On my way down a bridge ladder to do the shakes, the ladder suddenly disappears from under my feet. I cling onto the handrails, my feet flaying around until the same ladder comes back up at me with a hammer-blow that sends a vibrating shock through my entire body. *'Bermadoo'* trembles: the ladder slams and appears to slew sideways as once again it goes from under my feet. The night-lights hum, the ladder handrails rattle. The metal door of an emergency fire locker bursts open to my right and the emergency night-lights go out. There is a gush of air inside a ventilation trunking as the deck shudders, drops, then comes back up at me. It is pitch black. The ladder back vibrates tunefully. I make it to the Burma Road as *Bermuda* slams over to starboard and I lose my footing, ending up in a corner as, yet again, the deck drops away and then comes back up at me from an unpredicted direction.

The For'd Seamen's mess is in chaos. It is almost completely dark as only a couple of the emergency nightlights are working. The deck is awash with water, wildly rushing from one side to the other. Everybody is bailing out with whatever container they have to hand. Overflowing buckets are being passed from hand to hand up the main ladder and then to a line of others leading to the main bathroom. It looks as though the water is pouring in through the Punkah Louvres much faster than the balers can clear it. Only half the hammocks are slung: those that are under vents are soaking wet with curtains of water flowing from their bowed undersides. Suitcases, grips and caps that were stowed on the top of lockers, are floating: they are grabbed soaking wet and thrown into one of the hammock stowages. A number of people have torches which they flash about. It is cold and soaking wet – nobody speaks, only the grunts and coughs of people working flat-out to clear the water that noisily slaps into everything and everybody.

'THE ENGINEERING OFFICER IS REQUESTED TO CONTACT THE BRIDGE.

CHIEF SHIPWRIGHT AND THE CHIEF BOSUN'S MATE REPORT TO THE BRIDGE IMMEDIATELY.

FIRE AND FORWARD EMERGENCY PARTIES MUSTER BY THE FORWARD DAMAGE CONTROL LOCKER.'

I remove my shoes, slip them into my pocket and look in vain for the blokes I need to shake. I spot them all baling out just as *Bermuda* shakes herself as she hits something hard and solid.

'That's what's known as a milestone, young 'un,' says an unsmiling Yorky as he drapes a dripping arm over my shoulder. 'You can help get the hammocks out of the stowage and take them somewhere dry before the water rises anymore.'

'I'm on watch, Hooky. I only came down to shake the Ops Room reliefs.'

Bermuda hits another milestone. A pile of plates bursts out of the mess trap locker and crashes to the deck. Yorky leaps away to see if any of them are still in one piece.

'ASSUME DAMAGE CONTROL STATE ONE CONDITION ZULU ALPHA, CLOSE ALL WATERTIGHT DOORS AND HATCHES.'

'And all the upper deck ventilation inlets,' yells someone from the back of the mess.

'ASSUME DAMAGE CONTROL STATE ONE CONDITION ZULU ALPHA, CLOSE ALL WATERTIGHT DOORS AND HATCHES.

CHIEF SHIPWRIGHT REPORT TO THE BRIDGE IMMEDIATELY ... I REPEAT IMMEDIATELY!

THIS IS NOT AN EXERCISE ... I REPEAT THIS IS NOT AN EXERCISE.'

'We can ferkin' vouch for that!' yells Deeps.

On the table in the adjacent section of the mess sits Joe the painter with a pile of sardine tins cradled in his lap. Slowly he opens each tin, removes a headless sardine by its tail and gently drops it into the slopping water. Nobody worries him – he is obviously dealing with the emergency in his own peculiar way.

In the Capstan flat there is water slopping from one side to the other. There is a slight fore-and-aft slope and the water is flowing aft somewhere. All the hammocks are swaying empty: I suppose everybody is down below bailing out. I check that my hammock is dry and head back to the Ops Room. *Bermuda* hits another milestone as I open the Ops Room door and I nearly tear it from his hinges.

I explain to Tansy what is happening down the mess.

He says 'Shit!'

The journey back to the mess is an obstacle course. In the mess I find Yorky and ask him what I can do to help.

'Just bail, young 'un. Hopefully someone will eventually manage to stop the North Atlantic coming in.'

'CHIEF SHIPWRIGHT AND CHIEF BOSUN'S MATE MUSTER AT THE FORWARD MAIN DECK DAMAGE CONTROL LOCKER.'

It is 05:45 before the water stops flowing through the ventilation trunkings. *Bermuda* still groans as she battles headlong into the weather. She slams directly into milestone after milestone, mounts her peaks with heady grace and surfs the sides of her troughs with rattling abandon.

As I swing up towards my hammock the blasted thing swings the other way as I loosen my grip and I end up flat on my back on the wet deck of the Capstan Flat. I treat my hammock with a little more respect the next time and manage to land my damp backside in the perfect place. I don't sleep: everything about *Bermuda* is screaming and groaning. We continue to confront the worst that the North Atlantic can throw at us. According to the bridge ...

'DO YOU HEAR THERE ... YOU WILL BE INTERESTED TO KNOW THAT WE ARE SURVIVING THE WORST PENTLAND STORMS IN LIVING MEM ...'

'Oh ... that makes everything OK then,' says someone ironic.

'DO YOU HEAR THERE ... THERE IS NO FRESH WATER AVAILABLE THROUGHOUT THE SHIP.

THE JUNIORS' BATHROOM IS STRICTLY OUT OF BOUNDS.

CHIEF SHIPWRIGHT AND THE ENGINEERING OFFICER REPORT TO ....'

At breakfast we eat directly from the trays that a couple of the most capable ABs in the mess have managed to collect. Breakfast consists of hard-boiled cackleberries, cold tinned tomatoes and a pile of soggy, lightly toasted bread. From somewhere a large kettle of strong, milky tea arrives and there is a scramble for one of the few cups that are still available. I find my metal mug at the back of my shoe locker and eject a squatting cockroach.

The smell of cold salt water, damp men, sodden hammocks and hard-boiled eggs is a stomach-churning mixture. *Bermuda* rattles up to the top of a roller-coaster wave and stops for what seems like a minute before her bows drop and she crashes down into the solid wall of the following trough. There is a large bang and *Bermuda*'s armour-plated sides groan as though being tasked beyond their limit. Locker doors fly open. I hold mine closed with a bare foot that is blue, cold and wet.

By mid morning, *Bermuda* has been turned 'stern to' the weather which gives the Emergency Repair Party access to the Fo'csle. They rig life-lines so that they can safely install patches on the damaged areas. Apparently all the ventilation inlets have been ripped from the deck along with all the wash-deck lockers: fittings that have been part of *Bermuda* since her build.

'DO YOU HEAR THERE ... THE UPPER DECK IS OUT OF BOUNDS.

THE UPPER DECK IS OUT OF BOUNDS ... EXCEPT FOR SEAMEN. THE UPPER DE ...'

There is a crack and a blue flash as the main mess Tannoy explodes.

At dinnertime we learn that both whalers have been smashed beyond repair, most of the boats on the Boat Deck have been damaged and all the Carley Rafts have disappeared. Theoretically that information should have worried me: my Abandon Ship station has apparently disappeared into the ink-black maelstrom that is the North Atlantic. It doesn't yet occur to me to ask anybody 'How would I abandon a sinking ship now?'

That used to be a whaler!

Bermuda moans and groans as she battles onwards, showing all the other members of the fleet what can be done in the teeth of gale force conditions. The weather gets worse during the remainder of the afternoon but we get a brief respite that enables us to check the upper deck damage. It is true, we have lost all our Carley rafts, both of our whalers and one of the Boat deck launches. All the vent inlets on the Fo'csle are no longer with us. The washdeck lockers have been ripped from their foundations. It is at this point I realise just how powerful and destructive the sea can be. *Bermuda* was built to withstand the worst Mother

Nature could throw at her, yet she has been badly damaged. It is something that I will never forget.

The messdeck has the distinctive smell of the North Atlantic about it. The bared deckhead plates are running with condensation that falls like rain whenever *Bermuda* shudders. Streams of water snake across the deck from unknown places. All the black heaters are switched on, and thankfully work: we cover them with wet clothing in the forlorn hope that they will dry.

The main galley has been hit badly with large amounts of boiling fat and water thrown everywhere. A senior Cook has been burnt and is in the Sick Bay encased in wet blankets. The Catering Officer has ordered all cooking equipment to be closed down, so we are fed an exotic choice of sandwiches that we cobble together from whatever basic ingredients we can find.

Miraculously the tot makes it to the mess unaffected: two people from each mess have been sent to collect it. All those of us who are 'under age', and normally banned from anywhere near the rum, are unexpectedly invited to the starboard forward mess.

Yorky explains. 'For all the work you young 'uns have done during the past few days, the mess has agreed that you can all have 'sippers'.

The guy standing over the rum fanny with a glass in each hand takes over. 'If you take a good mouthful of rum, that is referred to as Gulpers. Half a Gulpers is known as a Wet; half a Wet is known as Sippers and if you pass your tot close beneath your mate's nose, that is officially known as Snifters.' Then he demonstrates the complexities of Sippers: it means just a little bit more that wetting your lips with the contents of the glass.

'Only two glasses have survived,' says Yorky.

A grimy glass is half-filled with rum and under the watchful eyes of the older mess members it is passed around us young 'uns. Initially I'm not impressed with my first taste of Pusser's rum. It isn't until it hits my stomach that I begin to appreciate its benefits. After we have all had Sippers we are ushered away so that the serious business of tot-drinking can continue.

I have the afternoon watch in the Ops Room on Thursday. I take up my position in front of the PPI – the screen is alive with white-grey splodges which could be other vessels or clutter caused by the raging seas.

Once I am settled and the official hand-over is complete, Tansy places his arm over my shoulder. 'Last watch but one in the Ops Room, lad.'

'Is it?' I ask, taken by surprise.

'Watch and Station Bill change-round. You'll probably be Watch on Deck as from your next but one watch ... with me.'

'Really?'

'Check the Watch and Station Bill.'

'Will do, Hooky.' I had got used to this Ops Room stuff. It is nice, relatively warm and dry, and I know exactly what is going on and where we are.

I check the Watch & Station Bill on my way to muster on the Quarter-deck. Tansy is right: as from the First Dog watch tomorrow I am part of the Watch on Deck. My last Ops Room watch is the Middle Watch tonight.

Despite the weather and damage, we continue to exercise. While we traverse the northernmost Scottish ledge, we have numerous four-inch shoots and an evening bombardment of the unfortunate Hoan Island that probably hasn't fully recovered from our last pounding. The fleet then forms a protective anti-submarine screen around ourselves and *Karel Doorman* as we enter Loch Eriboll to anchor for the night. When Vice Admiral J G Hamilton is satisfied that his entire fleet is safely secured to the bottom of a very deep Scottish Loch by using extra lengths of cable, he changes his mind and orders the fleet back to sea, as there is a sudden threat of attack and the weather is worsening.

'ACTION STATIONS.
ASSUME DAMAGE CONTROL STATE 1 CONDITION ZULU ALPHA.'

Some bastard has fixed the mess Tannoy.

20

HOLDING THE LINE AT SCAPA FLOW

I join the real sailors for the First Dog watch on Deck the following day. I muster in the Canteen Flat dressed in Number 8s with scarf, hat and gloves. While we all huddle on an empty part of the deck, our names are called and Tansy tells us our duties. I am detailed as starboard forward bridge lookout for half an hour. He tells Sugar, who is detailed as starboard after bridge lookout, to show me what to do.

'Never done bridge lookout before?' asks Sugar.

'No.'

He runs through everything.

Before leaving the relative warmth of the Canteen Flat, Sugar and I grab an oilskin from a pile in the corner. They are cold, stiff and smell of thousands of previous unwashed occupants.

My report to the Officer of the Watch on the bridge is hopelessly wrong. Although I am standing next to Sugar while he reports, I say a similar sort of thing but in the wrong order. 'Sir, Starboard lookout reporting forward ... sir.'

But I do manage to get my name and rank correct. Fortunately there are no other ships out in this weather on our starboard side. From the port side I hear one of the lookouts report a contact bearing red zero six zero intermittent flashing white light. The Officer of the Watch identifies it as a friendly lighthouse.

With my heavy Admiralty Pattern binoculars, which I eventually manage to focus correctly, I scan my patch of the North Sea from right forward to 100 degrees on the starboard beam but see absolutely nothing. I practise in my head what I have to say to the Officer of the Watch if I see something, but thankfully my sector remains empty.

I am relieved on time and wait inside the bridge to report to the Officer of the Watch that I have been relieved and that all visual contacts have been reported, when there is a flurry of activity. Mrs Lumby's husband arrives from behind a blackout curtain on the after bridge bulkhead. The Officer of the Watch salutes smartly and gives the Captain a run-down on what is happening: course, speed, weather conditions, the surface situation and communications from other ships etc. It goes on for ages and there is no mention of the waiting lookouts as the Captain slumps onto a large swivel armchair on the port side. A Steward arrives and presents him with a cup of steaming coffee on a saucer.

'Biscuits sir?' he asks, while standing to attention at his shoulder.

'Handful of those chocolate-coated digestives.'

'Won't be a moment, sir.'

Sugar spots a lull in proceedings and walks over to where the Officer of the Watch is standing someway to the right of the Captain, staring purposefully out of the bridge window while acknowledging the change of helmsman in the wheelhouse.

'Able Seaman Kayne, starboard after lookout relieved sir. All visible contacts reported and handed over.'

I am never going to get that lot right and I don't. It goes something like: 'Ordinary Seaman Broadbent starboard err lookout forward relieved sir. All reported contacts visible and reported.'

Thankfully the Captain notices at the same time that the gyro compass is ticking away to one side and tells the Officer of the Watch who immediately yells down the voice-pipe to the wheelhouse. 'Who is on the wheel?'

There is a mumbled reply that I can't hear clearly from where I am standing.

'Wheelhouse ... you are drifting off course. You should be steering zero seven five. Hand the wheel over to the senior helmsman of the watch.'

Mumbled reply.

Sugar nudges me in the ribs and nods towards the bridge wing door. Thus ends my first lookout session.

Down in the Canteen flat, Tansy is organising Kye. A couple of the lads are busy with their knives shaving curls of chocolate from large slabs.

I remove my oilskin, throw it onto the pile and plonk myself down on a spare piece of deck alongside the Kye shavers. I observe the experts of the watch as they blend the curls of Kye with 'tinned cow', sugar and water.

While one of the lads is dispatched to the Engine Room to steam-up the Kye, the rest of us rummage in the Watch on Deck locker for something to drink out of. Most of those on watch have brought a mug with them, but I haven't: I have to make do with a badly chipped enamel mug stained black-brown both inside and out. There is no bathroom near, so I do a bit of cleaning with spit and fingers, but the Kye stains are too well established. I have decided to have a go with my Pusser's clasp knife just as the steaming fanny of Kye appears.

I am one of the last to scoop my mug full of the oily brown liquid from the almost-empty fanny. It is brilliantly strong: the very best mug of Kye I have ever tasted.

All the empty mugs and cups are piled into the empty fanny and a couple of the lads are sent away to the bathroom to rinse them. I silently wish them the very best with mine.

I have a sudden reason to visit the heads.

Eventually we are relieved.

Someone mentioned the risk of contracting haemorrhoids from sitting on cold metal decks for hours on end. Makes no difference to me: I don't have a clue what Haemo-whatsits are.

I have the Saturday morning watch on deck. At 04:10 Tansy details me off to help one of the ABs check the Fo'csle for damage. Huddled inside a huge oilskin with a pair of someone else's seaboots on my feet I trudge up and down the Fo'csle looking for damage. I don't notice any and thankfully the AB reports to Tansy that there is no damage to be seen. *Bermuda's* Fo'csle on a cold, windswept October morning close to the Arctic Circle is not a comfortable place to be.

I do another half-hour stint as Bridge lookout: this time I spot a ship. The Officer of the Watch identifies it as 'Bogey Echo' that has been reported by the Ops Room and identified as a fishing vessel out of Peterhead with no nets out and displaying the wrong system of lights.

At 14:30 we anchor in Scapa Flow.

'DO YOU HEAR THERE … FOR INFORMATION *HMS BERMUDA* WAS LAST HERE IN SCAPA FLOW 19 YEARS AGO TO THE DAY, FRESH FROM THE BUILDERS' YARD.'

A full damage survey of *Bermuda* is carried out. The shipwrights are already busy repairing the damage to the boats on the Boat Deck. The shattered remains of both Whalers are stowed away somewhere to await expert examination. The remains of a few Carley rafts are found near to the after funnel.

'WATER RATIONING.

IT IS HOPED THAT FRESH WATER WILL BE AVAILABLE THROUGHOUT THE SHIP AS FROM 14:00.

SHIP'S COMPANY ARE TO REPORT ANY SERVICE LEAKS DIRECT TO HQ1.

CHIEF SHIPWRIGHT AND CHIEF ENGINEER REPORT TO HQ1 AND THE BRIDGE RESPEC …'

There is a Quarter-deck panic when it is discovered that some of our stanchions have been damaged. We scour *Bermuda's* bowels for replacements but none are found. This is a repair job that nobody has expected, and Goosie is beside himself with grief.

'Do ya know what haemor-whatsits are?' I ask Yorky.

'Do you mean haemorrhoids?'

'Yeah, something like that.'

'Piles lad, ferkin' piles.'

'What are they?'

'Beyond my scope of expertise, young 'un. Suggest you ask someone in the Sick Bay to explain that one to you.'

'Can I catch 'em from sitting on the cold metal deck?'

'Certainly can.'

Oh no! And I remember what was said about the CDA trap in the For'd heads.

During dinner on Friday a Royal Marine comes down the mess to tell Wiggy that 'Mad Mike', the Cocky they have been training up to challenge Bannister, has done a runner. One moment he was in his makeshift gym doing his daily circuits. The ship rolled and the next time they looked, he'd gone. They've searched high and low but can't find him.

'He likes cold baked beans and we've left loads around the mess but none have been touched. We're concerned for his safety.'

'We'll keep an eye out,' says an understanding Wiggy.

'How's Bannister?'

'Terrific. I'll break the news to him about Mad Mike after tea. He's got a training walk this afternoon and I don't want him upset.'

'I understand,' says the Royal Marine, tapping the side of his misshapen nose. 'I understand.'

'We'll keep an eye out for Mike. Does he have any distinguishing marks?'

'Yeah ... looks like a ferkin' cockroach.'

The gales abate slightly on Sunday and the day is spent repairing damage. I am boat's crew on one of the undamaged launches that *Bermuda* is using to ferry repair experts from ship to ship. I am bowman – I stand in the bows of the launch when she comes alongside other ships and wield my boat-hook to grab whatever is available to stop us from moving. Thankfully the launch's Killick Coxswain is brilliant. I don't know much about Scapa Flow but I do know that there are sunken ships and their crew below us: it is an eerie feeling.

When we are safely back onboard *Bermuda* and the launch is back on her cradle, the Killick coxswain gives my shoulder a squeeze. 'Well done, young 'un. That wasn't easy.'

'Thanks, Hooky.'

'You're in Yorky's mess, aren't you?'

'Yeah.'

'Good lad, you did well today. Did you enjoy it?'

'Yep.'

'Yes what?'

'Yes, Hooky.'

'I've got your name: I'll make sure you're in my crew in future.'

'Thanks, Hooky.'

HM Submarine Truncheon sails at 04:45 on a cold Monday morning with a south-westerly whipping the surface of a dark and forbidding Scapa Flow.

Once again the Fo'csle party are shaken out of their 'pits' early to disentangle *Bermuda* from the bottom and we weigh anchor an hour later. For some inexplicable reason we do a quick run up and down the west coast of the Island of Hoy as far as the phallic symbol of 'The Old Man of Hoy' before returning to Scapa to anchor once again. At teatime, we depart once again in order to refuel from RFA Wave Chief. It doesn't start smoothly – both ships have difficulty in keeping station with each other and Wave Chief's approach has to be repeated a few times. I am given the job of handling the Distance Line on the Fo'csle. The Distance Line incorporates a series of coloured canvas markers strung between the two vessels. The numbered markers are large enough to be visible from the bridge and indicate the distance between the two vessels. The guy on the Fo'csle of Wave Chief secures his end of the Distance Line to his guardrails and disappears. I work out that it is my job to adjust my end of the line to keep it as taut as possible. I am the only person on the Fo'csle. The wind is freezing, bitterly cold water has drenched everything. I should have got myself an oilskin. Within minutes my Number 8s are soaked through, my hands, my ears, my feet and my nose are freezing. I concentrate on keeping the line taut. A particularly aggressive goffer comes over the bows, splits in two and almost knocks me off my feet as it comes at me, knee high. I have never been as cold or as wet in my life, and I don't know how long it will be before I'm relieved. My hands have gone way past blue: I stuff them inside my soaking wet sleeves but it doesn't help. There is a continual stream of water rushing down the deck. My feet are sodden and it is difficult for me to keep my footing. Hanging on to the guardrails is the only way I can keep the Distance Line taut.

All of a sudden there is a series of blasts on our horn and the distance line fizzes through my hands. A series of stiffened canvas markers force their way between my frozen fingers. I watch as Wave Chief starts to turn away. I try to prevent Wave Chief from drifting away before deciding to let my end of the line go. I slip aft as I watch my line fly over the guardrail and disappear into the turbulent waters. Problem: I've lost the Distance Line, but all I can think about is getting dry and warm.

I stand in the mess with water pouring off me. Squinty tosses his empty can of beer into the gash bucket. 'What the ferk have you been doin'?'

'Distance Line on the ferkin' Fo'csle.'

'We've just done an emergency break away ...'

'Was that what it was?'

'Yeah.' He scoops the towel from my locker door and tosses it towards me.

'The Distance Line went.' I towel my hair.

'Don't worry about that, young 'un. Get yourself down to the bathroom before they turn the ferkin' water off.'

I stand in the hot shower, totally enveloped in hot steam and slowly remove my 8s, my shoes and my socks. My cigarette is a soggy mess in the scupper.

I am just about comfortable from the chest upwards when the water begins to dribble. I kick the shower partition. 'Thanks very ferkin' much.' I wang the shower control first one way and then the other but it makes no difference: the water has stopped. I towel myself dry and squeeze the water out of my number 8s.

'DO YOU HEAR THERE ... FRESH WATER TO THE LOWER DECK BATHROOMS AND HEADS WILL BE TURNED OFF IN TEN MINUTES TIME.'

I tip the water out of my soaked shoes. 'Bollocks,' I say to nobody in particular.

Back in the mess Squinty is explaining to Yorky that I'd been on the Distance Line.

'They've already turned the ferkin' water off.' I say.

'Get some clothes on,' says Yorky. 'Tug'll make you a wet.'

It's surprising how quickly a cup full of Pusser's full strength tea and a couple of cigarettes can get you back to normal. Within minutes I am cracking Distance Line jokes with about half a dozen other lads in the mess.

'Swing the lamp ... young Pete's got a sea story for us,' says Yorky.

As the sun is going down we once again anchor in Scapa Flow and the ship's divers are sent down to inspect our starboard propeller that someone suspects is damaged. Goosie has a few unfortunates over the side removing nothing serious.

That evening I have the Last Dog anchor watch and Goosie is Duty Petty Officer. Sugar explains to Goosie that I'd been on the Distance Line when we did the emergency breakaway from *Wave Chief*. Goosie confirms that I did exactly the right thing by letting the end go and says that I can take a Make & Mend tomorrow afternoon. A 'Make & Mend' is an afternoon off.

Next morning it is yet another early call for the Fo'csle part-of-ship and we are underway before breakfast. We carry out a forenoon jackstay transfer, taking onboard a bloke from *HMS Blackwood* who has assaulted a Senior Officer and has been sentenced to 49 days' detention. He is to be held in our cells until we reach harbour and he can be transferred to the Royal Naval Detention Quarters in Gosport.

HMS Blackwood supplies the Distance Line, as we no longer have one.

I never get my promised Make & Mend, of course. According to Goosie, we are far too busy to have Ordinary Seamen asleep in their hammocks during daylight hours. In the afternoon *HM Submarine Truncheon* disappears and we carry out Anti-Submarine exercises.

On the Quarter-deck, we drop the guardrails and huddle on the side out of the wind as a helicopter approaches, hovers directly above us and lowers a bulging blue nylon sack on the end of a line. It is rumoured that the sack contains mail. The sack is collected by a couple of Regulators and we re-rig all our guardrails.

The weather worsens once again as we hammer west along the top shelf of Scotland.

All the mail in the sack is official.

Goosie grabs me as we are getting the scrubbing-down gear out of the locker. 'To make up for missing your Make & Mend, I've decided to excuse you from scrubbing down today.'

'Thanks, PO.'

'The Regulating Office need someone to do cell sentry for an hour.'

'Cell sentry?'

'Report to the Regulating Office and tell them that you're the cell sentry until 16:00.'

'OK, PO.'

They're a miserable bunch in *Bermuda*'s Regulating Office. One of the Leading Regulators, totally lacking in conversational skills, escorts me into the dark and rank bilges. I know we're up forward about as far as we can go. The cell-block area is narrow and smells like a rarely cleaned toilet. The compartment itself is small and triangular with three solid steel doors on either side. One of the doors is slightly ajar and secured with a length of full-bodied chain and a monster of a padlock. Inside, curled up in a corner, is a bloke dressed in Number 8s with no shoes and no belt. There is a bucket in the corner of the cell.

The Leading Regulator speaks to me for the first time. 'You don't talk to the prisoner. You don't give the prisoner anything. You don't ask the prisoner anything. If anything happens and you require help, pick up the telephone and yell: it's a direct line to the Regulating Office.' He points to a typed notice on the bulkhead.' Those are your rules. Make sure you read 'em. OK?'

'OK.'

'Ok WHAT?'

'OK, Leading Regulator.'

'Someone will relieve you at about 16:00.'

'Thanks, Hooky.'

Once the Leading Regulator has closed the clipped watertight door behind him I am alone with the prisoner. I feel a little vulnerable despite the chain and the padlock being firmly in place.

'Got a smoke, mate? I haven't had one for a couple of days,' the prisoner asks.

I say nothing.

'Got a smoke, mate? You can talk to me you know ... really.'

I've got cigarettes, but I lie. 'Sorry mate, don't smoke.' I don't know what else to say.

'Do you know where the ship is?'

'Scotland somewhere I think.'

'What's life onboard this bastard like then?'

'OK.'

'Food's crap, isn't it?'

'Yeah the food's crap.' I lie.

It is a long hour and by the time I am relieved my sense of smell has completely deserted me.

Down the mess I tell Languid where I've been for the past hour and he sympathises with me. 'Who gave you that job then?'

'Goosie.'

'The shit, that's a Regulator's ferkin' job that is, boyo.'

In the camouflaging light of a Scottish dusk we make a 20-knot spurt to rendezvous with another helicopter.

Just before midnight, as it starts to hammer-it-down, we rig Quarter-deck safety lines and drop all our guardrails.

We wait until the young lad manning the Bridge telephone reports in a loud clear voice. 'Bridge reports that the helicopter transfer of a dummy Admiral has been cancelled due to the worsening weather PO.'

'Up guardrails,' yells Goosie. 'Unrig safety lines.'

Early morning, north east of Cape Wrath in almost gale force winds, *Bermuda* keeps a careful watch on her smaller escorts: in particular the frigate *HMS Blackwood* who has reported some structural problems.

At dinnertime we carry out another six-inch shoot.

'HANDS CLEAR OFF THE UPPER DECK.

WE WILL SHORTLY BE FIRING ALL SIX-INCH ARMAMENT.

SECURE ALL LOOSE EQUIPMENT.

CLOSE ALL UPPER DECK SCREEN DOORS AND SCUTTLES.

THERE IS A TYPOGRAPHICAL ERROR WITH THE TOMBOLA NUMBERS ON TOMORROW'S DAILY ORDERS: THEY ARE TO BE IGNORED.

THE CORRECT NUMBERS WILL BE PUBLISHED THE DAY AFTER TOMORROW.'

The For'd Seamen's mess has almost fully recovered from the flood and got its electrics back in full working order. The last thing we need now is for our electrics to be blown away again … and they are.

'HANDS ARE REQUESTED TO USE FRESH WATER SPARINGLY. THE SHIP'S COMPANY ARE REMINDED THAT THE JUNIORS' BATHROOM IS OUT OF BOUNDS.'

The weather improves slightly and the wind has dropped by the middle of the afternoon when a helicopter from *Karel Doorman* ditches. The fleet converges on its last reported position. All serviceable boats are launched and we manage to rescue all the crew. The helicopter is lost.

Later that evening the fleet anchors in Spey Bay. All available boats are in the water transferring Senior Officers onboard *Bermuda* for what is termed a Wash-up. Once again I am boats' crew, this time wielding the after boat-hook.

'WILL THE PADRE MAKE HIS EXACT WHEREABOUTS KNOWN TO THE OFFICER OF THE WATCH ON THE BRIDGE.'

Goosie scans all our faces as we muster on the Quarter-deck the following morning. 'Now then, my special lads, who's feeling particularly fit and strong this morning?'

Nobody responds. I have learned that admitting that you are feeling fit and strong is not a sensible thing to do.

'You, you, you and you. Report to Petty Officer Callard on the Fo'csle … Chop Chop!'

I am the penultimate 'you'. All four of us slope off forward and meet up with another group of four from the Top part-of-ship who are also on their way to report to the Fo'csle.

On the Fo'csle, the port capstan is the centre of attention. Petty Officer Callard, a large man with a lengthy black and grey beard, pale grey eyebrows and a ruddy, weather-beaten complexion, claps his hands as we arrive. 'Ha Ha! Help is at hand. Muster over there, my lovely lads.'

We do as instructed and gather in a bunch between the capstan and the port guardrail. We watch as members of the Fo'csle part-of-ship arrive with long wooden battens on their shoulders and slot them into the top of the port capstan as instructed by Petty Officer Callard and a couple of Leading Seamen.

'Right then lads,' Petty Officer Callard claps his hands enthusiastically. 'We've been instructed by the bridge to raise our port anchor by hand. I estimate that we have between 20 and 30 fathoms of anchor chain lying on the bottom, so that should be easy enough to bring up. However, we have no way of knowing how the anchor itself lies. Hopefully, it's not trapped under a rock or anything. I want four people on each bar initially. If extra muscle is required, we will add one extra person to each bar. Should it be necessary to replace tired or injured individuals we will have a reserve unit ready on standby. We have asked the bridge if they can supply a Royal Marine bandsman who can play a fiddle ... a violin ... so that we can hoist the anchor to the strains of a well-known and inspiring sea shanty. You, you, you, you, you and you ... one on each bar.'

I'm the second 'you' and I take my place on the bar between a large and a medium-sized Able Seamen.

Petty Officer Callard checks that we are distributed correctly on the outboard end of our respective bar and instructs us to 'Take the weight' as the capstan brake is released.

'On my order, left foot forward and in time,' yells Petty Officer Callard. 'Put all your weight onto the bar. Stamp it down lads. Ready ... stamp it down left foot first ... left foot first!'

The capstan moves surprisingly easily and the anchor chain begins to come inboard. The pawl arrangement, that prevents the capstan from running back on itself, clatters as the chain slowly wraps itself around the base of the capstan before disappearing down a pipe and into the depths of the chain locker. A couple of guys with hoses hang over the forward guardrails washing the anchor chain as it appears, dripping with interwoven strands of green Spey Bay weed. They continually report to Petty Officer Callard the alignment of the chain.

One of the blokes from up forward reports 'Cable up and down, PO.'

We are stopped. PO Callard orders the brake applied. From behind I hear the noise of a pair of out-of-tune instruments.

'No fiddles I'm afraid, lads,' says Petty Officer Callard. 'We've got a bugle and a clarinet instead.'

'Couldn't organise a bag-off in a brothel,' my bar neighbour says.

'Right then, lads.' Petty Officer Callard claps his hands. 'Let's give it a go. Best foot forward GO! Royal Marines PLAY!'

Nothing moves. Only the creak of solid English oak capstan bars and a few chesty coughs interrupt the strains of an unknown sea shanty.

The anchor chain doesn't move an inch. The brake is applied and Petty Officer Callard sends one of his Killicks away to find the capstan bar extensions. We rest with our backs leaning against our respective bars. A Royal Marine trombonist and a drummer arrive to reinforce the musicians.

The extension pieces are installed. We move to the ends and the 'reserves' join us.

'Right lads, this is the last chance. I don't want the bridge to log that we are unable to shift this anchor.' He waves an arm at the Royal Marines. 'Hope you have something uplifting in your repertoire.'

The Band go into a huddle and start to play 'Anchors Away'.

'They're taking the piss,' says my neighbour.

The brake is disconnected and slowly, very slowly, the chain moves.

'We're in sixteen fathoms of water, lads. Won't take us long. Put your backs into it and it'll be over before you know it.'

The cleaning hoses spray us, as circuit by circuit, the chain slowly comes in. Zombie-like we stamp our aching feet into the slippery wet green deck. The Royal Marines play a strange version of 'Hearts of Oak'.

One of the blokes up forward yells 'Anchor clear of the water, PO.'

'Just half a dozen more turns lads ... just a few more turns!' encourages Petty Officer Callard.

Eventually the anchor is hoisted home, the Capstan brake applied, slips and screws attached to the anchor chain and the anchor pulled home by a couple of lads on a long metal bar screwing a large black bottle screw. Wire anchor strops are rigged.

We unship the bars and extensions and stand waiting for our reward.

'Thanks, lads. Well done. Back to your parts of ship.' Petty Officer Callard turns to the musicians. 'Thanks, lads. Give my thanks to the Bandmaster. Tell him he can have 'snifters' of mi tot sometime next week.'

We've hoisted a ferkin' anchor by hand and it isn't Stand-easy yet.

The Fleet sails in formation during the Last Dog Watch to round Kinnaird Head before dispersing to their designated ports. *Bermuda*, once again, points herself towards the delights of Rosyth.

21

GAZING UP THE LADDER

We secure alongside the South Arm at Rosyth on Friday morning. The civil authorities in Rosyth are worried about *Bermuda*'s unruly crew. The local police were stretched to their limit during our last visit with the underground cells below Dunfermline's police station full of *Bermuda*'s unruly crewmembers most nights. The Rosyth authorities are worried what will happen when we are let loose after a stressful period at sea. The Regulating Branch liaise with the local police and some of the Duty part of the Watch go ashore to support the local constabulary.

During the afternoon, trucks loaded with Carley rafts appear on the jetty and a team of civilians swarm over our bridge superstructure to fit them. I feel a whole lot better once my Abandon Ship Station is re-installed. We also receive a couple of replacement whalers that take ages to fit onto the davits correctly.

Throughout the evening, the Naval Patrols bring back many drunken *Bermuda* personnel. Some have managed to convince the Naval patrol to give them a lift back to the dockyard and others are brought back against their will. All the police cells north of the Firth of Forth are occupied. Taxi firms report that they have taken large numbers of our ship's company over the bridge to Edinburgh.

Next morning, the ship is opened to visitors. We stand in anticipation as the official opening time of 14:00 approaches. The jetty is empty, and it remains empty until 16:00 when it is decided to cancel everything. Quite obviously Rosyth and her surroundings aren't interested in us. We replace all the ladder backs.

Back down the mess, Joe says that he had hoped for some Scotsmen in kilts to visit so that he could have a good ogle. He is serious!

Tug and I catch a bus into Dunfermline on Sunday. It is closed so we catch the same bus back to Rosyth. Fortunately, the dockyard canteen has no drinking restrictions and we are able to enjoy a couple of pints of Heavy and some games of snooker. I am proving to be an enthusiastic but less-than-average snooker player. It is a moment of some celebration whenever I pocket a ball.

Ammunition ship!

Flag Officer Flotillas (Home) Vice Admiral J G Hamilton CB CBE holds a Wash-up meeting onboard while we rig the dreaded coir mats and extinguish our cigarettes. My Ronson Varaflame lighter is confiscated because I didn't hear the broadcast telling us to leave our lighters and matches in our lockers. I wonder if those attending the Admiral's meeting are also banned from smoking: I doubt it.

By 17:00 all the ammunition is stowed, the Wash-up meeting has finished and we are allowed to smoke. My Varaflame is returned to me.

'OUT PIPES.

CLOSE UP SPECIAL SEA DUTYMEN.

CLOSE ALL UPPER DECK SCREEN DOORS AND SCUTTLES.

HANDS OUT OF THE RIG OF THE DAY CLEAR OFF THE UPPER DECK.'

We are off again and heading for the more temperate climate of Newcastle-upon-Tyne. Those down the mess who have been to Newcastle before give us the benefit of their experience. 'Unless you feel brave, don't drink more than one bottle of the local Newcastle Brown Ale and beware the women ... oh yes! ... be wary of the Geordie women,' says Prof.

We lower a couple of stages over the side to touch-up our stained paintwork before we enter the River Tyne. A small number of people waving black-and-white striped shirts and scarves can be seen on both banks.

Bermuda is secured on number 23 berth by mid morning. There is a smell about the place. One of the lads from Gateshead says it is a glue factory up-wind that processes the bones of dead animals.

By dinnertime we have the main awning and its pink-and-white striped companion rigged. The deck is scrubbed white and all the gratings and stainless steel covers installed. The Machinery workshop has done a brilliant repair job with our damaged stanchions. The after section is ready to receive official guests and the rest of the ship is being prepared for an influx of visitors.

Once again I am duty. As soon as I finish my dinner I change into my second-best suit and cap and muster on the boat deck. The queue of expectant visitors already snakes far along the jetty. I am given the job of offering a helping hand to anyone who requires assistance in negotiating the steps from the end of the brow down onto the boat deck. If I get a smile or a thank you, I respond with a smile. I say 'Hello' to anyone who greets me with the words 'Hello Sailor', which many do. There are lots of girls: it is a nice sunny day and they are all wearing summer clothes.

During a lull in the visitor flow I am enjoying a quiet period chatting with the Quartermaster and the Bosun's mate – cracking a few jokes and exchanging opinions on some of our female guests – when the Officer of the Day comes strutting over the Boat Deck. 'Who are you?' he bellows directly at me.

'Ordinary Seaman Broadbent, sir.'

'Are you on duty or are you just loafing around?'

'On duty, sir.'

'Have you seen what's going on over there?' He waves his telescope towards an area of the Boat Deck directly below the long open-backed zigzag ladder that leads down from the after Bridge Deck.

I look over and understand immediately what is going on. Our be-skirted visitors are descending the long open-backed ladder and a large group of appreciative crewmembers have gathered under the ladder in order to enjoy the view. As a relatively inexperienced chap, I'm pleased that I am able to quickly understand the situation, even if my Commissioned inquisitor can't.

'I think that the lads on the Boat Deck are looking up at the ladies who ...'

'I know what they are doing, lad. It's plainly obvious.'

'Yes sir.'

'Get yourself up that ladder and stop any more women from coming down.' He waves his telescope at the group. 'I'll dismiss that lot.'

'Do you mean only the ladies wearing skirts, sir?' I thought I'd ask.

'Yes, lad! Everyone in a blasted skirt!'

'What do I say to the... err ladies, sir?'

'Use your common sense, lad.' He glares at me. He is turning crimson. 'If you can't use your limited imagination ... just ... well, think of something!' He points upwards. 'Look there's a group of three coming down.' He cups his mouth and shouts. 'You lads over there at the foot of the ladder ... move well away. I say again ... move well away from the foot of that ladder!'

'Is there an alternative route for the ladies to take, sir?' I ask.

The Officer of the Day doesn't like that question. He splutters. 'I'll get that organised. You just get to the top of that ladder and stop those ...' He waves a trembling telescope at the group who are just about to begin their descent. 'Stop those ... those three women.'

'Shall I send them back to the top, sir?'

'Use your common sense, lad ... if you have any!'

Behind the Officer of the Day the Quartermaster and the Bosun's Mate are desperately trying to stop themselves laughing.

'Go on then, lad ... get up there and stop those ... those women.'

'Aye aye, sir.'

At the foot of the ladder I stop and look up to see what I can see. I cough, take a deep breath, look down and put my right foot on the bottom rung of the ladder. While climbing I try to stop myself looking up and ponder how I should deal with my fast-descending problem. The clatter of three pairs of high-heeled shoes on our metal ladder gets louder the higher I climb. At about the midpoint of the ladder I come face-to-stomach with a tight black-and-white checked skirt.

'Hello pet, 'scuse me,' she says from above me.

I look up at a face framed beyond a pair of large conical breasts. I look down, she has black nyloned legs and white high-heeled shoes. I look up again. 'Hello. I'm sorry but I've been told to tell you that you're not allowed down this ladder anymore.'

The tight black-and-white checked skirt moves to one side and positions itself on the same rung as me. I get a whiff of something overwhelmingly pleasant. I look into her heavily made-up eyes – she has a pointed nose and is wearing red lipstick. I swallow and try not to look at her intimidating breasts that are pointing directly at my palpitating chest.

'Why's that then, pet?' she asks.

'Because the Officer of the Day said I have to. I've got to stop anybody wearing skirts coming down this ladder.'

'Why's that then?' asks her friend who is wearing a pale blue cardigan over a flared yellow dress and is chewing gum. She blows a bubble and bursts it with her tongue.

'Because those lads down there are err ... looking up your skirts,' I blurt. I can feel myself going warm around my neck.

'Ger away,' says the girl chewing gum. She blows another bubble.

'If I had a flabber,' says the checked skirt, 'it would be well and truly gasted.' She inhales and I back off a few inches.

'The cheek of them young sailors,' says the third girl who has large, round eyes, dark curly hair and an unusually long nose. 'Looking up ladies' skirts indeed.'

'What could they see, do you think, Sandra?' the checked skirt asks the bubble-blower.

'Nothing much from this distance.'

'Have you got your pants on?'

'Not sure.' Sandra strokes her backside and looks to the heavens. 'Think so ... err yes!'

The checked skirt puts a cupped hand on my shoulder. 'Look, pet: we know what we're doing. You've been at sea for some time and if you lads are looking up our skirts then so be it. We consider it to be our patriotic duty, don't we girls?'

'Yes,' says Sandra.

'Certainly do,' says the lady with the extraordinarily long hooter.

Sandra is still checking herself out. 'Got mi bessie ones on!'

'What about you, Maggie? What's your pants situation?' the checked skirt asks the one with the dark curly hair.

'What day is it?'

'Tuesday.'

'Then it'll be the cherry-red ones, Brenda pet.'

'Is that the Officer who told you to stop us?' Sandra points to the Officer of the Day. 'That good-looking young Subby?'

'Yes. You're not going down, are you?'

Sandra pushes past me. 'I'm goin' to put 'im straight.'

Brenda taps my backside and gestures down. 'After you, pet.'

I've failed completely. I descend to the boat deck sandwiched between my three escorts. Sandra strides purposefully towards the Officer of the Day who is pretending to look at something on the jetty.

I hide behind one of the launches until the zigzag ladder is empty and scramble quickly to the top to try and redirect the rest of the be-skirted traffic down the internal ladders. It is one heck of a job.

Back down the mess, over tea, I tell the mess my story and it gives everybody a laugh. Yorky, Sugar and Prof give me a bollocking because I didn't follow things up in the prescribed Naval manner ... and got the contact details for any of the three girls. 'Can you confirm that one of them had her best pants on?' asks Sugar.

I nod. 'So she said.'

'Best pants. You know what that means don't ya?'

'Not really ... no.'

'She was on the pull.'

'No?'

Sugar puts an arm around my shoulder. 'We need to have a chat, young Peter.'

I am beginning to learn how this sea-story thing works: not only did you have to have a great story to tell, you also had to incorporate a few good jokes and have a great punch line.

The following day we are once again open to visitors. The zigzag ladder is properly 'roped off' and a notice saying 'Out of bounds. No ball games.' is hung at the top and the bottom. I hang around the boat deck to see if Sandra, Brenda or Maggie will make an appearance, but they don't and I get another bollocking from Yorky.

Visitors are ushered off before tea time and ...

'DO YOU HEAR THERE ... OPERATION THIMBLE HUNT. OPERATION THIMBLE HUNT.

ALL SHIP'S COMPANY ARE TO INSPECT ALL THEIR DESIGNATED COMPARTMENTS TO ENSURE THAT ALL VISITORS HAVE LEFT THE SHIP.

LEADING HANDS AND PRESIDENTS OF MESSES REPORT TO THE REGULATING OFFICE.

THE SHIP WILL SAIL AT 19:30.'

Joe throws a hardened paintbrush at the Tannoy. Yorky tells me and Tug to inspect all the 'traps' in the forward heads. We formulate a strategy when we notice that a few of the compartments are occupied. We knock on the closed doors and apologise to the occupants for the inconvenience. If an annoyed masculine voice tells us to go away in short, sharp, jerky movements that's exactly what we do.

Later in the afternoon, rumour has it that two professional ladies have been found in the Stokers' bathroom. They were both secreted in the aft' shower as they'd negotiated acceptable lower-deck terms for a lift to Rosyth. The Killick of the Stokers' mess is already explaining things to the Master-at-Arms.

We unrig awnings. Those of us who were duty on Saturday complain that we haven't had the chance of a 'run ashore' in Newcastle.

At 19:30 the tugs that eased us alongside just 34 hours earlier haul us off the jetty. At midnight we meet with *RFA Wave Chief* off Blythe and refuel for a couple of hours before turning purposefully north.

On Monday 6 November *Bermuda* berths at Rosyth and hosts a dinner party onboard for the Commander in Chief (Home Fleet). It is a day of Quarter-deck bullshit and the sloping and un-sloping of awnings on an unpredictably rainy day.

In the afternoon, and without any warning, I am instructed to go to the Ops Room where I am subjected to an oral examination by the senior Radar Plotter. Unsmilingly he asks me a series of awkward questions about the Radar systems onboard. Unfortunately I don't have the answers to any of his questions and I fail miserably. If I'd passed I would have been able to wear a spider's web badge with a star above it. I don't understand much about any of the Radar Plotting stuff apart from what I have experienced in the Ops Room and learned from Tansy: I am much more in-tune with the Seamanship part of my job.

Later that afternoon we salute *HMS Pellew*, who enters Rosyth with her long red-and-white Paying-off pennant flying. She is similar in appearance to *HMS Petard*, the frigate I'd first gone to sea on for a week while at *HMS Ganges*.

Lower deck is cleared for the reading of yet another Punishment Warrant on Tuesday morning. It is no surprise to those who understand the system, that the individual whose hat is taken off is the Killick of the Stokers' mess. He is charged with bringing female guests onboard in Newcastle without obtaining the necessary permissions and a number of other things.

Sugar, who is standing alongside me, whispers, 'So that's it then: there must be a special request form if you want to bring a couple of prossies onboard.' I miss the interesting details of the charges. The Leading Stoker is demoted to plain Stoker and given 42 days' confinement in the Royal Naval Detention Quarters.

'He was only trying to look after the needs of the lads in his mess,' says Sugar as we are dismissed.

Wednesday is a gold braid day. Goosie is forever moving us away from the after brow area, and bringing us back. Apparently J G Hamilton has once again invited onboard the Commander in Chief (Home Fleet) along with the Flag Officer Scotland, the Air Officer Commanding Scotland and their senior staff for a bite to eat and a few 'wets'.

During the course of the day, frazzled-looking Stewards appear occasionally on the Quarter-deck for a break and a quick smoke. Goosie keeps a close eye on them: if anybody stubs a cigarette out on his wooden deck they will be in serious trouble. Fortunately, even Stewards know to use the Firth of Forth as an ashtray.

The following morning the Commander in Chief (Home Fleet) revisits us, this time to carry out a Walk-round inspection. Fortunately the Quarter-deck isn't on his inventory. The For'd Seamen's mess is though, and every available mess member is put to work for the morning. I watch as buckets full of cockroaches are given a float-test. I bet nobody's found the big bastard who has taken up residence inside my shoe locker: I've been after him for weeks.

Sunday 12 November is Remembrance Day and a service takes place in the dockyard attended by Officers and men from all the ships. The Flag Officer Flotillas (Home) is in attendance, as is Mrs Lumby's husband. The customary two-minute silence is observed throughout the fleet.

In the afternoon we are Open to visitors. For a change I'm not duty and as I cross the Boat Deck I am disappointed to see that the 'No entry' notices have been hung at the top and bottom of the zigzag ladder and it is roped off. I am tempted to stay on the upper deck but it is bightingly cold and there is only a small cluster of potential visitors stood on the jetty wrapped in heavy Scottish coats and scarves.

Tomorrow we are due to pitch ourselves once again into the ravages of the Pentland Firth and the northern ledge of Scotland. We are all issued with paint pots and brushes. None of us take our painting tasks very seriously. I am far from a painting expert, but I know that whatever I apply will end up in the waters of the North Sea before it has time to dry.

We leave Rosyth and traverse the top ledge of Scotland during the night. The weather doesn't disappoint us. It has us rocking and rolling all over the place as we pound our way west, directly into the oncoming weather. All yesterday's hastily applied paint is washed away.

We slip past Cape Wrath in the early hours of Wednesday and plough south to anchor in Loch Scavaig on the south side of Skye at 19:00.

22

A SHARP-END SEAMAN

Today I am transferred to the Fo'csle part-of-ship and Tug is transferred from the Fo'csle to the Quarter-deck. My new boss is Petty Officer Callard. Because he sports a thick and very ancient black and grey beard, everybody calls him 'Scurze'. This is what I have been looking forward to – I am happy to leave behind all the bullshit associated with *Bermuda*'s Quarter-deck and get to grips with proper, down-to-earth, sharp-end Seamanship. Now I will be able to put all my theory into practice – anchoring, coming to a buoy and all that.

Tug says that he won't miss all the early Fo'csle mornings when *Bermuda* has to either haul in her anchor or unhitch herself from a buoy before breakfast.

I am beginning to understand that there are three types of Seaman in the Navy. There are those who like to work with the tiddly type of stuff and are well-suited to a life down aft. Then there are the hardened 'haul away mi hearty' types who work up forward getting their hands dirty, dealing with the masculine side of Seamanship. In the middle are those who are neither forward or after types: these are the Top men who look after that part of the ship that is neither sharp-end or blunt-end. In my opinion, I am most definitely a sharp-end type Seaman.

On the Fo'csle, I recognise many of the blokes from the mess. Scurze's Leading Seaman is a tall, rangy bloke who is known as 'Ginge' – not because he is ginger, but because his surname is Rogers. We have another Leading Seaman called Jock Stirling who is very definitely a Scotsman.

The following morning we are called to the Boat deck to witness the reading of yet another Punishment Warrant for a Leading Chef who has tried to smuggle a side of beef ashore inside his raincoat. In his defence he claims to have been 'drunk as a skunk' at the time.

We are expecting a reasonably quiet afternoon but we spend most of it rigging bottom lines in the teeth of a typical Scottish, November gale.

'HANDS TO TEA.

DIVING OFFICER REPORT TO THE COMMANDER'S CABIN.

ALL SHIP'S DIVERS MUSTER ON THE STARBOARD SIDE OF THE BOAT DECK.'

The ship's divers spend hours in the relative dryness of Loch Scavaig's waters as they carry out an official full-bottom search.

A purple-coloured Deeps, who flops down the mess with his long black flippers hung round his neck, gives us a geo-thermal assessment of the waters of Loch Scavaig.' That was a bastard of a dive, that was.'

'Was it cold then, Deeps?'

'Ferkin' freezing.'

'That's what you get the extra shillings for.'

'Piss off.'

The Fo'csle part-of-ship is mustered just before 21:00 to hoist our starboard anchor. As a new member without any practical experience in such matters, I am made to stand to one side with a stiff broom ready to scrub any Scavaig sludge from the anchor chain that the hoses don't dislodge.

There are no sardines left by the time all we cold and weary Fo'csle hands make it back down the mess.

Our overnight passage takes us south to round the Mull of Kintyre and to berth alongside Prince's Pier, Greenock on Friday morning. By dinnertime the United States 18th Carrier Division, led by the Aircraft Carrier *USS Essex*, arrives to the crash-bang-wallop of many ceremonial salutes. I can't believe the size of the American Aircraft Carrier: she's bigger than Leeds Town Hall.

The message must have been passed to 'Scurze' that I am an expert brass tally polisher as I am given a tin of bluebell and a fresh rag and told to shine the tallies on the forward screen bulkhead. The tallies are all new to me but I read them all and show them who is boss.

On Saturday *Bermuda* is opened to visitors in the afternoon. Celtic are playing Rangers and the majority of our visitors are heavily wrapped females. Newly issued 'clickers' are issued to those of us tasked with counting the number of visitors. Together we click 2,985 visitors in two-and-three-quarter hours.

When our gangways are eventually closed to new visitors, the entire ship's company is mobilised ...

'DO YOU HEAR THERE.

ALL VISITORS ARE REQUESTED TO LEAVE THE SHIP.

OPERATION THIMBLE HUNT.

THE SHIP'S COMPANY ARE TO INSPECT THE SHIP AND ALL HER COMPARTMENTS TO ENSURE THAT ALL VISITORS HAVE LEFT THE SHIP.

LEADING HANDS AND PRESIDENTS OF MESSES REPORT TO THE REGULATING OFFICE.'

Officially, nobody is found. There is a rumour that three ladies dressed in Lyons Corner House type waitress uniforms have been spotted in the after Senior Rates mess. After a lengthy investigation, the Regulating Staff discover that they are Petty Officers preparing to take part in a 'Waitress Night' Senior Rates party.

'DO YOU HEAR THERE.

THE WINNER OF THIS MONTH'S TOMBOLA IS THE PADRE, WHO WILL BE DONATING A SMALL PROPORTION OF HIS WINNINGS TO THE ROYAL NAVAL BENEVOLENT TRUST.

THREE CHEERS FOR THE PADRE ... HIP, HIP ...'

There is nobody in the mess inclined to cheer. We've never seen the Padre.

Tug and I decide that Saturday night is the best night to have our one and only run ashore in Greenock.

Once over the jetty our instinctive Sailor's nose leads us to one of Greenock's nightclubs. We have to climb stairs to get in and at the top we are patted down for things hidden. It is the first time that I have ever been frisked. The Club is packed, it is dark and the disc jockey keeps playing 'Walkin' Back To Happiness' by Helen Shapiro, 'The Savage' by The Shadows and for some strange reason, just for a laugh, 'My Boomerang Won't Come Back' by Charlie Drake. Unfortunately neither Tug or I can satisfy the financial demands of the girls, who are more interested in our American cousins. At about 23:30 the Americans start to leave, explaining that their 'Liberty' expires at midnight, regardless of age. There is a good deal of friendly banter, which almost turns violent when Soapy refers to them as 'Cinderellas'. When all the Americans have departed we try to impress the girls who are left ... but fail.

On Monday morning the experimental submarine *HMS Explorer* departs accompanied by *HMS Scorpion* and *HMS Broadsword*. More American ships arrive.

On Tuesday morning the American fleet begins to leave. The American 'Canteen Boat', the last to leave, salutes us as she passes us late in the afternoon.

The Admiral hosts a cocktail party for the Greenock glitterati which continues into the early hours. It is probably a co-incidence that he has waited until all our US cousins have departed.

As duty watch I am up early on Wednesday stowing awnings, gratings and covers away and scrubbing the Quarter-deck. At 08:00 *Bermuda* sails headlong into a week of intense anti-submarine exercises with *HMS Trafalgar, Finisterre, Jutland, Llandaff, Berwick*, and *Exmouth* along with US and Canadian ships *Essex, Robinson, Stribling, Noah, Jonas Ingram, Miller* and *Waccamaw*. All of us are supported by the tankers *RFA Wave Ruler, Wave Knight, Wave Chief* and *Tideflow*.

The exercises continue for the following eight days during which time we spend lengthy hours at Action Stations, eat stacks of dry corned beef sandwiches, wear our anti-flash gear to destruction, fight imaginary fires and repair hundreds of imaginary holes in our armour-plated structure.

The fleet anchors off Belfast in the forenoon of Thursday 30 November. Once again I am boats' crew and help to transfer senior Officers from all the ships to *Bermuda* in order for them to contribute their bit at the Wash-up meeting. *Bermuda* moves from her anchorage to Victoria Wharf in the city on Friday. We spread awnings, install gratings and stainless-steel covers.

I am duty once again and the ship is open to visitors. Either it hasn't been publicised or the good people of Belfast aren't interested, because we have fewer than 40 visitors, which isn't worth all our efforts.

As we are in Northern Ireland, armed sentries are deployed at vulnerable parts of the ship. Despite my protestations, I am given a rifle. I tell the Duty Petty Officer that I was rubbish on the Ganges shooting range but he gives me a battered old .303 Lee Enfield rifle anyway and pencils me in for the midnight to 01:00 watch on the Fo'csle.

Fortunately, Victoria Wharf, Belfast is quiet at midnight. With my rifle on my shoulder and dressed in my Number 8s, boots, gaiters, raincoat, cap with chin-stay down and target-white webbing, I resolutely pace up and down the Fo'csle examining pieces of Seamanship equipment and tripping over the anchor cable more than once. My recently polished brass tallies are dulled. By the time I am relieved, I am bored and cold.

'This is a load of bollocks isn't it? Anything to report?' Soapy asks as he relieves me.

'Nothing.'

'Did they tell you how to get ammunition?'

I look at him. The fact that I have a firearm but no ammunition hasn't occurred to me. 'Don't know.'

'It's a load of bollocks really. In the event of an emergency you would have to contact the Officer of the Day by telephone.' He points to the bulkhead mounted phone. 'He could be in the Wardroom or asleep in his cabin ... and he would verbally authorise the issue of live ammunition. You would then have to sign the 'Ammunition Issue Log' that is located in the small arms store and by the time you make it back to here the emergency would be ... well, you know ... no longer just an emergency.'

'That sounds ferkin' ridiculous.'

'It's the way things are ... when giving us rifles.'

I am freezing and confused by the time I haul my hammock up to the capstan flat.

We sail at 09:30 on Tuesday and immediately begin our quarterly Full Power Trial. Our compatriots in the Engineering Department manage to coax an exhilarating 29.9 knots out of our elderly engines. *Bermuda* rattles, screeches and squeals as we race down the Irish Sea, intent on arriving at Portsmouth's Pitch House Jetty as soon as possible.

Pompey Dockyard is full of ships. December is the time of year when everybody wants to be home with their families. Today I am duty on the brow and I note in the harbour movements log that *HMS Carron, Wizard, Urchin, Vigilant, Rocket, Loch Ruthven, Brighton, Lowestoft* and surprise, surprise ... *HMS Keppel...* have entered harbour. I was in Keppel Division at *HMS Ganges.*

During the morning Stand-easy, we are ushered into the starboard forward part of the mess for an impromptu ceremony. An upturned rum fanny is placed at the head of one of the mess tables and covered by a couple of grubby mess cloths. Placed centrally on the top of the fanny is a dried and polished tot glass.

Standing behind the make shift altar, grim-faced and facing the open mess, are a couple of Able Seamen dressed in their No 1 suits with caps and standing 'at ease'.

Once we are all assembled, Yorky steps forward. 'Today is a special day in the history of the United Kingdom.' The two ABs cough in unison. 'A special day that we of the For'd Seamen's Mess will not let pass without due ceremony. Able Seaman Eric Jasper, in civilian life a committed single man from Lee-on-the-Solent and schooled in Stubbington, will explain.'

Able Seaman Jasper nods his thanks to Yorky. 'Gentleman, we are gathered here this morning ... Thursday the 7th day of December in the year of our Lord 1961 ... to give thanks to our Health Minister Mister Enoch Powell. Able Seaman Soapy Watson will explain why.' AB Jasper steps to the side as Soapy gently raises the empty tot glass to the deckhead. 'In recognition of the service recently offered by Mister Enoch Powell, the Health Minister, to all single heterosexual men of the United Kingdom ...'

'Ferkin' get on with it. My coffee's goin' cold,' shouts someone from the back.

'Eject that man,' orders Yorky and there is a scuffle. 'Give him a rub down with a wet dishing-up cloth.'

Soapy continues. 'In recognition of services recently offered, we, the single heterosexual men of the United Kingdom, salute Mister Enoch Powell.'

Able Seaman Jasper calls himself to attention and states in a crisp and clear voice, 'As from last Monday, birth control pills for girls over the age of consent will be available on the National Health Service. My colleague Able Seaman Watson will explain the implications of this momentous ... er ... thing.'

'It means increased opportunities for single lads to have sex.'

A hearty cheer fills the mess.

'To Mister Enoch Powell, God bless 'im.' Soapy once again raises the tot glass.

'To Mister Enoch Powell.' We all reply.

'Three rousing cheers for Enoch ... Hip, Hip ...'

'Hurray.'

'Hip, hip.'

'Hurray.'

'Hip, hip.'

'Hurray.'

Then we go back to work and get a bollocking from Scurze for being late back from Stand-easy.

Jock Sterling sums it up for us in his own way while issuing us all with deck brooms. 'You young, single blokes have got it made now 'aven't yea? All those girls on the birth control pill will be skipping around toon waving their knickers in the air eh?'

Personally I am finding it all a bit difficult to understand. What do I do if the female population of the United Kingdom suddenly turns promiscuous? How will I deal with that?

23

GO WEST, YOUNG MAN

I am fortunate to be on the first Christmas leave party and at dinnertime on Wednesday 13 December I skip over the brow and away for a couple of weeks. I stroll along The Hard and up to Portsmouth Harbour Station without noticing any significant difference in the attitude and appearance of the females of Portsmouth. Maybe it will be noticeable in the more sexually liberated towns and villages of West Yorkshire.

I arrive home in Pudsey just before midnight. After telling Mum when I am going back, I tell her about where I have been since the summer. It doesn't take long to explain Invergordon and Rosyth. I decide that an extremely censored version of my time in Amsterdam is appropriate. I skip over Antwerp but spend some time making the story of the three girls on the zigzag open-backed ladder in Newcastle a little more amusing than it actually was. We've heard rumours onboard about a future trip to Bermuda in the Caribbean. It impresses both Mum and Tony and we dust off the *Reader's Digest World Atlas*.

I give Mum the four quid that I have been given for food and accommodation while on leave. She enjoys getting that and has got into the habit of buying herself something special with it.

Scanning the previous day's *Daily Mirror* I discover that the top of the hit parade is 'Tower Of Strength' by Frankie Vaughan: not my kind of singer. There is a small article on page five written by some old bloke urging girls not to rely on the birth control pill to prevent themselves from falling pregnant. I am more than a bit confused about this 'Pill' business. Apparently unmarried girls can't be prescribed the Pill except in special circumstances. I wonder what circumstances they are.

I bump into the attractive blonde who lives up the street. She is no longer a schoolgirl, having found herself a job at a

Building Society in Leeds somewhere. I explain to her about *Bermuda* the ship, the places that we have visited and our future trip to the Caribbean. Travel isn't her thing and she isn't impressed. Just for fun I ask her if she fancies a trip to Elland Road on Saturday to watch Leeds play Liverpool. As a netball-type gal, she emphatically refuses. We are both growing up in completely different directions. I wonder if she has any special reason to be on the Pill.

I go to Elland Road by myself on the Saturday before Christmas Day and watch a surprisingly in-form Leeds United overwhelm Liverpool 1-0. A new signing, Billy Bremner, scores. I'm not surprised to find that there has been no significant improvement to the toilets since my last visit: that's second Division football for you.

Christmas Day is one of the few days of the year when Mum can legally close the shop, although we still get people knocking on our back door asking for things and Mum never refuses to serve them. We enjoy a great Christmas dinner, pull crackers and Mum and I enjoy a couple of drinks. I tell her what I have heard about Newcastle Brown Ale and she says that she's never heard of it. I get clothes for Christmas.

On Boxing Day I once again go to Elland Road to witness an awful post-Christmas display as we are roundly beaten by the sophisticated and ultra-fit Scunthorpe United 1-4.

I pack some civilian clothes in my bag before going back off leave, hoping that I will be visiting places where I'll be allowed to wear them. I wonder what I will say if cross-examined back in the mess on what effect the Pill has had on the sexual attitudes of West Yorkshire girls. I decide that I will play it cool and pretend to keep the details to myself. Obviously it is going to take a while for all the girls in the country to understand the liberating benefits of the Pill: I just have to be patient.

The vast majority of us return from first Christmas Leave on the morning of Thursday 28 December. Most of the Scotsmen onboard have opted for second leave so that they can celebrate Hogmanay that apparently is important north of the border. On Sunday, New Year's Eve, we are instructed to bring all the paraphernalia associated with our brows inboard and stow them away. Apparently New Year's Eve is a traditional time when light-hearted theft is common between ships. Daily Orders wish us a Happy New Year for 1962.

I corner Lash as he is stowing his kit away in his new locker in the For'd Seamen's Mess. He has reached the magic age of 17½.

'Hiya mate.'

'This is a bit different isn't it?' He looks around.

'You'll get used to it.'

'Suppose so, but will they get used to me?

'What do you mean?'

'The farting.'

I place a calming hand on his shoulder. 'There are champion farters up here. I doubt they'll notice.'

'I try to hold 'em in you know ... but the pressure just builds and builds.'

'So you haven't worked out what's causing it, then?'

'No.'

Yorky appears as Lash is closing his locker door. 'Ordinary Seaman Trainer?'

Lash blinks. 'Yes, Hooky.'

'You can sling your hammock as far away from the mess as is possible. You have a reputation, I believe.'

'Err ... I have a prob ...'

'As far away as possible, young 'un.' Yorky taps him on the shoulder and departs.

'How did he know about it?'

'It's probably on your service documents.'

'Naah.'

'Probably.'

Early on Monday morning we are towed up to the ammunitioning jetty. Once again we smokers ingest as much smoke and nicotine as we can before ...

'OUT PIPES.

NO SMOKING THROUGHOUT THE SHIP UNTIL FURTHER NOTICE.

ALL MATCHES AND CIGARETTE LIGHTERS ARE TO BE STOWED IN LOCKED LOCKERS.'

The coir mats are rigged and it is the time once again for humping six-inch shells around.

By early afternoon we are back on our Pitch House berth and smoking again. The Captains of *HMS Loch Ruthven, Brighton, Rocket* and *Solebay*, among others, call on 'John-Jo' Hamilton ... as he is now referred to ... for Kye and Sticky buns. Something is going on.

Tug and I have a few runs ashore. Yorky tells us about a small place called The Gem on Commercial road where you can buy a pint of Scrumpy for 7½d. By the time we find it the price of Scrumpy has been increased to 8d. Despite the taste and all the bits floating around in it, it is a wonderfully cheap way of getting legless and we enjoy ourselves in what is probably the smallest pub in town. We have a last pint in the 'Immoral' where Tug notices that the Scrumpy is green. I say it is probably the reflection from the horrible olive-green curtains.

The following morning Tug is proved right. We are both suffering badly from a dose of the 'dog'. By the evening our young, healthy bodies have sorted the problem out and we are almost back to normal.

Once again the senior Radar Plotter onboard asks me a series of questions to which I don't have the correct answers. While the remainder of the RP basics onboard get their RP3 badges. I remain a basic.

On Friday the 12th I hear a familiar voice from the other side of the mess. I slink over and see Conkers stuffing his kit into a locker. Conkers was in the same mess as me, Lash and Tug at *Ganges*. He had a few problems while at *Ganges* and was back-classed. Consequently he didn't leave at the same time as the rest of us.

'Ferk me, if it isn't Conkers.'

He looks up from his locker. 'Hi Pete, mate.'

'How are things?' We shake hands in the mysterious fashion that ex *Ganges* boys do.

'Great ... or they were before I tried to fit everything into this ferkin' locker.'

'When did you arrive?'

He looks at his wrist: he isn't wearing a watch 'About half an hour ago. I'm relieving Borrowdale.'

'He got sick after having a tattoo ... tattoos.'

'I heard.' He shuts his locker door with his foot and whispers, 'got my sexuality problems sorted.'

'Good. What did you decide on then?'

'Bisexual.'

'What?'

'Goin' bisexual.'

'What does that mean ... up for anything?'

'Suppose it does ... yeah.'

'You better keep it quiet. There's a bloke onboard here called Joe who's a real queer. He's the ship's painter.'

'I'm not into painters. In fact I'm not into anything right now. I'm going through what you might call a celibate stage.'

'What's that when it's at home?'

'It's a period when you're not engaging in actual sex ... at all.'

'Right then,' I say. I am tempted to tell him about my encounter in Amsterdam, but I don't want to be cross-examined by Conkers.

'Good news about the 'Pill' isn't it?' I ask.

'Suppose,' Conkers snorts.

All Christmas leave is completed by mid January. Once again there are some absentees from the For'd Seamen's mess. The lockers of those who haven't returned are emptied and the contents logged and placed into kit bags. One of the lockers contains a couple of well-worn female wigs and a couple of pairs of stockings that get the Leading Regulator into a bit of a panic and he scampers away to find Master-at-Arms Foggo.

On Monday morning the tugs *Forceful* and *Capable* haul *Bermuda* off the jetty and guide us out of the harbour. Tug gives his Island his customary salute as we pass Seaview. We get wind of something before we hear those immortal words ...

'ACTION STATIONS.

ASSUME DAMAGE CONTROL STATE 1 CONDITION ZULU ALPHA.'

Surprisingly, we have a decent dinner although we have to eat it wearing our disgusting anti-flash gear. At teatime we secure ourselves to Portland No 2 Buoy. Our accommodation ladder is lowered and within minutes the Flag Officer Sea Training's barge is alongside and he storms up the ladder for a chat with John-Jo. Later that evening the Captains of *HMS Saintes, Solebay, Finisterre, Camperdown, Jutland* and *Trafalgar* join them ... for a game of something-or-other probably.

After an uneventful night we slip from No 2 buoy before breakfast the following morning as Her Majesty's assembled ships get down to some serious training. *Bermuda* starts the day with some gentle four-inch Anti-Aircraft tracking and then spends the afternoon transferring lumps of concrete backwards and forwards between *HMS Trafalgar* and *HMS Jutland* before returning to Portland to anchor just after tea.

Wednesday's training menu includes six-inch and four-inch firings and helicopter transfer operations. Anti-submarine exercises take us through to the early hours of Thursday with the submarines *Porpoise* and *Sea Scout* doing their best to break through and score a hit … for exercise purposes only.

The following day we carry out Damage Control and Atomic, Biological, and Chemical Defence exercises as well as a concrete block transfer with each of the six destroyers as we battle east. Eventually, as the sun sets beyond the skeletal masts of *HMS Victory*, we slip through the narrow harbour entrance, do an about-turn, assisted by a couple of tugs and berth, with our bows pointing out to sea, on South Railway Jetty. Leave is granted to those who are 'native' to Portsmouth. It doesn't include Tug because the Navy doesn't accept that the Isle of Wight is close enough.

On Friday, another Punishment Warrant is read, followed by a 'Captain's Address' during which he explains to us that we are, without doubt, the best ship's company he has ever had the honour to work with. We do, however, have more work to do to bring ourselves up to Flagship standard.

Instead of sailing in the afternoon as planned we are told that we are to stay in Portsmouth until an Engine Room technical problem is solved. This pleases all the locals in the Forward mess and they give the Stokers' mess an impromptu three cheers. Yorky even invites the Killick of the Stokers' mess around for 'gulpers' at tot time.

Tug and I take Conkers for his first run-ashore in Pompey. The Scrumpy in the Balmoral isn't green and Conkers, obviously in heterosexual mode, is fascinated with the ladies who appear from the neighbouring back streets. Tug and I can see that something is ringing-his-bell as he doesn't contribute to our table conversation like we know he can. We eventually manage to drag him away to the NAAFI Club where he is asked by a reasonably good-looking girl to sign her in. Conkers thinks he has been specially selected and is confused and upset when his Marilyn skips away once the entrance formalities are completed. Towards the end of the evening Conkers goes to the toilet and never comes back. We assume that he has met someone and we aren't that concerned.

As we are leaving, I spend some time explaining to Nora's mum behind the desk about Danny's and the Texas bar in Antwerp.

'You did tell Ralph that he is welcome at my place anytime didn't you?' she asks.

'I certainly did.'

'You, my young friend, are going to mature into a very acceptable young man indeed.'

That frightens me.

The following morning I see Conkers, still in his uniform, curled up on the deck of the Capstan Flat alongside his unopened hammock.

'Where the ferk did you disappear to last night?'

'Went back to The Immoral.'

'Why?'

'To see if that ginger-haired piece was still there.'

'Was she?'

'Eventually yes.'

'And then what?'

'I took her back to her place.'

'You didn't?'

'Did.'

'Didn't?'

'Did.'

'How much did that cost you?'

'Dunno.'

Later that morning, during Stand-easy, Conkers comes over to our side of the mess to ask Tug and I if we have seen his ID card and his wallet. We haven't.

'Must have misplaced it somewhere,' he says

I haven't much experience of this kind of thing, but I think I know where his ID card and wallet may have gone.

By the evening, Conkers is formally charged with losing his ID card. He has seen the Officer of the Day who has put him on Commander's report.

The following day Conkers is awarded seven days' number 9s by the Commander and has three shillings and nine pence docked from his pay. We confirm that it is an exorbitant price to pay for a replacement ID card.

Sugar comes ashore with me the next day and we go to the Balmoral specifically to track down the ginger-haired 'piece'. Sugar knows most of the ladies by name and makes a few inquiries on Conkers' behalf. After a number of pints each, we return onboard. Tug has slung my hammock for me and I pass an uncomfortable night.

Next morning my head hurts: it feels as though my brain is loose.

Sugar tells Conkers that the ginger-haired girl is keeping a low profile until *Bermuda* puts to sea: she knows that we will come looking for her. Conkers nods understandingly – from his expression I think his head hurts as well.

Bermuda departs Portsmouth just after 11:00. It is rumoured that we have three prisoners and a couple of Prison Officers onboard. The prisoners are apparently being returned to Bermuda to face the death penalty. I don't know if I believe that or not. As soon as we pass Nab Tower, we are straight into yet another series of Anti-Aircraft tracking exercises as we battle against the weather on our way west. In the late afternoon, the bridge receives a signal to divert to Plymouth with all speed.

In Plymouth Sound we rendezvous with an MFV just before midnight and transfer a rating who needs to leave us for compassionate reasons.

On Thursday morning we are in the internationally designated area for 'man overboard' drills.

'MAN OVERBOARD, MAN OVERBOARD.
AWAY SEABOAT'S CREW, AWAY SEABOAT'S CREW.
SICK BAY STAFF MUSTER ON THE PORT SIDE OF THE BOAT-DECK.'

The seaboat/lifeboat is launched to recover a dummy dressed in number 8s, over and over and over again!

By the end of the day *Bermuda* has rescued the dummy numerous times and the Sick Bay staff are becoming slipshod at administering first-aid to a lump of plastic.

In the middle of our 'man overboard' exercises we manage to fit in a short but serious series of four-inch shoots. We make a big hole in the Western Approaches.

Bermuda trundles her way south-westwards. The weather slowly improves and the long slow Atlantic swell is a welcome change from the choppy seas that we have become used to around the British Isles. This is my first journey outside Europe and I am excited.

24

BERMUDA WELCOMES *BERMUDA*

To stop us getting bored, Mrs Lumby's husband decides he will do weather deck rounds on Sunday morning. This throws Scurze into a flat spin and we are all allocated painting, scrubbing and brass-tally polishing tasks.

I am glad that I am no longer on the Quarter-deck, as I imagine that a visit to somewhere like Bermuda is sure to involve lots of cocktail parties and VIP visits. I learn that the capital of Bermuda is Hamilton and that John-Jo's family name is also Hamilton: I wonder if that is a coincidence.

Over the next days the weather improves significantly. It is February and the sun is shining warm and bright. Strong enough for me to find a shielded place aft of the aft funnel to take my shirt off and get a bit of colour to my anaemic upper body.

A list of excursions and visits that have been organised for us during our visit is pinned on the mess notice board. There is also a list of contact details for Bermuda residents who are prepared to offer hospitality to crewmembers. Older mess members explain to us youngsters that the list is known as a 'Grippo-list' and is quickly taken up by those whose main aim in life is to cadge and purloin as much free stuff as possible. All the other messes know about the list before we do – by the time the list arrives down our mess, all the places have been taken.

In the distance I see the outline of the Azores, but we don't get closer than a smudge on the horizon. I know that they are owned by Portugal and are located somewhere in the middle of the Atlantic.

Down the mess we have a group of people who had been to Bermuda before and who impart their knowledge to the rest of us. Apparently it is expensive and the policemen wear white uniforms similar in style to those of the UK. Blokes wear knee-length shorts. I don't believe that the sandy beaches are pink though – that is obviously a bit of messdeck exaggeration.

'Have you ever seen a whale?' Wiggy asks Languid.

'No.'

'Never?'

'Never.'

'I've seen a whale. In the Juan le Fuca Straits near Canada,' says Deeps.

'What Straits?'

'Juan le Fuca.'

'You're ferkin' jokin'.'

'Honestly.' Deeps looks offended.

'Piss off, Deeps man!' says the bloke from Gateshead.

Being the type of man who unquestioningly does as he is told, Deeps leaves the mess.

Later in the day, enjoying a quiet smoke on my washdeck locker, I see my first flying fish. A whole shoal of them keep pace with us, flying impressively through the air. The chefs have been given permission to stream baited fishing lines over the Fo'csle. Scurze fusses around making sure that everything is kept clean. Once or twice I see someone catch a fish.

Thursday is definitely a 'shirts-off' day. The Atlantic sun shines bright and warm and the deep blue waters through which we slice are glimmer-glass calm. The 'Grippo' list has been removed from the mess notice board. Best going-ashore uniforms are ironed, caps scrubbed and footwear polished.

We are up early on Friday to give the Fo'csle a good scrub. We have a hurried breakfast before entering harbour. There is a last-minute panic when one of the ship's crest tampons for the end of 'A' turret barrels can't be found. Everybody agrees that one of the visitors must have nicked it. Scurze is enraged.

'CLOSE UP SPECIAL SEA DUTYMEN.

HANDS FALL IN FOR ENTERING HARBOUR PROCEDURE ALPHA.

HANDS OUT OF THE RIG OF THE DAY CLEAR OFF THE UPPER DECK.

CLOSE ALL UPPER DECK SCREEN DOORS AND SCUTTLES.'

At 10:30 on Friday 9 February, we fire an 11-gun salute before being secured to the Commercial Wharf at Bermuda's Ireland island. Bermuda smells of lush green vegetation. Disappointingly, there are very few people to witness our arrival. I wasn't expecting crowds of excited flag waving people but I half-expected there to be a group of uniformed Commonwealth officials wearing feathered hats and carrying swords to welcome us.

I watch as the three prisoners and their guards shuffle over our brow and into a large open-backed van. So it is true then: we did have prisoners onboard.

We find gratings that we use to cover the more unattractive bits and pieces of Fo'csle equipment. Jock finds the missing tampon and he and Scurze publicly apologise to everybody in Northern Ireland and Newcastle. A long black American car arrives on the jetty and we all crane our neck to see who is coming onboard – maybe it is a film star. It isn't: it is a bloke in uniform wearing a very strange, feathered hat and carrying a long curved sword.

That evening we are banned from the upper deck as Bermuda's movers and shakers arrive onboard in their hundreds to enjoy some Royal Naval hospitality. A map of the islands appears down the mess and we realise that we are parked a long, long way from the capital city of Hamilton and any other place where we can get a beer. Some of the blokes go ashore, but return onboard within hours to report that we are stuck in the 'back of beyond' with nowhere to go and not one licensed premises to be found.

'DO YOU HEAR THERE.

HANDS ON THE UPPER DECK ARE TO BE DRESSED IN THE RIG OF THE DAY.

THE STARBOARD SIDE OF THE UPPER DECK AND AFT OF THE AFTER FUNNEL IS STRICTLY OUT OF BOUNDS.

NO GASH IS TO BE DITCHED UNTIL FURTHER NOTICE.'

Everybody is becoming a little disgruntled. Conkers has finished his punishment and is straining at the leash to get ashore.

We were expecting a quiet Sunday, but the lower deck is cleared of Seamen after breakfast to rig Hurricane hawsers. The weather forecast is bad. Needless to say the hawsers are stowed in a locker near the forward bilges and it takes ages to grapple them up to the Fo'csle. Then we rig a series of large rattan fenders down the entire ship's side. The island of Bermuda is telling us, in its own peculiar way, that we aren't welcome ... yet.

By Monday morning the tail of the hurricane has passed us. I expected a hurricane to be an interesting experience, but it wasn't. It howled at us, made us agitated and gave us a good buffeting, but now all is serene and we are undamaged. After breakfast we haul the hurricane hawsers in, stow the fenders away and at 10:15 drift away from Ireland island.

The moment we are clear of the island's fishing fleet we come under attack from aircraft of the Royal Canadian Navy's Aircraft Carrier *HMCS Bonaventure*. Our escort for the day is *HMS Londonderry* who races around trying to fend our attackers off.

Everybody is feeling a bit 'miffed'. We have battled our way across the Atlantic for a visit to a distant island of the British Empire: just to be attacked by our Commonwealth cousins.

At nightfall, all the ships are darkened for a night exercise.

'DARKEN SHIP.

RIG BLACK OUT SCREENS. CLOSE ALL UPPER DECK SCREEN DOORS.

CLOSE ALL SCUTTLES, DEADLIGHTS AND HATCHES.

BUFFER AND ENGINEERING OFFICER REPORT TO THE BRIDGE.

THERE WILL BE NO FRESH WATER FORWARD OF SECTION TANGO UNTIL FURTHER NOTICE.

CHIEF SHIPWRIGHT REPORT TO THE BRIDGE.'

Tug and I are detailed off as boats' crew and in the pitch blackness we crawl into the whaler along with an unidentified Officer. There is no moon. The sky and the waters are ink black. It is a strange, unnerving feeling to be lowered down the ship's side by two lines of men holding on to the whaler's falls. Eventually the waters lap below us and we are released. Our engine starts the second time and we gingerly tour our small fleet, doing a circuit of each ship while our Officer yells instructions over his loud-hailer whenever he spots an escaping sliver of light from somewhere. Thankfully, *Bermuda* is as black as pitch and almost invisible. *HMCS Bonaventure* isn't.

The following two days are spent running, screening, attacking and repelling everything that is flung at us. We use all our four-inch and six-inch shells, some of which I know individually.

We returned to Ireland island at 18:00 on Wednesday 13 February.

'THE WINNER OF THE TOMBOLA HOUSE FOR THE SECOND TIME IS THE PADRE.

THIS PROVES BEYOND REASONABLE DOUBT THAT THERE IS A GOD AND THAT HE WORKS IN MYSTERIOUSLY FISCAL WAYS ...THREE CHEERS FOR THE PADRE. HIP HIP ...'

We are in one of the most sophisticated countries in the world, the sun is shining and it is Valentine's day ... and what do we do? ... we paint the ferkin' ship's side. Joe arranges paint dumps throughout the ship where large drums of Pusser's ship's-side grey are placed alongside a pile of paint tins and brushes. Everyone without a believable excuse is given a section of *Bermuda* to paint, particularly the starboard side. Me and my stage companion slap thick glutinous wodges of paint on those parts of the port anchor where it will stick.

Friday 16 February. To celebrate my 18th birthday ...

'CLOSE UP SPECIAL SEA DUTYMEN.

HANDS FALL IN FOR ENTERING HARBOUR PROCEDURE ALPHA.

HANDS OUT OF THE RIG OF THE DAY CLEAR OFF THE UPPER DECK.

CLOSE ALL UPPER DECK SCREEN DOORS AND SCUTTLES.'

Dressed in my second-best uniform and my cap with chin-stay down, I man the side with the rest of the crew for the short journey through the Sound and our ceremonial arrival on Hamilton's waterfront. An 18th birthday is a milestone in any young boy's life, but the size of the welcoming, flag-waving, crowd on Hamilton's Main Street along with a white uniformed marching band is overdoing it a bit – I am understandably overwhelmed and grateful. Scurze knows it is my birthday and gives me the simple job of installing the white canvas dodgers to the brow and arranges for someone to swap duties with me so that I can go ashore. Down the mess, I implore Tug and Sugar to keep the fact that it is my birthday quiet as I don't know what the For'd Seamen's mess might do to me if they find out. I don't fancy messdeck 'bumps' or anything similar. Tug and I invite Conkers to go ashore with us.

Once all the ceremonial paraphernalia is rigged, our electricians rig floodlights on the ship's side. While Tug, Conkers and I skip ashore over the forward brow without any fuss, the Governor and staff arrive at the after brow with all the

Floodlit – for exercise

accompanying bells and whistles associated with such visits. Crowds have gathered to watch his arrival. Our Royal Marine Band stand expectantly to attention opposite the after brow. *Bermuda* looks magnificent.

We have been given rough direction to the Seamen's Mission, known worldwide as the Flying Angel, where we are assured the beer will be reasonably priced. We walk slowly down the main street with pink-and-white buildings on one side and a beautifully presented Royal Naval Battle Cruiser on the other. The roads are litter-free and the relatively small number of cars that are around are large American ones. People are friendly and greet us warmly: I suppose it is easy to be friendly when you live in such a place.

Eventually we find the Flying Angel. The beer is cold and reasonably priced, despite it not being British.

Tug tells the gentleman behind the bar that it is my 18th birthday. We hope that we will get at least one celebratory beer, but we don't. When we ask him what we can do in Hamilton that won't cost us a fortune he suggests that we do what most young, first-time visitors to Bermuda do – hire a moped and go for a ride around the island.

We find the place where we can hire mopeds. Between us we have zero experience on anything motorised. I have driven a car illegally for about 20 minutes, Tug is experienced with power boats and has stripped down a few outboard engines. When asked, Conkers admits that he once lived near a garage. Surprisingly the rental formalities are extremely simple: we have to confirm that we are each over 17 years old and not suffering from anything that will prevent us from understanding Bermuda's road-traffic signs. He makes us walk a white painted line, sniffs our breath and concludes that we are all reasonably sober.

Eventually, the Hamilton branch of 'The Hells Angels' are ready to hit the roads of Bermuda. With bell-bottoms flapping, collar streaming and chin-stay firmly in place, we splutter up the street, past the Flying Angel and away ... at an impressive eight miles per hour. By the time we clear the Hamilton suburbs we are the undoubted masters of our respective machines. Thankfully Bermuda's traffic is light and we spend the afternoon calmly scouring the island, stopping now and then to give our delicate groins a break. We stroll on many a beach. Bermuda's most prominent colour is definitely pink. Many of the houses are painted pink ... and there is more than one pinkish beach. On a particularly beautiful beach, we hold a brief, but poignant, ceremony. Sat gazing at the deep blue sea that laps gently not far from our feet we say a joint thank you to Her Majesty the Queen and the British taxpayer for our Bermuda day. I say a heartfelt thank-you for a memorable 18th birthday before re-straddling my machine and motoring back to Hamilton ... at about six knots.

Conkers suggests we have another beer once we have returned the bikes and got our deposit back. In fact what happens is that we have more than one and we stagger back onboard well after dark, awash with foreign beer that we reckon is as weak as gnat's water.

18 years old eh?

I'd have been proud of yesterday's achievements if it wasn't for the mother of all hangovers. It isn't just me: Conkers and Tug are similarly afflicted, and we all spend much of the day somewhere quiet. That evening we recover enough to once again put on our suit and cap and stand on the jetty to watch our Royal

Marine Band perform. From the jetty *Bermuda* is an impressive sight, perfectly floodlit and not a speck of rust or a blemish to be seen anywhere. Immaculately dressed and drilled, the Royal Marine Band play all the familiar rousing British marching music to a large and very appreciative crowd who have gathered to witness a good slice of British ceremonial. It all ends with the playing of 'Ceremonial Sunset', a tune that always makes the hairs on the back of my neck stand up.

None of us relatively young Ordinary Seamen have sufficient money to 'do the town' more than once. However I do go ashore for a stroll during the day to buy and send some postcards and to buy some things to remind me of my visit. I buy a glass ashtray for Mum and a black leather billfold type wallet for myself with the name 'Bermuda' and an outline of the island embossed in gold on the outside – if that doesn't impress the Pudsey girls, nothing will. Bermuda is a magical place: it smells wonderful, everybody is so friendly and the weather is pleasantly warm.

Apparently there'd been an open invitation to a 'Grand Farewell Dance' at Hamilton Hall with 'Dancing to Maud Fox's Band' until midnight. The invitation arrives in the For'd Seamen's Mess the day after it's happened.

On Tuesday afternoon Scurze tells me to report to Sub Lieutenant Bracegirdle's cabin. I have to ask a Wardroom Steward where it is. Apparently, the fact that I once shared a wooden bench with Len Hutton qualifies me to play cricket for the ship.

Sub Lieutenant Bracegirdle doesn't look directly at me; he speaks to the after bulkhead of his cabin. 'We have organised a game against the Bermuda Sailing Club tomorrow,' he says, while rummaging in a large brown paper sack of a bag. 'I hear that you come from Pudsey.'

'Yes sir.'

'And that you knew Leonard Hutton.'

'Yes sir ... err did. Yes sir.' It is an outrageous exaggeration.

He holds up a pair of white trousers. 'Got any whites?'

'No sir. Sorry sir.'

'I thought not. Try those for size.' He tosses the trousers to me while staring into the bag. 'Got a white shirt?'

'No sir.'

'I'll put you down to bat at four.'

'OK sir.'

'The Gunnery Officer and myself will open.' He finds a shirt, holds it up to the light from his very own scuttle, folds it up and hands it to me. 'Might need to run an iron over that.'

'Right sir. Thank you sir.'

'Can you bowl?' he asks the bulkhead.

'Yes sir.'

'What would you describe yourself as?'

'Err ... fast sir. Not much of a spinner.'

'So I could give you a few overs early on then ... depending on the state of the wicket?'

'Yes sir. Thank you sir.'

He writes something on a sheet of paper. 'Transport at fourteen hundred tomorrow afternoon, give you time for your lunch to settle.' He glances at me but doesn't smile.

Lunch? We don't do lunch in the For'd Seamen's Mess.

I leave with a pair of trousers and a shirt tucked under my arm. Bloody hell, I'm in the ship's cricket team, and where am I going to find a ferkin' iron?

Thankfully Yorky has the key to the locker where the mess iron is kept and Scurze gives me half an hour off to iron my 'whites'.

Today there is a ceremony on the Quarter-deck that attracts many of Bermuda's movers and shakers. 16 years ago apparently the island of Bermuda had presented *HMS Bermuda* with four silver bugles and a silver ship's bell. Now we are ceremonially returning them. To signify the official hand-over, the ship's bell is rung 16 times and a final farewell is blown on the bugles. Despite having spent many hours polishing the Quarter-deck's brightwork, I am not invited to the hand-over ceremony, but I am told that the Quarter-deck looked good.

The following day I muster at the gangway after dinner in my whites and my newly scrubbed white plimsolls. Alongside a group of Officers is a pile of cricketing equipment.

'If you can take all that stuff onto the jetty Broadbent, the transport should be along soon,' says Sub Lieutenant Bracegirdle

I realise why I have been selected: someone has to do the humping.

The Supply Officer is late and it isn't until 14:20 that our full team, a scorer and a volunteer umpire are ready to go.

The pitch is immaculate. There is a good crowd of onlookers lounging around the boundary. Both the local umpires are wearing floppy hats. To a man, the Bermuda Sailing Club wear perfectly ironed whites and proper cricketing shoes. The Bermuda sun shines brilliantly and there are trays of small triangular sandwiches and other nibbles on a table in the visitors' changing room.

To cut a long cricketing story short – we lose. I have the third highest score and am the first to hit a boundary before being run out for twelve because the Supply Officer at the other end isn't paying attention and fails to run when I call. I bowl a couple of overs but without success: it isn't a good wicket for those of us who can't spin the ball.

Back in the mess I tell Yorky that I had a 'Horse's Neck' after the game.

'You'll be eating in the ferkin' Wardroom before long, you will, young 'un.'

'I was the second highest scorer.'

'With how many?'

'Twelve .. and the first to hit a boundary.'

'You're Wardroom-bound you are, young Broadbent ... You'll be eating in the Wardroom trough before long.'

The following day I return the whites to Sub Lieutenant

Bracegirdle's cabin.

'Did you enjoy the game, Broadbent?' he asks the bulkhead.

'Yes thank you sir.'

'The Supply Officer didn't actually hear you call. He has a hearing problem.'

'Right sir.'

'Next game is in Gibraltar.'

'Right sir, thank you sir.'

He smiles as I hand him my whites, but he still doesn't look directly at me.

All too soon it is time for us to leave. I shall always remember Bermuda – pastel-coloured Bermuda, sophisticated, warm and pink Bermuda where the population celebrated my 18th birthday ... and you only get one of those in a lifetime, don't you?

The crowd assembled on Hamilton's Main Street to wave us farewell isn't as large as that which had celebrated my 18th birthday. At precisely 09:00 our bows gently swing away from Hamilton. We salute a fond farewell and the Royal Marine Band play as we make our sedate way up the Sound and back out into the Atlantic.

Much to Scurze's annoyance, and once we have stowed all the ceremonial stuff away, The Civil Defence Platoon is assembled on the Fo'csle for rifle and Bren gun training using live ammunition.

Conkers has been given the job of manning the ship's telephone exchange which is located down below the wheelhouse somewhere. I go down there and actually connect a few lines for him. It is a panel full of holes and festooned with wires. There is always someone onboard wanting to phone someone else. Personally I have never had cause to use a telephone onboard *Bermuda*, but now I know how they are connected, maybe I will ... if I know anybody who would appreciate a call.

Saturday wouldn't be Saturday without an inspection to prepare for, and John-Jo has apparently threatened to inspect some of the messes. As we don't know which ones he will choose to inspect we all prepare ourselves for the worst.

The morning is spent in making the mess presentable. Anything that can't be cleaned is removed and I witness real naval bullshit at its most sophisticated. Miraculously, within a couple of hours, the place is transformed into something a little bit more than presentable and everybody is told by Yorky to 'Make yourselves scarce until rounds are finished.'

It is a nice warm day so I sit on my washdeck locker and smoke numerous cigarettes while gazing out over placid turquoise waters … great!

Wiggy brings Bannister up for some fresh air. Bannister doesn't look to be his normal energetic self.

'Bannister doesn't look too great today,' I say.

'I think the atmosphere in his locker is a bit oppressive.'

'In what way?'

'All those rotting pants.'

'Not rotting, surely?'

'You don't have to go in there, young 'un. I've got to do a lot of delving to find him sometimes.'

'Why don't we wash them, then?'

Wiggy flicks Bannister's lead and he flips over onto his back, legs and antennae flaying. 'He likes that, does Bannister.'

'Right then.'

'I don't think the mess would agree to washing them.'

'Why not?'

'I think most people consider them to be sacred in some strange way. They're like ancient manuscripts, I suppose. Historical artefacts.'

I don't know what to say. Artefacts! What were artefacts when they were at home?

Both Wiggy and I notice the bank of fog that is like a white wall ahead of us. Within minutes it has enveloped the entire ship. From where we are sitting by the after funnel I can't see the short distance to the forward funnel. The temperature drops alarmingly. Looking over the side I see a shoal of flying fish alongside, some blindly bashing themselves into the ship's side. I hope they don't damage the paintwork.

Wiggy flicks Bannister back over onto his feet, picks him up and puts him in his pocket. Then we retire to the relative warmth of the mess.

Gibraltar is to be our next port of call. The mess is full of stories of Gib' as most of the blokes have been there many times before. Apparently, it is a great place to buy watches, jewellery and electrical goods, as it is a duty-free port. There is also a great Naval canteen and loads and loads of pubs down the main street that sell English beer. One major disadvantage is that all the young Gibraltarian girls are chaperoned until marriage, so the prospect of meeting a Spanish senorita is less than nil.

Despite the fog, the Civil Defence Platoon practises shooting at the Atlantic from the Fo'csle. When they leave, Scurze scours the deck and scuppers for empty shell cases and to his delight finds some and struts away, jangling the empty shell cases in his pocket – no doubt on his way to have a 'friendly' word with the bloke responsible for tidying up.

25

FALLING IN LOVE WITH GIB

On Friday we wake in a fog-free environment. *RFA Tidereach* rendezvous with us early and *Bermuda* fills her fuel tanks.

The afternoon is spent getting everything ready for docking in Gibraltar tomorrow. Scurze, who of course has been to Gib many times before, knows that dockyard assistance to berth something as large as *Bermuda* cannot not always be guaranteed – so we make sure that we are ready and have all the necessary equipment to do it ourselves.

Saturday 3 March 1962. Seeing Gibraltar for the first time is quite an experience. North Africa to starboard, Spain to port and the sentinel of the Rock of Gibraltar towering tall and proud in the clear distance.

We fire an 11-gun salute as we make our way through Gibraltar's North Entrance.

Scurze is right. 'There's no Dockyard-mateys. That's ferkin' typical. You, you, you and you report to the boat deck. Tell Petty Officer Kelly that you are the Fo'csle contribution to the berthing party.'

With three others I am encapsulated in a cage and craned over the side and onto Gibraltar's jetty. We receive heaving-lines thrown at us and toil doggedly to haul over *Bermuda*'s heavy berthing ropes and wires. I am gaining respect for Dockyard-mateys with every pull and clearly understand why they aren't too keen to berth something the size of us at this time in the morning. We notice that the Dutch Frigate berthing behind us has loads of dockyard staff to help with their delicate berthing ropes and wires. We stay on the jetty for as long as we can while the brows are secured. We earn ourselves a 'loud hailer' bollocking from someone when we sit on a couple of the berthing bollards: apparently, that's not allowed.

The Navy's reason for being in Gibraltar is to carry out maintenance. The crew's reason for being in Gibraltar is to get drunk and buy some 'rabbits'. Don't ask me why souvenirs are called 'rabbits' – I don't know and nor does anyone else I ask, even Prof.

We know a number of the older lads well enough by now to accept their invitation to go ashore with them, and Yorky nods his approval. Dozens of other ships are due to descend on us over the next few days, so it is sensible to get ourselves ashore now before the place is swamped and the price of beer shoots up.

I immediately fall in love with Gib. The Naval Canteen is the first important 'watering hole', conveniently located at the top of the steep rise from the Dockyard. Its beautifully tended gardens of palm trees and exotic flowers mask an imposing white building that contains a number of comfortable bars and warm English beer at duty-free prices. It is the perfect place to start my first Gibraltar experience.

The narrow crowded Main Street is full of bars and open-fronted shops where we can haggle for the price of everything. Haggling is something new to me, and I don't take to it immediately. I pay over the odds for a small, brown plastic clock before one of the older lads tells me never to pay the asking price.

We call into a few bars: they are cool, dimly lit places, full and noisy. The blokes we are with, however, are determined to show us the most popular bar in town – the notorious Trocadero Bar situated on the corner of a small square about halfway down Main Street. The Troc's shuttered, glass-free windows open out onto the narrow street and square. Inside it is huge and already heaving with 'Bermudas'. Long bare wooden tables and straight-backed wooden chairs are placed with barely enough room to squeeze between them. In the centre of the room is a raised area where an elderly dark-haired lady in a red and black ensemble and clumpy black shoes performs an energetic Flamenco dance while row upon row of 'well oiled' sailors from Her Majesty's Ship *Bermuda* try to look up her swirling skirts.

My first tentative visit to the heads is an eye-opener. I've tried to put it off for as long as possible because it requires a lengthy and potentially dangerous series of zigzags between tables piled high with glasses. It is my first experience of a multi-sex toilet. For the first time in my life a woman holds out her hand for money before she will let me enter. As we gentlemen relieve ourselves in the prescribed manner we are jostled by a number of women dressed in colourful Flamenco dresses. One lady in a yellow dress with black spots is particularly attractive. None of the ladies pay any attention to us at all – no matter what we are doing.

Once back on my table I am keen to watch the lady in the yellow polka-dot dress perform. A couple of pints and a second trip to the toilets later, I see the lady in yellow eventually take to the 'stage'. Although still attractive, she does adopt a rather severe expression while dancing. She does, however, have a habit of raising her skirts to give us all a glimpse of her well-browned thighs and shiny black knickers.

It is Prof once again who starts the singing. Stomping up and down one of the tables while miraculously avoiding the stockpile of glasses, he sings ...

> 'Oh please daddy will you take me to Gibraltar,
> I want to see the rock and the big baboon,
> I want to go out there at night to see if what I've heard is right,
> I want to see if the Buffer can fly around the moon.'

Big cheers for the Buffer.

> 'Oh please daddy will you take me down Main Street,
> I want to spend my money in the flashy stores,
> I want to buy a postcard of a Geisha looking neat,
> And when you turn it sideways, she winks and drops her drawers.'

Everybody cheers.
Squinty takes over from Prof on the tabletop ...

'This is my story, This is my song,
I've been in the Navy too ferkin' long.
So roll on the Rodney, the Repulse and Renown;
This flat-bottomed bastard is getting me down.'

From the far end of the room someone else jumps on a table, raises a glass and ..

'No, No, No.
This is my story, This is my song,
I've been in the Navy too Ferkin' long.
So roll on the Rodney, the Repulse and Renown;
This two-funnelled bastard is getting me down.'

The ladies stop dancing.
Squinty responds ...

'No, No, No.
This is my story, This is my song,
I've been in the Navy too Ferkin' long.
So roll on the Rodney, the Repulse and Renown.
This armour-plated bastard is getting me down.'

Everybody cheers in agreement.

The fight starts later. A three-badge chef is halfway through a version of 'This Old Hat Of Mine' on the stage and has got down to his underpants and socks when the Chefs' table and the Stokers' table collide. They bounce off each other with fists and glasses flying everywhere.

Someone jabs me in the ribs and yells 'Out of the ferkin' window, young 'un!' I drain my glass, grab my brown plastic clock and crawl out of the window onto Main Street's pavement. I scuttle over to the other side of the street where I stand while the mayhem inside the Troc spills out onto the pavement, then into the centre of Main Street itself and then into the square.

Bodies are thrown out of the windows and drunken scuffed bodies try to climb back in. Some of the bar staff are involved and surprisingly some of the dancers. The lady in the yellow dress packs a tremendously effective kick to the groin area. When someone pulls her wig off it is apparent that she is no lady. I should have realised something wasn't right when I saw 'her' standing in front of a gent's 'pistol' earlier. I am fast realising that I will have to be careful about things in the future, a pair of well-shaped thighs and a pair of shiny black knickers aren't a guarantee of anything.

'Did you see that? The piece in the yellow dress is a bloke,' I say.

'That's Norman,' explains one of the older blokes standing next to me. 'Ex RAF, been performing here for yonks.'

We all make it back onboard eventually. I haven't arranged for anyone to sling my hammock for me, so I sleep fully clothed in a quiet corner of the Capstan Flat draped over my lashed-up hammock ... at least I think it is mine.

Next day the harbour begins to fill with British, French, Canadian and Dutch warships. Because of the number of ships now in Gib, leave is restricted to one part of the watch only, that means only a quarter of the crew are allowed ashore each day. Conkers, Tug and I swap duties so that we can go ashore in the afternoon. We take advice from the older lads and find the entrance to a tunnel that is carved through the rock and stretches from one side of Gib to the other. We emerge on the other side of the island at a small fishing village called Catalan Bay where there are a few bars and a hotel called the Catalan Bay Hotel. But there is no action.

Back on Main Street we have a beer or two at the Canteen and then buy our postcards and local postage stamps before hitting the shops for 'bargains'. Our haggling skills are undeveloped and we probably pay too high a price for whatever we buy. The first of The Troc's customers to be ejected through the window lands at our feet while we cross the square on our way back onboard.

Back down the mess, when asked how much we have paid for our souvenirs, we promptly halve the amount we've actually paid.

It is four days before we can go ashore again. We have a few beers at the Canteen before catching the lift up to an area near to the peak that is the playground for the army of Barbary Apes. They prove to be cheeky little buggers with the habit of trying to pinch our white lanyards. Eventually we get bored with trying to bond with the apes, who have the better of us intellectually, and we return to sea level.

My plan is to have a quiet Sunday but the Senior RP onboard is duty and decides it would be a good day to re-examine me. Our dislike for each other is well-ingrained and he fails me again. He writes the following on my Radar Plot History Sheet (S-1245 C Revised-May 1955) ...

'Ordinary Seaman Broadbent has failed his RP starring examination three times and has been warned that he is in danger of losing his Specialist Qualification. He is not at all bright and has great difficulty in remembering the necessary details. A pleasant young man who tries hard but is not very reliable.'

Bollocks to him then.

I still feel a little delicate on Monday morning. Collectively Tug, Conkers and myself have run out of money. None of us has yet mastered the art of budgeting.

The morning is full of activity as the various ships put to sea and straight into Exercise 'Dawn Breeze'. *Bermuda* sits and watches with parental pride as her fleet departs, each ship respectfully saluting us. We wait until the harbour is empty before leaving. We have dockyard-mateys to flick the eyes of our mooring lines and wires from dockside bollards.

After battling into a severe westerly swell for a couple of hours we suddenly stop. One of the Dutch destroyers establishes a tow and tries unsuccessfully to pull us into wind. Apparently, once more, we have forgotten to take our brake off. At mid-afternoon the tow is logged as a failure and we make our way back to Gib, where we anchor in Blackstrap Bay just before tea. No leave is granted: it would have been nice as all the other ships remain at sea.

On Tuesday we are underway early and we spend the next three days practising action, defence and security exercises as well as landing Civil Disturbance Platoons on difficult parts of Gibraltar before returning to port late on Friday evening.

I still don't have any money so I go for a quiet stroll on Friday afternoon which costs me nothing. At Rosario Bay I find a badly maintained plaque on a wall that explains that this is the place where Lord Nelson's body was brought ashore after the battle of Trafalgar to be preserved in a cask of spirit, before being taken back to England. I wonder how many people know about that. That's a story for the mess.

Yorky hands me a folded sheet of paper. 'Internal mail for you, young 'un ... from your friends down aft ... in the Wardroom.'

I unfold my sheet. It is the team list for *Bermuda* First XI against a select Gibraltar XI. I am down as thirteenth man. Batting at number 4 is someone called Lieutenant Commander Dorrington-Tweed. 'I'm thirteenth man.'

'Let's have a look.' Yorky holds his hand out. As a fully-fledged Yorkshireman he instinctively understands everything cricket. 'Thirteenth man, young 'un – you'll be carrying the bags and taking drinks to any of the team who wants one. You're the team's dogsbody. The twelfth man is Sub Lieutenant Oscar Alan Smith.'

'I was the second highest scorer in the last match in Bermuda.'

'Who's taken your place, then?'

I point at the fourth name on the team list.

'Lieutenant Commander Dorrington ferkin' Tweed – who's he?'

'The bloke who's taken my place.'

'You happy being thirteenth man then?'

'Not really, no.'

'Then phone Brace bloody Girdle, or whatever his name is, and tell him you can't play.'

'I can't do that ... can I?'

'Tell him you're under punishment. He won't dare to check with Foggo.'

'Will you do it for me ... please.'

'If you were old enough to draw your rum it would cost you 'gulpers'.'

'Would it?'

'Don't worry. I know where Bracegirdle's cabin is. I'll go and tell him. He's a wimp really. I'll make some excuse for you.'

'Thanks, Hooky.'

'You're 'Cook-of-the-mess' for the next three days.'

'Thanks.'

'Thanks what?'

'Thanks, Hooky.'

'That's better.'

On Saturday I perch myself on my washdeck locker and watch the cricket team as they stroll over the brow. Sub Lieutenant Bracegirdle is carrying the bags and has to make numerous trips backwards and forwards. I am miffed to have lost my place and I hope *Bermuda* loses.

On Sunday, the result of the First XI cricket match is posted on the sports notice board. The select Gibraltar XI declared at 130 for 8. In reply *Bermuda* scored only 29 all out. Lieutenant Commander Dorrington-Tweed was out for a duck and Sub Lieutenant Bracegirdle, batting at number three, scored only one before being 'caught and bowled' by a bloke called Jesus Hernandez.

The following Saturday we are subjected to a serious mess inspection by an Officer who has a real dislike for the For'd Seamen's Mess. We are picked up for almost everything. Even the deck underneath the port forward hammock stowage, that Tug and I have cleaned, isn't considered clean enough.

On Sunday 1 April Tug and I decide to visit the 'proper Spain'. Despite being told by those members of the mess who have been to mainland Spain before that the village of La Linea de la Conceptión, known as La-Lin, doesn't have anything to offer, we decide to go anyway. We think it is an April fool.

In La-Lin we drink far too much and get to the Spain-Gib border just after it closes at midnight. We find an empty and unlocked Spanish bus and crash out on the back seat. In the morning we are awakened by screaming schoolgirls and swiftly arrested by the Spanish Guardia. After spending most of the forenoon in the cells at the border we are escorted back onboard in the afternoon to face the wrath of the Regulating branch.

Our reception committee at the top of the brow could have been friendlier.

'Where's your cap, lad?' asks the Officer of the Day.

'A Spanish lady pinched it – couldn't stop her sir,' I lie.

'Likely story.'

The Master-at-Arms in particular is beside himself when I ask for my Station Card. 'It will be a long time before you see your station card again, my son. Get changed and fall in outside the Regulating Office in five minutes with a cap! You do have another cap, don't you?'

'Yes sir,' I lie.

Down the mess, I manage to borrow a cap that almost fits and doesn't have a name inside it. Unfortunately, it has a couple of large ship's-side grey paint splodges on one side.

Outside the Regulating Office the Master-at-Arms homes in on my cap. He looks inside for a name: there isn't one. He taps the paint splodges. 'Best you got, lad?'

'It's my working cap sir.'

'How Dare You Come To MY Defaulters' Table Wearing Your Working CAP!'

'Sorry sir.'

Both of us are charged with being five hours and 25 minutes adrift while the ship is under sailing orders. I am also charged with returning back onboard out of the rig of the day.

The Officer of the Day is busy, so we are put on Commander's Report for tomorrow.

The ship is being ammunitioned and every fifteen minutes we were reminded ...

'NO SMOKING OR NAKED LIGHTS THROUGHOUT THE SHIP.'

We don't even have the comfort of a cigarette to relieve the pressure. After a hurried dinner of cold leftovers I muster on the Fo'csle to help with the ammunitioning, and – surprise, surprise – I am placed in the bilges of one of the ammunition lighters.

During a short break between lighters, I watch the French aircraft carrier *Clemenceau* leave.

Eventually the ammunitioning is finished and we smokers enjoy a life enhancing smoke. At 17:00 we change into number three uniforms, fall in on our parts-of-ship and *Bermuda* sails sedately out of harbour and straight into yet more air and submarine 'attacks' as we, along with our escorting 5th & 7th Destroyer Squadrons, head north.

Tug and I agree our story so that we can tell the Commander the same thing. We will say that we were at the border before midnight but that it was already closed. The story about the Spanish school-bus could possibly amuse the Commander.

For the second time I muster in the passageway outside the Commander's cabin in my second-best suit. I have borrowed a half-decent cap that is a size too large for me. Master-at-Arms Foggo accuses both Tug and I of making a habit out of leave breaking.

I tell the 'bus and cap' story to the Commander and receive

the mandatory 'leave is a privilege' lecture. I am part-way through an explanation as to why we were onboard the bus when the unsmiling Commander tells me to stop. He reminds me that this is the second time I have been up in front of him for leave breaking and as such I will be awarded 14 days number 9s. If I break leave rules again I will be in serious trouble.

The Master-at-Arms is not amused. 'Defaulter on caps. 14 days number 9s ... right -aah tin ... quick march!'

Back down the mess Yorky can't believe that I've got 14 days number 9s. Then I tell him that it is the second time I have broken leave and that I left my cap in Spain, he nods understandingly. I am slowly joining the For'd Seamen's messdeck Defaulters Club.

Tug only gets 10 days number 9s because he didn't lose his cap.

Air and submarine attacks continue throughout Tuesday. On top of everything else I spend an extra hour and a half cleaning the forward Senior Rates' bathroom and heads: they are a manky lot.

Without any warning, I am told on Wednesday morning that I will spend the day being examined on my Seamanship knowledge. It starts in the cabin belonging to an Officer I've never seen before. He asks me all sorts of questions that I answer to the best of my ability. Then I spend some time with a Petty Officer from the Bosun's party who tells me to tie a series of knots and to do the first tucks of an eye-splice in a length of coir rope. Scurze examines me on Fo'csle stuff – anchoring and coming to a buoy. Goosie examines me on towing on the Quarter-deck. After dinner, a Petty Officer from the Communications branch sits me down on a locker on the flag deck and tests me on what I know about international signal flags and their meanings. I have time to sneak a quick cup of coffee before my final examination of the day: half an hour with another member of the Bosun's party being tested on what I know about ship's husbandry. Ship's husbandry is all about scrubbing, polishing and painting – I know loads about that.

Thursday 5 April we spend battling through the Bay of Biscay, a notorious stretch of water that is particularly ferocious today. As the weather deteriorates we rig safety lines and ...

'DO YOU HEAR THERE ... THE UPPER DECK IS STRICTLY OUT OF BOUNDS.
CLOSE ALL UPPER DECK SCREEN DOORS, ALL SCUTTLES AND ALL DEADLIGHTS.'

Once we have rigged all the safety lines most of the lads are given jobs down below. I am given the job of Lifebuoy Ghost and handed an elderly lifejacket to wear. I huddle myself alongside the after emergency telephone on the Quarter-deck, ready to call the bridge if I see anybody, or anything fall over the side. I have absolutely no authority to stop anyone wandering out onto the Quarter-deck.

Biscay's waters are smashing over our guardrails and swamping the wooden Quarter-deck. Water is cascading down the ladders from the deck above. Out of the screen door on the port side emerges an Officer who has either not heard the recent pipe, misunderstood it or thinks the upper-deck restrictions don't apply to him. I don't know exactly what to do: I can't leave my telephone and the wind is so loud that I won't be heard if I shout. Then things happen quickly. The Officer looks over the side at the foaming water. A wave comes from forward and hits him, lifting him off his feet. A following wave curls and flings him over the side. I reach for my phone – I am about to crank the handle when a third, or maybe a fourth, wave lifts him back over the guardrails and dumps him on the deck. With arms and legs flaying he slides, amid grey foaming water, and smashes into the after jack staff base. I tell the voice on the other end of the phone that an Officer has just been thrown overboard and then back inboard again and is presently lying, soaking wet against the after guardrails. As I place the telephone back in its cradle, the soaking-wet Officer slowly scrambles to his knees and, taking advantage of a slight lull, staggers forward towards the screen door. He manages to open it and disappear. I call the bridge again and I'm asked who the Officer is. He is surprised when I say that I don't know ... sir.

I repeat my story to the bloke who relieves me an hour later. He has no sympathy for whoever comes out on the upper deck unprepared in this weather. I never heard any more about the Officer who I saw cheat death: I bet he remembers it, though. During the night we lose another whaler and half of our Carley rafts.

Once we are north of Biscay the seas calm to a long roll and the wind drops to a sensible British Isles level.

In the evening I *am* summoned down to the Officers' cabin flat and told officially that not only have I passed for Able Seaman, but I have done it with an extraordinarily high percentage. However, I can't be promoted to Able Seaman until I pass the dreaded RP starring exam ... so I have to apply myself to that from now on. I am also told that I will be transferred to the Top part-of-ship as from tomorrow, where I can learn more about boats.

At 05:00 on Friday we are preparing everything for entering harbour. On the horizon is the now-familiar sight of the Isle of Wight with the Nab Tower just visible in the early morning mist.

The big dipper on the end of the pier at Billy Manning's is clear as we muster for entering harbour. We stand in perfectly straight lines as we silently enter Portsmouth harbour, too early for the firing of the normal salutes. There are no waving crowds to welcome us. It takes a couple of harbour tugs to manoeuvre us so that we are facing bows-out-of-harbour on South Railway Jetty. As a new Top part-of-ship member, I'm not surprised when I find myself in a basket being craned over onto the jetty to receive *Bermuda*'s berthing ropes.

A small group of dockyard-mateys arrive just as we are putting the finishing touches to everything and installing the rat-guards. At 08:00 a fleet of official wagons arrive on the jetty and we are invaded by HM Customs & Excise. Guards are placed on both brows to prevent anybody sneaking ashore. Each mess has been given a pile of customs declaration forms for those who have bought anything abroad to fill in. I don't think that a brown plastic clock, a glass ashtray or a black leather wallet is what HM Customs & Excise are interested in, so I don't bother filling in a form.

The uniformed gentlemen from HM Customs & Excise set up their desks in the Forward Capstan Flat. A couple of hammocks belonging to lads who are Special Sea Dutymen, and who haven't had the chance to stow them away this morning, are left hanging and this upsets someone. Before the end of the day, a couple of Dockyard workers with grinders remove all the slinging bars within the Capstan Flat ... that have been there since *Bermuda* was built. All of us who have been sleeping in the Capstan Flat now have to find ourselves somewhere else to sling our hammock.

Tug and I had planned on going ashore but instead we spend the early evening searching for a replacement slinging-place. We both find a space that is vacant at 23:00 and we sling our hammocks. Today is the beginning of a wandering month or so during which we move 'slinging' places dozens of times.

I receive a letter from Wilco. She is going back to *HMS Dryad* in September. She has been promoted slightly and has recently done a NAAFI course on the newly acquired frothy-coffee machines. For the first time she has spelt orgasm correctly: I bet she had to ask someone.

I enjoy writing to Wilco – I don't have to worry about my spelling – and I can write anything I want. I am beginning to write things that my Mum wouldn't approve of.

On the first Wednesday after we complete our period of punishment Tug and I go ashore. We make it to the NAAFI club an hour before closing time and for the first time, there are no Marilyns waiting outside to be 'signed in'. We have a quick couple of pints and stroll back onboard well before midnight. I wonder if I am growing out of the Ponderosa.

On Thursday morning I oversleep and stumble onto the Boat-deck five minutes late, without having had a wash or a shave. Petty Officer 'Paddy' Kelly isn't impressed with my appearance or my posture.

'Welcome to the Top part-of-ship ... eventually. I hope this isn't to become a habit, young man.'

'No, PO.'

'Are we feeling a little delicate this morning?'

'Not really, PO.'

'Fancy a nice quiet and relaxing job do we?'

'Yes, PO.'

'Bilges of the port launch need cleaning out.'

'Thanks, PO.'

'Away you go. Grab some cleaning gear from the locker and get on with it!'

'Aye aye, PO.'

Boats bilges are awful places – particularly when they haven't been cleaned for a while.

We are paid after dinner. Both Tug and I have money in our pocket again and we want to go ashore. We have heard that there is a Dockyard Canteen somewhere, but neither of us know exactly where it is.

Down the mess I ask Languid if he knows where the Dockyard Canteen is.

'It's payday, boyo. What the ferk are you goin' to the Dockyard Canteen for? Tonight is 'Grab a Granny Night'.'

'Wha?'

'Grab a Granny Night at the Mecca.'

'Where's that then?'

'The Mecca?'

'Yeah.'

'Arundel Street.'

Tug looks at me, I look at Tug. The word Granny doesn't inspire us. My grandmother is a lovely woman, but I don't fancy spending an evening with the likes of her.

'So Grannies go down to the Mecca do they?' Tug asks.

'Not really Grannies. Every other Thursday the Mecca fills with all the town's available women: they know when Navy payday is. Tonight is the night for getting amongst it. If you can't pick up a bit at the Mecca on pay day ... there's something wrong.'

'Right then.'

'Me and Wiggy are going down there – you can come with us if you like.'

'OK then.'

In the company of Languid and Wiggy, The Ship Anson pub on The Hard isn't as intimidating as I had been led to believe. It is dark, crowded and the beer is excellent, particularly as Languid puts his hand in his pocket to buy the first round.

We stop at a few other hostelries on the way down Queen Street. Wiggy, Languid or both of them know the names of all the barmaids. Wiggy in particular has an admirer called Barbara behind the bar at The Standard.

As we approach the Mecca, Languid warns us. 'No pissing about now. If the bouncers suspect that you've been drinking they won't let you in. So it's shoulders back and mouth shut.'

The moment I step inside the main doors I am overpowered by the smell of perfume, the click-clack of hundreds of stiletto-heeled shoes and the sheer number of women. Upstairs we find ourselves a corner table in the main bar. It is my round.

By the time I get back to the table with the drinks Tug has already been told all about the Thursday night routine.

'Apparently it's every man for himself out there on the floor,' Tug explains. 'No muscling in on anyone else's partner.'

'There is a game we sometimes play,' says Wiggy.

'Go on.'

'Dragon hunting.'

'Eh?'

'Dragon hunting. All you have to do is find the ugliest girl you can and bring her back to this bar at exactly 22:30.'

'Why the ugliest?'

'Because it's a dragon competition. The one with the ugliest wins.'

'Wins what?'

'That's not important.'

'Wiggy's good at it. He normally finds the really grotty ones.'

'I ferkin' don't,' an indignant Wiggy replies.

Languid winks at me and Tug. 'He does.'

Tug and I stand on the side of the dance floor that's awash with dancers, mostly girls dancing with other girls.

'We've only got forty minutes to find an ugly one.' I point to a couple of mature individuals dancing around their handbags about ten feet away. 'What do you reckon, then ... split those two up then, shall we?'

'Yeah, right then.'

I totter over and tap the tallest of the two ever so gently on the shoulder. 'Excuse me, can we interrupt you for a dance ... just the one dance.'

The smaller of the two stops gyrating, looks at Tug and shakes her head. Her partner looks at me, adjusts her shoulder strap and says, 'piss off.'

As we walk back to the edge of the floor, I say: 'Lesbians.'

'Yeah.'

Back in the bar at the prescribed time of 22:30, Wiggy is sitting with the peroxide blonde lady who rejected me ten minutes earlier. Languid is all by himself, but alongside his half-empty pint glass is a drink with a small blue umbrella sticking out of the top.

'Sorry,' I say, holding my arms out. 'Unsuccessful I'm afraid.'

'Never mind,' says Wiggy. 'You can do the vote.'

'Vote?'

Wiggy takes me by the shoulder and marches me away from the table. 'You have to decide which of us has managed to find the ugliest one.'

'Right then.'

'But I think Languid's lady might be taking him back to her place, so I don't mind you voting for mine. Quietly, of course – don't say anything in front of the girls. Understand?'

'I think so.'

He nudges me in the ribs. 'Here she comes. He nods over my shoulder. 'Languid's latest conquest.'

I turn and watch an extremely well-developed lady of indeterminate age wobble between the tables until she reaches Languid. She drapes a beefy arm over his shoulder and sits herself down with a thump.

'He likes big women,' explains Wiggy.

'Christ,' I say.

The peroxide blonde finishes her pint in one and barges past Wiggy. 'I know what you bastards are playing at,' she says as she heads towards the exit door.

Wiggy looks at the ceiling. 'Win some ... lose some. Only cost me a pint after all.'

I look over to where Languid's large lady has almost completely enveloped him. All I can see of him is the fingers of his left hand and the lower part of a juddering leg.

'Best leave them to it, I reckon,' says Wiggy.

All three of us make it back onboard well before midnight. Wiggy asks the Quartermaster to make a note of the time Languid returns onboard. It will be an indication on how successful he has been with his new conquest.

Nobody has slung our hammocks because we haven't asked anyone to do it for us. Eventually we manage to get them slung: it is almost second nature by now.

According to the Quartermaster's unofficial log, Languid returned onboard bleary-eyed at 06:37 this morning. Thankfully, no underwear is offered in evidence. Wiggy manages to keep the details of Languid's latest conquest to himself over breakfast.

I spend the morning 'Stand-easy' packing my little brown case for leave. This afternoon I am heading home for Easter. I get another letter from Wilco and she starts it by calling me her 'cheaky, cheaky boy': she isn't the best speller in the world.

Portsmouth Harbour Station is relatively clear. Yorky is also on second leave and we share a carriage. We smoke our way to Waterloo where we have to wait for a couple of hours due to some kind of problem on the line north. Yorky takes me to the Union Jack Club where we enjoy a cup of excessively strong tea and a sausage sandwich. It is a strangely derelict place staffed by morose individuals dressed in maroon coats. Yorky once dated a girl who lived in London and so spent a lot of time in the UJC. It is a cheap alternative to a London hotel for those in the services, but not recommended for young lads on their own.

'If you ever stay here, young 'un, make sure you have something strong to put behind your cabin door. Pass keys are easily obtained hereabouts.'

'Right then.'

'Great place for a run ashore in London, though.'

'Right then.'

On the journey north we have a good discussion about Leeds United and we are both disappointed that the football season is now over. If we'd taken leave earlier, we could have enjoyed a 0-0 home draw against Derby County.

Yorky tells me that we are going to Stockholm next and adds that it is an 'interesting' run ashore – or it was three years ago when he was last there. His last ship had been stationed in the Far East and he tells me all about his experiences in Singapore, Hong Kong, Tokyo, the Philippines, Australia and New Zealand. If only half of it is true ... I can't wait to get out there.

'Did you buy anything in Bermuda?' he asks.

'A wallet.' I don't tell him I bought Mum a glass ashtray.

'Nice place eh?'

'Terrific, yeah.'

'Did you hire a moped?'

'Yeah.'

'Enjoy yourself?'

'Yeah.'

The subject of Blacky crops up as we enter Doncaster. Apparently he has upset almost everybody in his part of the mess. Yorky says that he has reported the problem to his Divisional Officer. It is possible that he could be subject to a psychiatric examination and drafted off.

'What was he like at *Ganges*?'

'Pain in the arse.'

We say goodbye to each other as the train draws into Leeds City Station and wish each other a good leave. It is after midnight so I get myself a taxi home. That is an unexpected expense.

At home, everyone is in bed and I wake up the next door neighbours as well as Mum.

'Hello love, I thought I'd left the door open for you.'

'It was locked.'

'Was it?'

'Yeah.'

'Sorry then.' She offers me her cheek. 'When do you go back?'

'Two weeks.' I give her a kiss. I love my Mum.

'Fancy a drink?'

'Beer?'

'Tea!' She taps my hand. 'Cheeky young man. It's way after closing time.'

'No thanks.'

I wake my brother as I dump my grip in the corner of our bedroom. After all the pleasantries are out of the way he asks me where I have visited and is impressed with Gibraltar and Bermuda. He gets the *Readers Digest World Atlas* out from underneath his bed and we find both places easily.

'What was the Atlantic like then?'

'Wet.'

'Don't be stupid.'

Then I tell him all about the hurricane in Bermuda which impresses him.

I snuggle down into one of Mum's specially made beds: clean everything and a soft, sweet smelling pillow. It is a change from the hammock.

The shop is busy the following morning. Tony and I are kept busy re-stocking the shelves and it isn't until dinnertime that I have the opportunity to formally present Mum with her glass ashtray from *Bermuda*.

'How many cigarettes do you smoke a day?' she asks me.

'No more than ten,' I lie.

'That's OK then. Have you brought any of those big Woodbine Export cigarettes home with you?'

'I've got two hundred.'

'Can I have one?'

'No. They're for service personnel only.'

'Don't be silly.'

'They're all marked 'HM Forces only' on the paper. All of them.

'They're not, are they?'

'If you're caught smoking one we'll both be behind bars.'

'Don't be silly.'

Tony asks if he can have one and Mum and I say 'No' at the same time.

Mum examines her Woodbine. 'You're right.' She points to the cigarette paper 'HM Forces only.'

'Told ya.'

We both enjoy a duty-free smoke. Tony glares at us.

I explain all about Bermuda and how nice it is. I also tell her about the 'Trocadero Bar's toilets in Gib'. Mum isn't surprised because 'it is abroad. isn't it?' I don't want to confuse her, so I don't mention anything about the bloke in the yellow Flamenco dress, or my morning spent in the cells at the Spanish border.

My trip back to London is uneventful. I don't mind going back – we are going to Stockholm.

I meet up with Yorky at Waterloo.

'Had a good leave then, young 'un?'

'Yes thanks. You?'

'Rubbish. Get a bit?'

'No.'

'Looking forward to getting back onboard then?'

'Suppose so. Only problem is that I haven't got a permanent place to sling my mick.'

'Try the Cinema.'

'The Cinema?'

'Port side forward door from the Boat deck.'

'I know where it is. Can I sling in there then?'

'Think so, yeah.'

'I'll give it a go, then.'

Yorky taps his pockets. 'Got any DF's left?'

'No.'

'Suppose I'll have to buy a packet of normal fags then.'

Yorky moans all the way back to Portsmouth harbour station about having paid 3/9d for a packet of Senior Service untipped. He offers me only one during the hour-and-three-quarters journey.

Tug, Lash, Conkers and I transfer our hammocks from the mess stowage area to the one in the Cinema. The mess is almost empty tonight and Tug and I have 'nine-o-clockers' almost to ourselves. We tell the duty chef that there are a dozen of us left in the mess and we are given a dozen tins of 'sardines-in', a sliced white loaf and some butter: so we gorge ourselves.

Saturday 19 May is a non-smoking day from 10:00 onwards. I inhale as much smouldering tobacco as I can before a couple of tugs arrive to tow *Bermuda* off the jetty and up the harbour to the dreaded ammunitioning area.

'DO YOU HEAR THERE.

NO SMOKING OR NAKED LIGHTS THROUGHOUT THE SHIP.

ASSUME DAMAGE CONTROL STATE 1 CONDITION ZULU ALPHA.

CLOSE ALL UPPER DECK SCREEN DOORS, HATCHES, SCUTTLES AND DEADLIGHTS.'

It is almost teatime before a couple of tugs plonk us back onto South Railway Jetty. The tug crew aren't too happy about working a Saturday afternoon despite the Dockyard's overtime rate.

Before we stow all the coir mats away we Top part-of-ship smokers huddle on the side opposite the jetty and have a ceremonial 'smoke'. We ingest cigarette after cigarette in order to get our nicotine levels up to something approaching normal.

The Daily Orders for Monday are published on Sunday. We are scheduled to leave Pompey early the following morning. Those of us in the For'd Seamen's mess who have pen and paper 'knuckle down' to writing letters. I write to Mum saying that we are sailing the following day but we know not where. It is a little more adventurous than 'we are going to Stockholm'. I also write some 'steamy' lines to Wilco who I know likes that sort of stuff. I feel all unnecessary when I've finished and have to have a cold shower.

Those in the mess who live locally go home 'to give the missus one' before leaving. Those of us who have no carnal reason for going ashore, and who are saving money for the impending delights of Sweden's capital city, stay quietly onboard ... smoke and play Crib.

Monday morning is cold and misty. *Bermuda* is hauled off the jetty by two tugs, which we dispatch as soon as we reach the centre of the harbour. Apparently, we are being filmed and John-Jo doesn't want *Bermuda* leaving harbour with tugs attached. On the Round Tower are a small group of well-wishers waving us farewell and God speed.

As we make our way sedately north without being 'attacked' by submarines or aircraft, we get down to the seriously technical business of painting ship. Never has the saying 'If it doesn't move paint it!' been better applied. Before the end of the day *Bermuda* gleams with badly applied but shiny Pusser's grey paint. Her brass-work shines in the watery spring sun and her decks are salt and dog-end free. It is the first time for many months that we have been at sea for days without subjecting ourselves to a series of complicated drills or exercises.

26

TRIANGULAR SANDWICHES FOR A STOCKHOLM GIRL

On Wednesday afternoon we are on Stockholm's M19 berth. Rumour has it that the King of Sweden and Princess Alexandra are among the expected guests next week. I can imagine the 'flap' the Quarter-deck part-of-ship will be in as they rig awnings etc. The Top part-of-ship has no such bullshit to rig: all we have to do is to make sure that the forward brow is rigged and the white canvas dodgers are installed the correct way up.

Those who have been to Stockholm before recommend the Tivoli Gardens as a good place to visit for those of us Ordinary Seamen who don't have much money to spend. Apparently Stockholm's beer, and just about everything else, is ultra-expensive. Tug and I change what money we have into Swedish Kroner and stay onboard for the first night while the Quarter-deck plays host to Stockholm's finest who have an invitation to quaff alcohol at the British taxpayers' expense. While most of the mess are ashore enjoying themselves, Tug and I, along with a few others, crack open a couple of cans of beer and a celebratory tin of Spam.

The King of Sweden, Princess Alexandra and numerous military and political dignitaries are due onboard on Saturday and *Bermuda* is in the middle of a massive 'flap'. Top part-of-ship hands are seconded to the Quarter-deck where I am employed polishing brass tallies. The inside of 'Y' turret is crawling with cleaners, polishers and painters just in case any of Saturday's dignitaries want to inspect the insides of a Second World War, triple six-inch turret.

Inspection by King Gustav VI. Note the striped awnings overhead

Conkers, Tug and I have a conference and decide that, as Tug and I are duty on Thursday night, we will all stay onboard and 'hit' Stockholm on Friday evening. We will buy postcards first and spend the rest of the evening and night in cultural, liquid pursuits.

On Friday morning we are told that we can no longer sling hammocks in the Cinema. In the afternoon, I have the important task of making sure that the underwater hull of the ship's barge, that is up on boat-deck chocks, is clean.

After tea, we shower, get changed into our best suits, hand our station cards in at the brow and skip ashore. None of us arranges for our hammocks to be slung.

We decide against taking one of the long line of waiting taxis into town: we have been told it will cost us a week's wages. So we walk, we walk and we walk. By the time we make it to anywhere remotely interesting, we are knackered ... but we have unspent Swedish Kroner in our pockets. We buy, write, stamp and post our postcards before shuffling around a few bars, spending an unreasonable amount in each for a small glass of barely acceptable Swedish lager.

I am scanning the play-list of a Bal-Ami jukebox when an attractive young lady taps my shoulder. 'F17 please ...press F17 for me ... please.'

I find F17 and press the button firmly. The record I have been asked to select is 'Stranger On The Shore' by Acker Bilk.

'He's English, you know,' I say to my companion as she snakes an arm through mine and ushers me to an empty table in the corner. As I sit down I look over towards Conkers and Tug who are staring at me open-mouthed. It looks like I've been 'picked-up'.

'I know,' she says. She is wearing a chunky knitted jumper over a flouncy striped skirt. On her feet are fur-lined boots. 'I am what is calling a jazz freak. Anything from America or England I am liking ... a lot.' She smiles a wonderfully welcoming full-faced smile. She is attractive: wonderfully attractive. It is the first time I've ever been 'picked-up' and I have to make adjustments, both physically and mentally.

I hold my hand out. 'I'm Peter.'

She tickles the tips of my fingers, 'My names is Gunnel. Nice meeting you, Peter.'

'Your name is Gunnel?'

'Gunnel ... yes.'

'Nice name.' I am tempted to tell her that it sounds exactly like the top edge of a boat, but I don't. I examine her face. She has shoulder-length blonde hair, sparkly blue eyes and a flawless complexion. She is beautiful and her mouth appears to have a permanent smile.

'Do you live in Stockholm?'

'Yes.'

'Have you lived here all your life?'

'Yes.'

'If you don't mind me asking, how old are you?'

'Eighteen.'

'Me too.'

'Pardon?'

'Me too. I am also eighteen.'

'Can I buy you a beer?' she asks.

A woman buying me a beer! 'You certainly can ... yes please.'

She stands up and hands me a woolly hat she has been holding in her lap. 'Look after that for me Peter, I'll be returning back soon.'

The hat is warm. I look over at Tug and Conkers. Tug leers at me, Conkers gives me a double 'thumbs up' signal. I watch Gunnel's backside as she meanders to the bar – it is brilliant. While she waits for the beers to be poured she goes over to the jukebox, presses a few buttons and turns round to look at me as the strains of 'March Of The Siamese Children' by Kenny Ball and his Jazzmen fills the air.

The beer she brings me is different. I offer her an Export Woodbine and she accepts it with a wonderful smile. 'Cigarettes are expensive in Sweden,' she says as she rolls the unlit 'Woodie' between her fingers. I make sure that the flame on the Ronson Varaflame is turned down before lighting her cigarette for her. She inhales deeply and holds her hand out for my lighter. She examines it from all angles before handing it back to me. 'That's nice.'

'Just a lighter.' I casually reply.

'That would cost...' she places her forefinger on her lips. 'Cost a week of wages to buy.'

'Blimey.'

'Pardon?'

'I'm surprised.'

'It's true.'

'Your English is very good.'

'I work for an English company, and I learn English at school for two years.'

'What do you do? Work I mean.'

'Secretary.' She taps her fingers on the table. 'I type letters. Not that much ... er, very interesting.'

We spend the next couple of hours talking and drinking and occasionally putting Acker Bilk or Kenny Ball on the jukebox.

Conkers and Tug come over to say that they are going

back onboard. Tug asks, with a wink, if I want him to sling my hammock for me. I can't be that lucky so I ask if he will and to let the Quartermaster know where my hammock is.

I am surprised to learn that apart from jazz, Gunnel enjoys 'Let's Twist Again' by Chubby Checker, and she drags me to my feet and we 'twist' in the middle of an almost-empty bar before the bloke behind the bar says something to us in Swedish that brings our dance, and my very first 'twist', to an end. The jukebox is unplugged.

Gunnel has a car. Travelling on the wrong side of the road for the very first time in my life, I enjoy the trip back to the port. She parks the car in a dark secluded corner and we enjoy a fondling session in the limited area of the front seats. It is a typical first-date exploratory session, ending with sloppy wet chins, disturbed clothing and a throbbing, troublesome appendage in my uniform trousers. Gunnel lowers both front windows that are dripping condensation. With my forefinger I draw a tick on the windscreen. She laughs. A smell is invading the car – a fishy type smell that reminds me of the glue factory in Newcastle.

We arrange that Gunnel will pick me up from the ship at 19:30 tomorrow. She knows exactly what time the King and Princess Alexandra are due to visit *Bermuda* and wants to see them both. She also wants us both to go to the Tivoli Gardens tomorrow as Louis Armstrong and his All-Stars are performing.

The fish smell has gone as I 'limp' back onboard. Tug has slung my hammock in the passage outside the bakery. Everybody is asleep: there is nobody I can brag to, so I spend a fitful and disturbed night.

The following morning the troublesome appendage is still much in evidence. The news of last night's 'pick-up' is common knowledge in the mess before I stow my hammock.

Skid, with a wicked glint in his eyes, leans towards me as I slice up a couple of tepid hard-boiled eggs. 'We have a rule in this mess, young 'un.'

'Mmm?'

'Whenever any of us enjoys a casual 'one-nighter' with a member of the opposite sex we have to produce tangible evidence of sexual activity.'

'I know. I know all about the knicker locker.'

'So ... did you dip your wick then?'

'Not exactly.'

'I heard you were dragged away to a quiet corner of a bar,' someone from the far end of the table confirms.

'What was her name then?' asks Yorky.

'You won't believe it,' I say as I lay slices of boiled egg onto a slice of white bread and sprinkled them with damp salt.

'Name, young 'un. Name?'

'Gunnel.'

'Gunwale?' says Skid.

'Yeah, Gunnel.'

'Well,' says Yorky. 'You know the mess rule. If you manage to have your wicked way with Gunwale ... when you put your oar into her rowlock so to speak ... you are required by the rules and regulations of the For'd Seamen's Mess to bring back to the mess an item of intimate clothing to confirm the act.

'We like knickers best,' says Prof.

'He only says that because he's never had his hand on a pair himself,' says a serious-looking Languid.

'I'll try my very best.' I take a bite of my egg sandwich: it tastes awful.

'Fresh Swedish knickers,' says Squinty, staring at the deckhead.

'Are you seeing her again, young 'un?'

'Tonight. We're going to see Louis Armstrong ... in the Tivoli Gardens.'

'And afterwards?'

'OUT PIPES.

BOTH WATCHES OF THE HANDS WILL FALL IN ON THEIR PARTS OF SHIP IN FIVE MINUTES.'

I ditch the remains of my egg sandwich in the gash bin.

'Tell the Top PO that you're mess sweeper this morning, young 'un,' says Yorky.

'But I'm not on the list.'

'It's a mess rule, young 'un. Anybody who almost gets his leg over does mess sweeper the following morning.'

So I do mess sweeper, spending half the morning in the mess cleaning and scrubbing.

The ship is open to visitors this afternoon so those of us who are interested struggle into our second-best suits and go up to the Boat Deck to watch the first crowd of visitors negotiate our brow. I am at the inboard end of the brow ready to offer a helping hand to any attractive young lady who finds the steps a little difficult to manage. I am disappointed at the large number of Swedish girls who wear trousers.

I am having a sneaky cigarette round the side of the Fo'csle that is out of bounds to visitors when I hear someone call my name. Gunnel, wearing last night's bobbly jumper and a pair of tight green trousers tucked into calf-length furry boots is leaning on the starboard side winch.

I flick my cigarette into Stockholm's harbour and duck under a boundary rope. 'Didn't expect to see you here.'

She gives me a peck on the cheek. 'I didn't know we could come onto *Bermuda* until I heard in ... on the radio this morning.' I get a whiff of something unpleasant – maybe it is something on the Swedish breeze.

'Can you show me everywhere?'

'Around the ship?'

'Yes.'

'Of course.'

We stroll up and down all the ladders and passageways open to visitors: the familiar, unpleasant smell comes and goes. On the bridge I notice a bright red rash on Gunnel's neck that spreads from below her chin round her starboard ear. I assume it is caused by her scarf that she is continually adjusting. The smell of the Tyne glue factory is stronger on her starboard side than the other. I am a little disappointed – maybe she actually works in a fish processing plant.

We part as the visitors are required to leave, promising to meet at the agreed time of 19:30.

Back down the mess I am subjected to the opinions of those who had noticed Gunnel and I together.

'Nice arse.'

'Lovely arse.'

'Didn't like her jumper much.'

'But she had a great arse.'

'Yeah a great arse.'

'Too good for young 'un.'

'Much too good.'

'Give her one from me, young 'un.'

'And a really good one from me.'

'And from me.'

'Nice arse.'

'Don't forget the proof. We require proof,' says Skid.

At exactly 19:30 Gunnel, wearing the same jumper and trousers, is waiting at the bottom of the brow. Standing alongside her car, she waves at me as I hand my station card in. The Petty Officer of the watch gives me a narrow-eyed smile. 'Have a nice time, lad.'

'Thank you, PO. I will.'

We find a spot at the far end of a roped-off area opposite *Bermuda*'s stern where we wait until the King of Sweden and Princess Alexandra are piped onboard with all due ceremony. As Gunnel's scarf slips I notice that her neck and ear is blemish-free. But to be on the safe side I position myself on her left side. I am convinced there is a connection between the rash and the fishy smell. When all the invited guests are aboard, and the Royal Marine band has taken up its performance position on the jetty, we wait a while for something to happen. When it doesn't, we leave.

The Tivoli Gardens is full of strolling people. We find a standing position in front of a shell-shaped stage and listen to Louis Armstrong and his All-Stars for a couple of hours. On the drums is Danny Barcelona ... apparently.

Gunnel says that Kid Ory is also on stage, but I don't know who Kid Ory is, so I pretend to be impressed. It is dark as we leave the open-air theatre. Gunnel says she knows somewhere quiet where we can have some private time together. An important section of my body is 'up for it' so I allow myself to be dragged towards a deserted circular structure with a roof, walls and lounger-type seats.

'A friend told me about here,' she says as she unwinds her scarf to reveal a bright red rash.

We get down to some serious snogging. For a while I am able to ignore the smell but it gradually intensifies and quickly becomes a distasteful and off-putting problem. With her dribbling mouth wide open, it becomes a stomach-churning distraction. Both my nose and my appendage are beginning to question what I am doing. As a Yorkshire lad I have grown up surrounded by strange industrials smells, but this one is Scandinavian and is making me feel sick.

I wind my window fully down on the trip back. I give what I think is her starboard breast a squeeze as I kiss her for the final time, but the bobbly jumper complicates everything. It is possible that I missed my target completely.

It is a while before the interior surface of my nostrils return to normal. I can still taste the smell and once again, part of me doesn't sleep well.

The following morning I am cross-examined in the mess.

'Got a bit of Swedish last night then, did we young 'un?' asks Skid.

'Bit of a grope in the Tivoli Gardens somewhere.'

'Good lad ... good lad.'

'But she's got a problem.'

'What?'

'Personal problem.'

'She's not a bloke, is she?' asks Skid as he scrapes the remnants of a partially eaten egg into the gash bin.

'No, definitely not.'

'Not with an arse like that she ain't, boyo,' says Languid

'What then?' asks Squinty as he passes me a slice of bread and a couple of rashers of fatty bacon.

'She smells.'

'All women smell, young 'un.'

'Great smell ... smell of woman,' gasps Squinty.

'The wonderful, erotic smell of woman,' drools Languid.

'No.' I try to explain. 'She smells awful ... fishy rancid.'

'Never.'

'Yeah. Smells like that glue factory near Newcastle.'

'You've got to ignore smells, young 'un.'

'Can't. It's too strong.'

'So no knickers then.'

'Sorry no. We were outdoors.'

'That's a feeble excuse, young 'un.'

'Sorry.'

'We'll put it down as a 'possible' then.'

'Not bad.' Yorky winks. 'Not bad, young 'un.'

'Thanks.'

'You going to give it another crack tonight then?' asks Deeps.

'I'm duty.'

'I'll do your duty for you if you want,' says Tug.

'Thanks but no thanks.'

'You've given up on it then?'

'Definitely.'

'Not seeing the girl with the wonderful bum again then?'

'No ... definitely not.'

'I hope that the smell isn't an excuse, young 'un,' says Yorky.

'The smell's a real problem.'

'Explanation accepted,' says Yorky as he stands up. 'Do 'Cook-of-the-mess' this morning. I need Squinty with me for a couple of hours.'

'Will do.'

I have a good long shower as we are connected to unlimited, crystal-clear Swedish fresh water.

At just after twelve the Leading Seaman who has spent the forenoon watch as Quartermaster on the brow, pokes his head into the mess. 'Ordinary Seaman Broadbent, there's a young lady on the brow asking the Officer of the Day if she can see you.'

All eyes turn to me.

'Well well well,' says Yorky.

'Has she got a nice arse?' asks Languid

'All women have nice arses,' says the Quartermaster.

'That's the first this trip,' says someone else.

'That'll be Gunwale then ... Gunwale,' says Squinty.

'ORDINARY SEAMAN BROADBENT REPORT TO THE FORWARD GANGWAY.

ORDINARY SEAMAN BROADBENT, FORWARD GANGWAY.'

'I'm not going.'.

'Chicken,' says Squinty.

'Get up there,' says Deeps.

'I haven't got any money left.'

'She doesn't charge does she?'

'Of course not.'

'ORDINARY SEAMAN BROADBENT REPORT TO THE FORWARD GANGWAY IMMEDIATELY.

ORDINARY SEAMAN BROADBENT.'

'I'm not ferkin' going.'

'There's a woman on the jetty standing next to a pale blue Volvo,' one of the lads in the next mess, who is looking out of one of the scuttles, says. 'Great arse.'

'That's probably the Gunwale then,' says Languid.

Within minutes all the scuttles are occupied. They are in line with the upper surface of the jetty.

'Come on, young 'un, give her a wave.'

'Not ferkin' interested.'

'She's coming over.'

'Come on, young 'un, give her a wave.'

'No.'

'She's getting closer.'

'Are you Gunwale?' the bloke leaning out of the nearest scuttle shouts. 'She's here, young 'un. Come and say hello at least.'

'No.'

'Come on.'

'I'm going to the heads,' I say, and leave.

I take the long way up to the bridge wings and peer over the edge down at the jetty. I can see her car parked at the bottom of the brow. I can see the bobbly jumper and tight green trousers approaching the mess scuttles. I watch as something triangular lands at her feet – then a second one.

Back down the mess, Sugar says that he made her a couple of sardine sandwiches. He thinks that the fish is appropriate.

'ORDINARY SEAMAN BROADBENT REPORT TO THE FORWARD GANGWAY IMMEDIATELY.
ORDINARY SEAMAN BROADBENT.'

I just sit there, the centre of messdeck attention for the first time. I am quietly enjoying myself: I haven't 'stood a woman up' before, and I feel strangely mature about it.

My messmates continue shouting to her out of the open scuttles.

'He's in here love...' etc.

Eventually Gunnel gets the message and leaves.

Later that evening I go ashore with some friends. I keep my eyes skinned for Gunnel as I walk along the jetty, but she has gone and I never see her again. At least I have another sea-story I can relate when sitting around the mess table on future ships.

Early on Wednesday morning we are pulled away from Stockholm's jetty. It has been an interesting visit to say the least. Among the small crowd on the jetty to wave us farewell is Gunnel wearing the bobbly jumper and tight green trousers. She stands alongside her car enthusiastically waving her scarf.

Bermuda test-hoists her long red-and-white paying-off pennant which we will be flying as we enter Portsmouth for the very last time on Saturday. The length of the pennant is calculated by how long an individual ship has been in commission: *Bermuda*'s is so long that she needs to use a series of red-and-white gas-filled balloons to keep the pennant flying horizontally.

In the North Sea we refuel from *RFA Wave Prince* without incident and set a southerly course for Portsmouth. The rumour is that the entire *Bermuda* crew are to be transferred to *HMS Belfast* shortly after our arrival.

27

IT'S ALL OVER FOR *BERMADOO*

As we pass Nab Tower at 11:00 on Saturday 2 June a group of Wardroom Stewards carry a piano out onto the Quarter-deck and with due ceremony toss it over the side. In years to come, a diver may find a piano in the waters near the Nab Tower and wonder what it is doing there.

We hoist our paying-off pennant that flies horizontal and proud with the help of our cluster of balloons. There is a small crowd on the Round Tower to welcome us back – not that many, but we've only been away for a couple of weeks. I think that I spot a bobbly jumper waving a scarf ... I panic ... but it is my imagination.

By 13:00 *HMS Bermuda* is firmly berthed on Pitch House Jetty within the depths of Portsmouth Dockyard – this time her bows don't point towards the harbour entrance, but point north towards Cosham and Portsdown Hill.

The Royal Navy starts to strip *Bermuda* early on the morning of Monday 4 June. For some unknown reason we aren't towed to the ammunition jetty to return our unused ammo. Instead a trio of ammunition lighters come to us.

'DO YOU HEAR THERE.

NO SMOKING OR NAKED LIGHTS THROUGHOUT THE SHIP.

CLOSE ALL UPPER DECK SCREEN DOORS, SCUTTLES AND DEADLIGHTS.'

I volunteer to do 'Cook-of-the-mess' and get out of humping ammunition. I realise for the first time that volunteering can have its advantages.

We can't officially smoke until well after tea when the last of our explosives is safely overboard. An ammunition-free *Bermuda* is enveloped in a cloud of grey, exhaled tobacco smoke within seconds of the smoking ban being lifted.

A number of the lads in the mess have received draft chits which means that they will be leaving *Bermuda* during the next few days. Many are going to Naval establishments in the Portsmouth area to do courses, others have drafts to ships operating in other parts of the world. Conkers receives a draft chit to *HMS Drake* in Plymouth. The mess is becoming less crowded.

Tug goes over to the Isle of Wight for the weekend. I am duty on the Saturday and Sunday so I have to stay onboard. Goosie is duty Petty Officer on Sunday: he is leaving *Bermuda* tomorrow and wants to say goodbye to his beloved Quarter-deck with a good scrub. So it is on Sunday afternoon, the Duty Watch along with Men under Punishment and some of us who have worked on the Quarter-deck over the year, scrub *Bermuda*'s Quarter-deck for the final time. When we are finished and it gleams sparkly white in the June sunshine, we form a guard of honour with our squeegees and make Goosie walk under our arch.

'You bunch of ferkin' idiots,' he says as he walks away from the Quarter-deck, possibly for the last time.

Did he have a tear in his eye?

Oh yes … he did.

I don't know exactly when it occurred but we reportedly received a visit from the Chief of Staff, whoever he is. Flag Officer Flotillas (Home), Vice Admiral J G Hamilton CB CBE and his staff leave us without so much as a farewell wave.

Each day *Bermuda* sits a little higher in the harbour waters as bits of the old lady are removed. We are awash with men in brown overalls stripping down and taking large amounts of complicated-looking machinery ashore. The Naval Stores branch organises large teams of men to form human chains throughout the ship to unload all kinds of other stuff into wagons and containers that line the jetty. The trick is to avoid being detailed off as de-storing party when we muster each morning. I often avoid it by saying I am 'Cook-of-the-mess': whether I am or not.

The Regulating Staff continue to be busy and lower deck is cleared one day to witness the reading of our final Punishment Warrant. I am surprised to learn that Squinty has been caught trying to smuggle a holdall full of tins of tobacco ashore and that he physically assaulted two of the Dockyard Police when apprehended. He goes down on record as the final person to have his Warrant read onboard *HMS Bermuda*. He is given three months' detention to be served in the Detention Quarters near Haslar hospital in Gosport. I am near to the front and I think he smiles at me as the details of his sentence are read out: but you can't be one hundred percent sure who Squinty is looking at.

Tug and I find the Dockyard Canteen up by the other Dockyard Gate. It is OK – reasonably cheap beer and plenty of spare snooker tables. Neither of us has improved our snooker skills but it is an enjoyable way to kick off a Portsmouth run ashore. We spend at least three evenings a week exploring the hostelries of Portsmouth, occasionally visiting the popular bars along Commercial Road. We never stay in the Lennox, Sussex, Criterion, Golden Fleece or the Albany very long. As soon as the Pompey girls arrive, they make a beeline for me and Tug ... and frighten us to death. We make our excuses and leave.

Tug finds himself a girlfriend in the NAAFI Club and for a few weeks I lose him. It all comes to an undignified and sorrowful end when she tells Tug that she has another boyfriend onboard *HMS Broadsword*.

On Thursday 21 June *HMS Belfast* is towed up the harbour flying her paying-off pennant and berths alongside us. She is our size and looks as though she has suffered some paint damage during her recent trans-Atlantic trip. Numerous gangplanks are rigged between the two of us and a steady stream of *Belfast*'s crew, with kit bags on their shoulders, cross our decks and onto a line of waiting blue buses on the jetty.

On Thursday 28 June *Bermuda* is officially stripped of her removable stores. Rumour has it that the Dockyard bottom between ourselves and *HMS Belfast* is littered with bulky and unwieldy stores items that have been considered too awkward to carry and which have been given a float-test in the hours of darkness.

We are given the day to pack all our kit and notices are posted detailing our new *Belfast* messes. We strip our hammocks and carry them onto the jetty where we toss them unceremoniously into an open-fronted container. I wonder what the Navy does with second hand, well-used hammocks.

All the members of *Bermuda*'s For'd Seamen's Mess are mustered on the Fo'csle with our kit bags. Yorky does a final inspection of the empty mess to make sure that everything has been removed. Then we are ushered over the short gangplank and down through a hatch in the after part of *HMS Belfast*'s Fo'csle and into her For'd Seamen's Mess. A list is posted on the mess notice board detailing our locker and bunk number.

I have a BUNK!

On Monday 2 July *HMS Belfast* is re-commissioned with a short morning ceremony under the command of Mrs Lumby's husband and with most of *Bermuda*'s ship's company.

Belfast assumes the role of Flagship when John-Jo reappears on Wednesday. I am part of the Fo'csle part-of-ship and, along with all the other Seaman, prepare to take *Belfast* to sea. Having taken *HMS Bermuda* through a 'Work-up' that lasted almost a year, we aren't surprised to learn that we are heading north to Invergordon in preparation for *Belfast*'s 'Work-up' that will start on Monday 9 July 1962.

Along with some others, I lounge silently on the upper deck as a couple of dockyard tugs tow us away from *Bermuda*. I try to ignore the lump in my throat. It is the last time I will see the old girl that has been my home for the past 14 months. According to the Navigator's Yeoman, we have travelled 34,152 nautical miles together: we had ploughed effortlessly through most of them, but some had damaged us.

'Ugly old bugger isn't she?' says Tug.

I think about it. 'No ... there's something about her.'

'What?'

'Dunno exactly. Some good memories.'

'Like what?'

'Ooh ... Joe the painter sitting cross-legged on the mess table dropping headless sardines into the flood water ... for one.'

'I didn't see that.'

'Being adrift after going to your place in Cowes that time.'

'I remember that.' Tug pulls a face.

'And the sandwiches, the triangular ones the mess made for that girl in Stockholm.'

'I remember that.'

'I won't forget her, she was a learning-ground for me.'

We continue to look at *Bermuda* in silence as we are pulled further away. Now she's an empty, partially denuded ship, home only to her native inhabitants. I wonder if what I think is a noticeable line of rust at the bottom of the long zigzag ladder, is actually a dense mass of cockroaches waving their antennae in a respectful, farewell salute.

Once *Bermuda*, always *Bermuda*.

A partially scrapped Bermuda *in Thomas Ward's shipbreaking yard, South Wales, 1965. She spent three years shackled to head and stern buoys at the top of Portsmouth Harbour before being towed away to be scrapped*

Lightning Source UK Ltd.
Milton Keynes UK
UKHW021115300821
389711UK00013B/992